Motivation Management

Motivation Management

Sheila Ritchie
and
Peter Martin

Gower

Published by
Gower Publishing Limited
Gower House
Croft Road
Aldershot
Hampshire GU11 3HR
England

Gower
Old Post Road
Brookfield
Vermont 05036
USA

British Library Cataloguing in Publication Data
Ritchie, Sheila
    Motivation management
    1. Employee motivation 2. Personnel management
    I. Title II. Martin, Peter, 1941–
    658'.044

ISBN 0 566 08102 4

Library of Congress Cataloging-in-Publication Data
Ritchie, Sheila.
    Motivation management / Sheila Ritchie and Peter Martin.
        p.   cm.
    Includes bibliographical references and index.
    ISBN 0–566–08102–4 (alk. paper)
    1. Employee motivation. 2. Psychology, Industrial. 3. Industrial management. I. Martin, Peter, 1941–   . II. Title.
    HF5549.5.M63R58   1999
    658.3'14—dc21   98–40509
                                                               CIP

Typeset in Times by Bournemouth Colour Press and printed in Great Britain by MPG Books Ltd, Bodmin.

Contents

List of tables

List of figures

Preface

This book was conceived in frustration. We as trainers felt that motivation as a topic had failed to mature. Managers were still being taught as if Maslow, Herzberg and McGregor were the only writers of note. True, all were pioneers who had made a significant contribution, but there has been no work since which is as accepted, or taught so widely, as these. And their work was undertaken in the 1940s to 1960s. Surely, we reasoned, the world had moved on? In our view, it needed to move on not only in theoretical terms, but in providing motivational tools for practical managers to use.

Despite extensive research, we could find nothing we felt comfortable with. The only solution was to do the work ourselves. A daunting prospect, but the only possible route that we could see to provide managers with the help they told us they wanted. We had an important advantage as trainers. We had access to large numbers of managers at all levels in a range of industries, in commerce and in government. What we had not realized, of course, was just how big the task was going to be.

The first question was, how to go about it? We wanted work that could be as valid as possible when based on non-parametric statistics and in the field of social and individual research. We wanted something that was relatively simple to use, but could develop depths of sophistication. We wanted to show the individuality of people, as opposed to 'people in the mass', and we wanted the tools to show how people in teams interacted with each other. Finally we wanted to build a model that subsequent research could sharpen and refine.

We were aware of course that there was no simple theory that could possibly give a complete explanation of individual motivational needs. We had to accept that, ultimately, people defy complete analysis. Indeed, that was a fact we were happy to accept. It is the guarantee that, for example, Berlin walls will tumble and that seemingly intractable disputes are capable of resolution. The task, then, became to simplify complexity and to amass enough useful data for practical application.

We decided to proceed, not by ignoring the previous work, but building on it. We looked at the factors that research and experience seemed to show were motivators, and we added some others that our own observations suggested were under-emphasized. The stance we took was that, in the absence of a complete explanation, we should provide as many motivators as we thought could reasonably be handled by busy managers. Eventually we settled on 12. Some of these turned out to be more important than others, so that in practice the 12 can sometimes be reduced.

Later research may show that the 12 do not provide the best insight. That does not worry us: we have to start somewhere and using the best available current thinking seems a good place to start. In practice, our approach provides an additional benefit. It is that as managers use the tools and develop awareness, so they can modify our motivators in line with their own observations and experience. They can modify our model, and even build their own. We would be happy to help them and would certainly like to know about their insights.

How were we to achieve this task? The first step was to find out what people thought motivated them. The second was to see whether or not they accepted our findings. Then we had to find out if other people recognized their view of themselves. We could do this both by asking people directly and by refinements such as asking them to obtain profiles of people they found easy to work with and difficult to work with, and so on. We have done such work, but clearly further research along these lines will be fruitful. So far, we have been encouraged, not only by the formal research, but by the 'oo...ah!' factor. People recognize themselves. Even more pleasing for us was that teams of people recognize themselves and are excited about the implications for their development. Teams and people seem to feel they have a tool which enables them to talk constructively about themselves and their relationship with each other. Though more work has still to be done, our frustration with the lack of motivation tools that caused us to write this book is starting to abate.

How did we reach this point? The first stage – asking people what they felt motivated them – was tackled by developing a self-assessment profile. In time-honoured fashion a forced choice approach was used, asking people to weigh the 12 motivators, one against the other. The chapter on The making of the Profile describes how the instrument was piloted and developed, and how the final version was refined. The result of this exercise is a unique Motivational Profile for each person which gives the relative 'strength', one to the other, of each of their 12 motivators.

We were, of course, unable to measure people's 'absolute' motivational needs. That is to say to measure, for example, their objective need for variety on some sort of motivational Richter scale. Such measurement is not possible, although in the chapter on Selection, we move some way in that direction. Nor is it possible to say, for example, that somebody's need for achievement is five times as great as somebody else's need for power. What we can say with certainty is that each person has weighed the 12 motivational factors relative to each other, and this provides a realistic and acceptable insight into their relative motivational needs. Thus a person could learn that his or her need for variety, for example, outweighed their need for achievement, and have some measure of the differences between them.

The practical benefit to managers is to give them some understanding of how to manage people who have different relative motivational needs. And it is more likely that those people will differ than that they will be very similar. In developing the research, the first task was to try to draw conclusions about what, in general, motivates managers. Statistically, a data bank was needed with a good number of responses, about one thousand profiles, and that took four years to achieve. We collected a further 412 at a later date to test a theory about increases in stress caused by increased competition and downsizing in organizations. To put this in perspective, Herzberg's original database was 200. The participants were managers we met in the course of business and managers who attended courses that we ran. Then the number crunching started. We looked at the mode, median and range for each factor. Satisfied that the instrument yielded reasonable results and seemed to be both valid and reliable (for more on these issues see the chapter on The making of the Profile), we collated the 'best' of the original 1 054 and the second set of 412, yielding 1 355 usable and complete responses.

Interestingly, we were unable to find any significant differences across the different occupations. Part of the problem was that we were unable to find a sufficiently precise way, say the standard industrial classification, of defining occupations. We had to fall back on broad categories: architect, engineer, finance manager, civil servant and so on. We concluded that the differences between individuals were more significant than the differences between professions. We also discovered some interesting results. For example, bearing in mind that we were working with a managerial audience, the drive for power and influence was relatively lower than we might have expected. The need for recognition and achievement was higher than the need for influence, which sets in train a great debate about the selection, development, role and effectiveness of managers. All of this we explore.

We pondered the significance of the remark made to us by a clinical psychologist that very many people were in the wrong job and that their motivational needs could not expect to correspond to the motivational needs of the job! Interviews with respondents reinforce this psychologist's views: so many people seem to feel that their work does not suit them – or worse, is actually stressful – that we wonder if most of the jobs available will ever be filled by people who find them rewarding, or even achievable without strain.

Another dimension in which we expected differences to occur was in national motivational tendencies. After all, Hofstede (1994) and Trompenaars and Hampden-Turner (1997) have reported significant differences in attitudes on their scales of measurement. We found none: in fact the differences between individuals in any group or in any one country were dramatic; inter-group and international differences were not discernible. The database revealed many other aspects of individual motivation, which we discuss at length in the chapters that follow.

How are managers to use the insights we provide? We consider the nature of motivation which we see as the satisfaction of a person's needs. When something motivates a person they feel and act in particular ways. To put it in a nutshell, they smile more and carp less. Therefore the task of the manager is to find out what it is that motivates people. Is it providing that person with opportunities for, say, achievement, or variety in their work, or a heavy dose of structure? How does the manager find out? Our Motivation Profile is a good start. It provides the wherewithal for a structured discussion and, together with the Profiles of other team members, gives some indication of how the team should be managed. The exercise must be presented in a non-threatening way. The self-assessment exercise works if people fill it in honestly because they want some perception of what motivates them. This question of honesty in Profile completion is covered in more detail in the chapter on The making of the Profile.

The other way, either alone or with the self-assessment exercise, is for the manager to use observational skills to try to establish when people are motivated and then to observe the cause of the motivation. Thus, the manager observing a smile in the eye and a relaxed gait might enquire, 'Why?' If the answer is that the person has had the opportunity to be creative and has been successful, then creativity would seem to be a motivator. Over a period, managers can build up a systematic picture of what motivates the people working around them. Similarly, the book provides a framework for people to start thinking about themselves. But for whoever is doing the thinking, each of the 12 motivators is examined in detail and the interaction between people in groups and how teams should be motivated are all explored. We believe we have provided powerful tools for busy managers. With practice, the lessons of this book will become second nature to them. Then we shall feel that our work has been truly useful.

Sheila Ritchie
Peter Martin

Acknowledgements

Writing this book was fun, though it seemed to take a long time. It began with our dissatisfaction with what was currently available for applying motivation theory to the real world of work.

Sheila had created a questionnaire which went through several revisions to the point where more revisions would not create any improvement and we wished to proceed with data collection. We then started to collect scores, not only from participants who attended courses we ran in the UK where we both live, but in Western Europe, many of the ex-Soviet states and the Middle East. We collected 1 000 usable responses and, cheered by our progress, analysed and checked them. We collected more responses and became bolder about using the results to inform and to develop training and management development materials and sessions.

Peter started and bore the brunt of writing the book, and the drafts began to pile up. Our initial intention was to write an airport book, designed for travellers who could use their long hours in the sky to gain some insight into what motivated them. We more or less finished that book in draft form and showed it to Malcolm Stern at Gower. He was enthusiastic, but wanted it re-focused as an aid to motivation for practising managers. So back to the drawing board for a complete rewrite. At the end it seemed we were totally absorbed, passing drafts back and forward to each other by the magic of e-mail. The book became a truly collaborative effort.

The 'number crunching' under Sheila's guidance was undertaken by Jacqueline Wieczorek, of ELM Training, over the period 1993 to 1998. Successive tranches of feedback forms were handled by her with patience and accuracy; the Profile was also put on to an Excel file, saving future respondents all the pain of adding up and of transferring scores from one table to another.

Of course, we were not alone. Our families had to put up with long conversations about 'the book' and although it is traditional in the acknowledgements section to talk about the forbearance and long suffering of the immediate family, it is true. Sarah and Duncan probably had to hear more about the book than they had expected, and Jeremy and Michael were wise not to let paternal preoccupations distract them from the demands of school and university. They were all very tolerant and their support deserves our recognition.

They may not be immediate family, but by the end of this long project some of them feel as if they are: we acknowledge a debt to those writers and researchers who contributed to the vast body of literature which we were able to use as a base for our work. Most of these are given their appropriate place in Appendix 1 on The theoretical framework of motivation or in the References section at the end.

SR
PM

How to use this book

We have written this book to be read with enjoyment and profit by people with three different sets of interests: by the busy manager seeking practical guidance on how to motivate his or her staff; by the human relations professional who likes to keep abreast of thinking in this area; and by the specialist who wants to look at the basic work we did and satisfy themselves that what we are saying is valid and statistically supportable. To all these readers we suggest that the first thing to do is complete and score the questionnaire on pages 5–12, one of the pillars on which the text is founded. Not only will this give you an insight into your own motivation, it will also provide the basis for thinking about other people's. It will whet your appetite, too, for understanding the impact of factors like the need for achievement, power, structure and so on.

For the busy manager, we suggest that either you encourage all the members of your team to complete the profile or you rely on your experience and powers of observation to form your own view as to what motivates each of them. Start with what you regard as their significant motivators, then refer to the corresponding chapters. If, for example, you think their high motivators are need for achievement and for structure, turn to the chapter on Achievement and read the section 'High factor 7, factor 3'. If you think they have a very low need for a particular factor, at least read the introduction to the relevant factor. Sometimes that will point you to other parts of the text as well. Thus if you consider your staff member to be low on factor 6, recognition, read the introduction to the chapter on Recognition.

In this way you will have acquired some knowledge of the personal motivators of your team. Now read further about how they are likely to cope with change (Managing change on pages 163–73) or stress (Coping with stress on pages 175–87) or the direction in which you should help them develop themselves (Training and development on pages 203–22); how their motivational needs are likely to influence their relationships with others (Working with others on pages 247–54); and the dynamics of teamworking (Teamworking on pages 189–201). In each chapter you will probably want to consult only the factors that relate to their personal profile.

If you are a manager who wants to become fully informed on the subject of motivation, you will benefit from reading all the chapters. There is a great deal of material to contend with, so you might prefer to keep the book to hand and browse as and when you have time or when you have to deal with a particular motivational problem. Reading the complete text straight through could produce information overload! Similar remarks apply to the human relations professional. Finally, if you are a specialist you should find the entire book valuable, including Appendix 1 on The theoretical framework and Appendix 2 on The making of the Profile which describes the research on which this book is based.

We hope all of you will gain fresh insights into the fascinating world of motivation, and enjoy a good read into the bargain.

Part I
The Motivation-to-work Profile

How to use the Profile

This questionnaire has been designed and tested to show you which factors you rate high and which you rate low as potential sources of work satisfaction. It allows you to project your needs and feelings, and thus acquire some understanding of your own motivation. It works by comparing a number of factors of importance to managers.

For best results work through the questionnaire quickly, without thinking too long about each question. Your first, unconsidered judgement is probably the truest reflection of your real feelings.

The Profile takes about one hour to complete and score.

Read each Statement on the Questionnaire (pages 5–9) entering points directly on to the Score Sheet (page 10). Be sure to allocate *exactly 11 points* to each set of four phrases A–D.

Example

You have 11 points to allocate to each set of four factors – coded (a), (b), (c) and (d) – under the 33 Statements, a total of 363 points. If you feel that one factor is of overwhelming importance, give it all 11 points; if you think it is insignificant, give it no points at all; otherwise share out the 11 points between the four factors as you wish, ensuring that you use all 11 points. An example would be the following Statement:

I would want to work in a job where

(a)   the salary and benefits were good   ......
(b)   I could develop the work as I wished   ......
(c)   other people would recognize and appreciate my work   ......

3

(d)   there was plenty of variety and change   ......

Use *all 11 points*, entering them directly on to the Score Sheet.

If you felt that factors (a) and (b) were very important, you could give them, say, **6** and **5** points, respectively, leaving **none** for factors (c) and (d). The way you allocate the points is for you to decide, but you must use **all 11** on each Statement. The points you give each Statement are entered on to the Score Sheet.

Questionnaire

Use *all 11 points* for *each* set of (a), (b), (c), (d)

Statements

1. **I think I could contribute well in a job where**
   - (a) the salary and rewards were good
   - (b) there were opportunities to form good relationships with colleagues
   - (c) I could influence decisions and demonstrate my worth
   - (d) there was a chance to develop and grow as a person

2. **I would *not* like to work where**
   - (a) there were few guidelines about what was required of me
   - (b) little feedback was given on my performance
   - (c) my job seemed to be of little use or value
   - (d) working conditions were poor, noisy or dirty

3. **It is important to me that my job should**
   - (a) have plenty of variety and change
   - (b) provide opportunities for working with a wide range of people
   - (c) have clear guidelines so that I know what is expected of me
   - (d) allow me to get to know the people I work with well

4. **I *don't* think I would be very interested in work which**
   - (a) allowed me few contacts with other people
   - (b) was unlikely to be noticed by other people
   - (c) was unspecified so that I was unsure of what I was meant to do
   - (d) was subject to a certain amount of routine

5. **Work appeals to me when**
   - (a) I am clear about what is expected of me
   - (b) I have a comfortable working area and few interruptions

(c)   the rewards and the salary are good
(d)   the job allows me to develop as a person

6.   I think I would enjoy
(a)   good working conditions and lack of pressure
(b)   having a very good salary
(c)   work that was intrinsically satisfying and useful
(d)   appreciation for my achievements and work

7.   I *don't* feel that work should
(a)   be loosely structured so that it is unclear what has to be done
(b)   provide few opportunities for getting to know other people well
(c)   have little value or use, or be uninteresting to do
(d)   go unrecognized or be taken for granted

8.   A satisfying job
(a)   has plenty of variety, change and stimulation
(b)   allows me to develop myself and to grow as a person
(c)   is intrinsically satisfying and rewarding
(d)   lets me be creative and allows me to explore new ideas

9.   It is important that work should
(a)   be recognized and valued by the organization I work for
(b)   provide opportunities for the person to develop and grow
(c)   have plenty of variety and change
(d)   allow the worker to influence others

10.   I *don't* feel that a job would be satisfying where
(a)   there was little contact with a variety of people
(b)   the salary and the rewards were not good
(c)   I could not form and sustain good relationships with colleagues
(d)   I had little autonomy or room for manoeuvre

11.   The most enjoyable jobs are those which
(a)   have good working conditions
(b)   are clearly specified and explained
(c)   are interesting and useful
(d)   provide recognition for a person's achievements and work

12.   I would probably *not* work well where
(a)   there was little chance to set targets and achieve them
(b)   I could not develop as a person
(c)   hard work went unrewarded and unrecognized
(d)   there was dust, noise or dirt

13.   It is important when designing a job to
(a)   provide opportunities for people to get to know each other well
(b)   ensure that a person can set goals and achieve them
(c)   build in opportunities for creativity

    (d)   ensure that the working conditions are comfortable and clean

14. I would probably *not* want to work where
    (a)   I had little autonomy or chances to develop as a person
    (b)   exploration and curiosity were not encouraged
    (c)   there was little contact with a range of other people
    (d)   perks and benefits were not good

15. I would get a lot of satisfaction from
    (a)   influencing the decisions others made
    (b)   plenty of variety and change in my work
    (c)   having my achievements valued by other people
    (d)   being clear about what was expected of me and how I should do it

16. I would find work *less* enjoyable if
    (a)   I could not set and achieve challenging goals
    (b)   I was unclear about what the rules and guidelines were
    (c)   the salary did not seem to reflect the level of work I was doing
    (d)   I had little effect on decisions made or on what people did

17. I think a job should have
    (a)   a job description and clear guidelines about what is expected
    (b)   opportunities to get to know colleagues well
    (c)   chances to do challenging assignments which stretch the person
    (d)   variety, change and stimulation

18. A job would be *less* satisfying if
    (a)   it did not allow for any creative input
    (b)   it was isolated so that the person worked alone
    (c)   it did not have the right climate for the person to grow or develop
    (d)   it did not let the person influence decisions that were made

19. I would like to work where
    (a)   other people valued and appreciated the work I did
    (b)   I could have an effect on what other people did
    (c)   there were good perks and benefits
    (d)   I could explore ideas and be creative

20. It is *unlikely* that I would want to work where
    (a)   there was little variety or change of task
    (b)   I had little influence on the decisions made
    (c)   the salary was not very good
    (d)   working conditions were unpleasant

21. I think that satisfying work should offer
    (a)   clear guidelines so that a person knows what is expected of them
    (b)   chances for creativity
    (c)   opportunities to meet a range of interesting people
    (d)   fulfilment and intrinsically interesting tasks

22. Work would *not* be enjoyable where
   (a)   there were few benefits or perks
   (b)   working conditions were uncomfortable or noisy
   (c)   the person could not compare their work with other people's
   (d)   exploration and new ideas were not encouraged

23. I feel that it is important for work to provide me with
   (a)   plenty of contact with a range of interesting people
   (b)   chances for setting and achieving meaningful goals
   (c)   opportunities to influence decisions
   (d)   a high level of salary

24. I don't feel that I would like a job if
   (a)   conditions were dirty, noisy or uncomfortable
   (b)   there were few chances to influence other people
   (c)   there was little in the way of challenging goals
   (d)   I could not be creative and contribute new ideas

25. It is important when organizing work
   (a)   to ensure that working conditions are clean and comfortable
   (b)   to build autonomy for the person into the work
   (c)   to provide opportunities for variety and change
   (d)   to give the person plenty of contact with other people

26. I would probably *not* want to work where
   (a)   conditions were dirty, noisy or uncomfortable
   (b)   I had few contacts with other people
   (c)   the job was not interesting or rewarding
   (d)   the job was routine and rarely changed

27. A satisfying job would probably
   (a)   be one where people recognized and appreciated good work
   (b)   allow me plenty of room for manoeuvre
   (c)   let me set challenging targets
   (d)   be one where I could get to know colleagues well

28. I would *not* like a job which
   (a)   was not useful and did not offer me fulfilling work
   (b)   offered little stimulation and change
   (c)   would not allow me to develop friendships with others
   (d)   was unfocused and had no challenging goals

29. I would tend to want to work where
   (a)   the job was interesting and rewarding
   (b)   people could form lasting friendships
   (c)   I could meet a range of interesting people
   (d)   I was able to influence decisions

30. I *don't* think a job should
    (a)   require a person to work alone much of the time
    (b)   give little chance for a person's achievements to be recognized
    (c)   prevent a person from forming relationships with colleagues
    (d)   consist of a lot of routine

31. A well-designed job would
    (a)   have good benefits and plenty of perks
    (b)   have clear guidelines and an up-to-date job description
    (c)   offer chances to set goals and achieve them
    (d)   provide encouragement for new ideas

32. I might find a job *unsatisfying* if
    (a)   I could not do challenging work
    (b)   there were few chances for creativity
    (c)   little autonomy was possible
    (d)   the work itself was not rewarding or useful

33. The most important things to build into a job are
    (a)   chances for original thinking and creativity
    (b)   intrinsically interesting and fulfilling work
    (c)   opportunities for forming good relationships with colleagues
    (d)   meaningful goals for the person to achieve

Score sheet

Statement	1	2	3	4	5	6	7	8	9	10	11	12
1	(a)......											
2		(d)......	(a)......		(b)......	(b)......		(c)......			(d)......	(c)......
3			(c)......	(b)......								
4			(c)......	(a)......	(d)......	(b)......						
5	(c)......	(b)......	(a)......						(a)......		(d)......	
6	(b)......	(a)......				(d)......			(d)......			(c)......
7			(a)......		(b)......	(d)......						(c)......
8				(a)......	(c)......	(a)......		(d)......	(a)......	(d)......	(b)......	(c)......
9									(c)......		(b)......	
10	(b)......										(d)......	
11		(a)......	(b)......			(d)......						(c)......
12		(d)......			(a)......	(c)......				(c)......	(b)......	(c)......
13		(d)......					(a)......			(b)......		
14	(d)......			(c)......			(b)......				(a)......	
15			(d)......			(c)......		(a)......	(b)......			
16	(c)......		(b)......		(b)......		(a)......	(d)......				
17			(a)......	(b)......			(c)......		(d)......			
18								(d)......		(a)......		
19	(c)......	(d)......				(a)......		(b)......	(a)......	(d)......	(c)......	
20	(c)......		(a)......	(c)......				(b)......				
21		(b)......										
22	(a)......			(a)......			(b)......	(c)......		(b)......		
23	(d)......						(c)......	(c)......		(d)......		(d)......
24	(a)......	(a)......				(a)......		(b)......	(c)......			
25	(d)......	(a)......		(d)......					(d)......	(d)......		
26		(a)......		(b)......								
27					(d)......		(c)......				(b)......	(c)......
28				(c)......	(c)......		(d)......		(b)......			
29				(a)......	(b)......	(b)......		(d)......			(b)......	(a)......
30			(b)......		(c)......		(c)......		(d)......			(a)......
31	(a)......						(a)......			(d)......	(c)......	(d)......
32							(a)......			(b)......		(d)......
33					(c)......		(d)......			(a)......		(b)......
TOTALS	......	......	......	......	......	......	......	......	......	......	......	......

Key

After completing the Profile, you will have a total score for each of the 12 factors. High scores for a factor indicate a high level of need, low scores indicate a low level of need, *relative* to other factors. The mode (most frequently occurring number), median (the mid-point of the range or spread) and the range (the lowest through to the highest score) recorded by 1 355 managers and professionals on our database are given after each factor description below. It is also useful to look at the histogram at the start of the chapter for each factor. You can then see the shape of the distribution curve, plotting your own score on it for comparison.

Factor number

1. Need for high salary and tangible rewards; desire to have a job with good benefits and perks. This need tends to fluctuate throughout a working life, heavy outgoings will send it higher (debts? new family responsibilities? new or heavy financial commitments?). Mode 27, median 19, range 0–96.

2. Need for good working conditions and comfortable surroundings. Mode 17, median 17, range 0–83.

3. Need for structure, feedback and information; need to reduce uncertainty and to establish rules and guidelines. (A measure of need for direction and certainty which can be an indicator of stress or anxiety and often rises or falls when person is facing important changes at home or at work.) Mode 26, median 25, range 0–69.

4. Need for social contact: wide range of people, light level of intimacy. (A measure of liking for working with others, not to be confused with how well someone relates to colleagues. It is possible to score very low, but still to be socially adept.) Mode 27, median 25, range 0–81.

5. Need to form and sustain long-term, stable relationships, small number of people, intimate level. (Need for deeper level of contact with others. As with factor 4, a low score does *not* indicate poor social relationships.) Mode 18, median 19, range 0–45.

6. Need for recognition and appreciation from others. (This is not a measure of liking for others, or of good social relationships, but of a person's need for others to give their attention, a desire for personal significance.) Mode 35, median 36, range 0–88.

7. Need to set oneself challenging goals and to achieve them; measure of need to be goal directed and self-motivated. (A measure of the drive to seek out challenges and to conquer them.) Mode 36, median 36, range 2–81.

8.   Need to influence and control others; competitive and power drive. (A measure of the competitive drive as it involves comparison with and influence over others.) Mode 31, median 31, range 0–79.

9.   Need for variety, change and stimulation; avoidance of routine (boredom). (Measure of tendency to keep oneself at a high level of arousal/vigilance; liking for change and stimulation.) Mode 34, median 35, range 0–78.

10.   Need to be explorative, creative and open-minded. (Measure of tendency to be curious and to think divergently. The ideas sought or contributed need not be original.) Mode 32, median 33, range 5–81.

11.   Need to develop and grow as an individual. (Measures desire for autonomy, self-determination and self-development.) Mode 35, median 32, range 7–84.

12.   Need to feel that one's work is intrinsically interesting, useful and rewarding. (A measure of the need for meaningful work with an element of social utility.) Mode 41, median 43, range 15–97.

Copies of this Profile, and licences to copy and use it, may be obtained from:

Sheila Ritchie
ELM Training
Seaton House,
Kings Ripton
Huntingdon PE17 2NJ
Telephone: 01487 773238
Fax: 01487 773359
E-mail: elm@ndirect.co.uk

Part II
The twelve factors

Factor 1

Money and tangible rewards

Highest score recorded = 96
Lowest score recorded = 0
Mode 27 Median 19

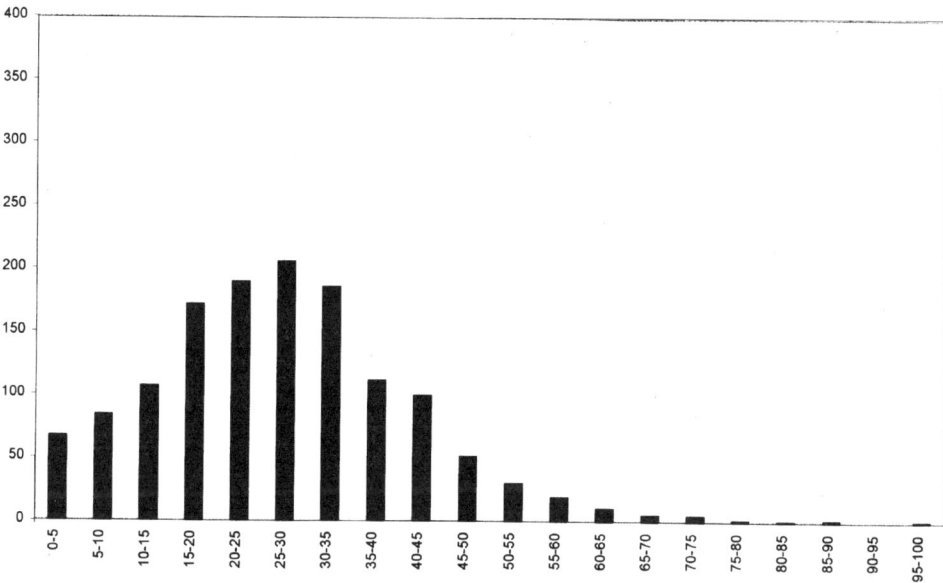

Figure 1   Factor 1: histogram of scores

Motivating staff with an above average need for money is, in principle, simple. The simplicity is deceptive. On the one hand, the business may not be able to meet the staff members' monetary aspirations. On the other, motivating with money is pregnant with difficulties, the two most significant of which are a loss of management control and the problem of deciding on a fair rate of reward. Managing money motivation is a balancing act between the need of the staff for money and the need of the business for protection.

Some managers, when faced with stress, unhappiness or disaffected staff, reach for the cheque book. It is the classic response when the employee says that he or she is unhappy in the job. Although it is occasionally the right response, paying out more money is often pointless, either because the problem is not susceptible to this type of solution or the member of staff does not value tangible rewards as highly as the manager thinks.

Let us first of all look at the situation where factor 1 dominates, scores on the other factors are evenly spread and there is no dominant second factor.

Factor 1 high, other factors evenly spread

High factor 1 means that money is the overwhelming driving force. In the most pronounced cases, the need for earnings is insatiable. Money is required not only to provide for home and family, but for its own sake. There will be no sense that 'enough is enough'.

The first consideration is that to earn high sums of money, people so motivated must be competent. Before even considering how to motivate, we need to be confident that there is competence. If we fail to do this, then we will either fail to achieve business potential or even suffer loss. The issue then will not be motivation but resuscitation. Secondly we should consider the other motivators to see how these might have an impact on performance. We discuss this later in the chapter. Third is a full understanding that high scorers have an almost pathological need for money. At the extreme, they will do anything for money. In some cases 'anything' will include ignoring the need to comply with statutory or contractual requirements, and in other cases will include illegal behaviour. It is wise to assume that a member of staff with this profile will be tempted to behave improperly. The corollary is that it is necessary to design systems that will quickly detect non-compliance or illegality. Beyond this, at or approaching the point at which earnings are seen to be threatened by management action, management will be resisted.

Managers will be in a difficult position. They will welcome the sales or whatever else is required, but they need to be sure that in taking action they know what they want and that, unless they so intend it, earnings will not be adversely affected. But, in practice, management of high earners is a battle for control with little quarter given. Management's most effective course of action is to nip in the bud quickly any deviations from acceptable behaviour, possibly linking action to financial penalties which will have been provided for in the contract. For example, if the boss wants to introduce a new product, service or way of working which the staff member suspects will interfere with earnings, they may well not want to co-operate and may even be tempted to obstruct. Consider, for example, a foreign exchange dealer faced with a boss who wants to introduce new financial instruments, that is, new ways of making deals.

The dealer will immediately ask the question: 'How will this affect my earnings?'. If the effect, even in the short term, appears to be detrimental, there will be a temptation to resist its introduction. At the very least, the dealer will ask the firm to guarantee his or her earnings. If the manager refuses, the dealer will find the temptation not to co-operate almost overwhelming. And, of course, he or she will be in a strong position. The firm pays well but it relies on the dealer's skill to earn it profit.

There are some rules of engagement. The first is that such staff are motivated when they see a direct correlation between their effort and their reward. That is to say, the reward they receive is a direct result of their own effort and is not dependent on anybody else. To make the point clearly, because it is an important point, if they are rewarded for selling something in a territory that has been assigned to them, then what is sold in that territory is sold only by them and by nobody else and the reward received depends only on their own sales. This means that managers need to make strenuous attempts to ensure that there is a strict causality between effort and reward. If there is not, there is a strong possibility of manipulation to ensure that personal earnings are achieved, though it is likely to be at the expense of management. Management will pay the commission, or the share options, but not necessarily receive the business benefit to justify it. Similar considerations apply if the scheme is weakly constituted, though in this situation there will be no need for manipulation. Unearned commission will be paid anyway. If causality is established, both sides can benefit, although in practice, causality is difficult to establish and so-called payment by results may well motivate staff but may not benefit the organization in proportion to the reward.

People motivated by money prefer to be rewarded for their own effort. They do not particularly like to work in teams. Team mates will be seen as possible competitors and as possibly undermining individual achievement. For example, time taken to help colleagues can be seen as time taken away from earning. If management wish to encourage team work, they must ensure that incentive payments include a factor which relates to team performance.

A good example of the resistance that can be expected from such high earners is the security company which was concerned that its salespeople did not help each other and were competitive over customers and territory. The sales staff thought that staff on administrative and telephone support should form allegiances with them as individuals, excluding and even obstructing colleagues as a way of expressing loyalty. The company felt that it was worth investigating means to change their salespeople's selfish attitudes and behaviour. They called a meeting with a consultant to see if the 'Sales Team' could be reorganized to work more co-operatively; to try to change their attitudes towards each other so that the firm as a whole could benefit from collaborative exchanges of customer leads and other helpful 'team-like' behaviour.

Exemplifying the group mood, a salesman called 'Mr Million' (because he sold more than that value every year) stated right away that he could see no advantage in changing his style of working, and certainly not his attitudes. For him all other sales staff were potential threats, capable of scooping a portion of what he perceived as a limited market. As he was rewarded by a low basic salary and a large personal commission on sales, he could only be motivated to change by some suggestion that would guarantee an increase in his income. He was unmoved by the idea of group commission or bonuses; declared others useless when it came to earning serious money; stated that he would rather depend on the income of Mother Teresa as a partner than most of his colleagues; and would not even consider the possibility of sharing leads or other forms of mutual support. He liked things just as they were and would regard anyone else getting more money as detrimental to him. He not only wanted to earn large amounts of money, but he also did not want others to earn as much, and that fact was of as much satisfaction to him as the absolute quantity of his own earnings. As you may guess, the group did not progress far towards establishing new methods of working.

Where money is the motivator, there is one sense in which management is easy. People so inclined will be prepared to tolerate any amount of boredom, work long hours, undertake repetitive tasks over periods of months and years and put work before family. Provided they are earning what they see as a satisfactory amount of money, such matters as job design are likely to receive scant attention. If these issues are raised, they may even be regarded with suspicion on the grounds that they might adversely affect earnings. If management insist on introducing the subject, they will need to do so on the basis that, at worst, they will not impair earnings or, at best, they might increase them. As a general rule, unless the situation is currently fraught with problems, managers should endeavour to introduce good job redesign on the grounds that it will be beneficial.

How do we motivate these people when they fail to deliver, or when their performance deteriorates? As a rule we will not have much time. The poor performers will not be allowed to retain important territories or activities if they are failing to deliver the required business. That means that we must have thought out in advance how we intend to deal with poor performance. In doing this we will obviously need to be aware of the requirements of employment law. The first step will be to check the rewards and make certain that they are still capable of providing the motivational incentive required. The second will be to check if there are any personal factors that are creating temporary problems, for example, family, bereavement or divorce. More permanent factors are likely to include a deterioration in personal health, and drug and alcohol abuse. There may even be a matter of updating skills or retraining.

The remedies to be applied depend on the causes of the deterioration. Short-term factors are the most susceptible to treatment or to the healing powers of time. Depending on the business situation, people with these sorts of problems are likely to return to good performance and to continue to earn the high sums that they require. Longer-term factors almost certainly mean taking people away from the job and probably removing them from the high-earning environment. What happens to them after that is a matter of career counselling or other appropriate action. Their need for money might remain, but the sad fact is that their capacity to earn it has diminished and they will need to look to their secondary motivators. If they are particularly lucky, they might be able to become high earners again at a later date.

What happens to those people who want high material reward and who are successful in obtaining it? Will they want even more or will they give up and aim for something else? The answer is that it depends on the person, but it seems that those who strive for more and more money are fewer in number than those who, having achieved a good level, decide to seek other rewards. Most professional and managerial people in our study who score high on this factor seem to relax their attitude after attaining what they perceive as a good level of financial reward.

> *There is no absolute sum that satisfies; each person just knows when the level that satisfies them has been reached. In interviews, sums as low as £20 000 per annum (slightly above the then UK average) satisfied one public sector worker aged 34, although he scored 41 on this factor (he referred to this as a 'living and comfortable wage'), whereas one 28-year-old IT professional (scoring 42) felt that her current £75 000 plus car and benefits could be much improved (now that she had been 'nearly fourteen months in the job').*

Factor 1 low, other factors evenly spread

Low factor 1 means that money is not a significant motivator. Other factors are more important. However, people with a low money drive do not expect to be exploited. On the contrary, if they are paid below what they think is 'fair', they will be de-motivated (Herzberg, 1966). Their approach to pay will be governed by the concept of 'felt fairness'. That is, their relativity to the outside world and to those within their own world must feel fair. If they are seriously out of line and they feel underpaid, for example, at the time of writing, university lecturers, they will tend to feel de-motivated. Motivation will then require strenuous attention to the other motivators.

In summary, money may not motivate these staff to greater effort, but they will be seriously de-motivated if paid less than the 'fair' rate for the job. Serious and prolonged discrepancies in earnings will undermine effectiveness and commitment. One of the most likely responses to such a situation would be for lecturers to secure as many 'moonlighting' opportunities as they can in other organizations. Acceptable in moderate degree, these 'consultancies' and other means of augmenting a low income can adversely affect a lecturer's work for his employer if they take too much of his time and effort.

Factor 1, factor 2 (physical conditions)

Generally people who have high money needs will regard their physical conditions at work with complete indifference. To use an historical analogy, we could call it the Klondike effect, after the early gold miners in the Klondike gold rush who spent days and even months panning for gold, looking for 'paydirt'. The modern equivalent is dealers who work in crowded and noisy conditions, possibly allowing themselves a hasty sandwich at lunchtime.

This does not mean that these same people, when they have made the money, will not want to spend it on luxury furnishing and accommodation. They might, but in work terms, physical conditions are irrelevant, except when they impair performance. In that context, managers may want to provide, for example, luxury 'power' offices and furniture where these are necessary for the right ambience for the business in hand. Otherwise, the conditions should be those that are appropriate and acceptable for the business being conducted.

By an odd quirk, those with low money needs but high physical comfort needs are the least likely to be able to afford, or receive, the comfort they want.

Factor 1, factor 3 (structure)

In motivating people with a high need for money we need to look particularly closely at their need for structure. For some jobs, a need for structure or at the very least an ability to work with structure is essential. For other jobs, structure needs are an impediment.

Structure needs are helpful where there is statutory regulation such as in the insurance or financial services industry. In those industries, failure to comply can be exceptionally damaging to the organization and the individuals concerned. Our motivation is concerned with balancing the tensions between the drive to accumulate, regardless of how it is done, and the need to conform.

People with high structure needs will be the easiest to motivate. They will find themselves unable to proceed unless they have done it the correct way. Indeed, they may take pleasure in demonstrating their compliance to clients. They will naturally build conformance into their approach to business. A large part of the motivation of such people lies in training and testing them on conformance and giving them the personal security they require to do business. Indeed, the business of training can be made enjoyable, with games and tests to demonstrate their competence, with particular emphasis on speed and accuracy. If they are launched into business without that confidence, they are likely to feel de-motivated and will either be unsuccessful or make mistakes.

Those with low structure needs should be steered away from such jobs. When the pressure is on, it is likely that the need to make the sale will dominate the need to comply. People who are in these jobs need close conformance supervision, something they will find irksome. The ideal situation would be to make checking conformance automatic, so that activities cannot be completed until the necessary acts have been undertaken. The problem is that such people will be tempted to cheat and there are probably few activities where such automatic checking is possible.

People with low structure needs are better in unregulated, *caveat emptor*, environments. They will be empathic, will twist and turn and do whatever is necessary to achieve the sale or complete the activity. There will be no fulfilment of needs in any sort of orderly manner. Motivating them will involve giving them maximum discretion and freedom. However, they will need to be precisely targeted to ensure that what they sell or do is in line with what the business requires and they will need first-class backup and support because they will be unable to supply that for themselves. Better still, they should be spoiled and pampered, but watched like hawks!

Factor 1, factor 4 (people contact)

It seems curious that people will do serious business involving large sums of money with those with whom they do not expect to maintain a long-term relationship. They do so, of course, either because those with whom they are dealing are very persuasive, because the organization they are dealing with has a reputation for honourable dealings, or because there is some body of law or custom which will protect them if things go wrong. Thus one of the ways in which we can motivate those with high money needs and a high need to work with large numbers of people is to ensure that the reputation of the company is valued, that the systems and backup administration work and that, if they go wrong, the mistakes are rectified quickly.

Another way to motivate is to focus on their relationships needs. Obviously, people with high money needs and a high need to rub shoulders with people should be steered in that direction. If their money need is very high, they will want to be able to achieve sufficient average earnings from their many contacts or they will not be able to achieve their financial targets. They attain satisfaction from doing little more than 'rubbing shoulders' and the more people they can do this with, the better they like it. Motivating them will involve talking to them at regular intervals and listening to what they say about their contacts and about their continuing satisfaction in working with a range of other people.

If their need for longer-term relationships is also high, we will see the conversion of casual into deep relationships and can help motivate them by discussing the relationships side of their work and facilitating moves they want to make. People with an above average need for short-term relationships are more likely to have an above average need for longer-term relationships. Having said that, the scores for long- and short-term relationships in our survey are relatively low.

If their need for people contact is low, we should establish how they relate in the longer term. If that is also low, we should establish whether they can relate to people at all. If they cannot, they need work which makes few demands on their social skills. However, many people have low needs but are perfectly functional in the working environment. They can manage to get along with people though they may take an instrumental view of relationships; that is, do what is necessary to get the work done. We motivate these people by concentrating on the other factors. They do not need to be brought into contact with large numbers of people, nor do they want to build longer-term relationships. They want to achieve, to develop themselves or to make money. That is where we should concentrate our effort. In fact, if they are motivated by, for example, a longer-term share option scheme, they may not want our motivational help at all.

Factor 1, factor 5 (relationships)

Those who are high factor 1/high factor 5 probably put considerable effort into building a reputation for reliability and integrity. They will want the people with whom they are dealing to be comfortable with them and to trust them. Every statement and action will be tested for probity. The benefit of all possible doubts will be given. Immediate gain will be forgone in the expectation that future gain, over and above those that would come from shorter-term relationships, will be forthcoming. Playing the long game involves risks, of course. The relationship may not develop as hoped; the people with whom they are trying to bond may move on or not be capable of delivering.

An important part of motivating such people is to make certain that the organization supports their integrity and does not allow them to be embarrassed by lack of support. Another part is to reassure them in those dark days when they work at building a relationship but are not yet receiving any financial reward. It can be done both by re-confirming organizational commitment and by being available to talk with them when progress seems slow and uncertain. It can be supplemented by giving them the opportunity to achieve satisfaction in other areas which, though possibly of lower priority, provide sufficient stimulus to occupy them and maintain their motivation. When the relationship flourishes and becomes rewarding, we will respect it, but at the same time maintain sufficient contact so that the prime focus of loyalty remains the organization for which we both work and not the client.

Factor 1, factor 6 (recognition)

Those who have a high need for money and make money have, in effect, already achieved the recognition they required. However, our research showed that about half of those with an above average need for money also have an above average need for recognition. That is, they want somebody to tell them how well they have done. Obviously, we motivate these people by giving them explicit recognition from somebody whom they see as significant. We consult them as to the form in which they would like to be recognized, making suggestions for such approaches as reporting their achievements in the organization's magazine, having dinner with important senior managers and so on.

We should be curious about the recognition they seek from customers. If they have no concern about personal recognition from this quarter, we should try to ensure that this is not reflected in carelessness, leading eventually to problems. We can explore attitudes in conversation, motivating a change in stance by reflecting to them the more positive attitudes of those from whom recognition is important; and having those people do it as well. If there is an excessive need for recognition from clients, this can be beneficial because it will lead to the wish to provide high quality goods or services. We can motivate by supporting this approach and seeking their views on the quality of the goods and services they provide. We may, however, need to maintain the balance between the interests of the client and our organization. If the client gives recognition, and we do not, then the balance may tilt to the client and our interests may be neglected in favour of the interests of the client.

People with low money needs but high recognition needs will probably do whatever is required for recognition regardless of the personal financial cost. They are motivated by allowing them the opportunity to work towards recognition through certain tasks.

Many people in the public sector, who are often not particularly well paid, are motivated by a sense of public service. Those who have a high recognition need will benefit from explicit recognition. In the UK one of the more explicit forms of public recognition is the Honours List. Here people who have given good service, often for little or even no monetary reward, are offered public and permanent recognition.

Factor 1, factor 7 (achievement)

According to this research, of those with an above average need for money, twice as many have a below-the-average need for achievement as an above-the-average need. That is to say, there are significantly different approaches to making money, requiring two different methods of motivation.

Those with a high achievement drive are possibly the easiest to motivate. They require targets, measurement and they want to do it themselves; the achievement has to be theirs. The target does not need to be set by them, nor do they require a large input into setting it. Their effort will lead to their reward. They will probably thrive in a sales environment where at the end of every sales period they can look with satisfaction on how well they have done against target, preferably beating it. If they have a high recognition need as well, they will require explicit recognition of their achievement.

Those who have a high need for money and a low need for achievement are best kept out of a targeted environment. They will not enjoy making the effort to achieve 'artificial' targets and will be de-motivated very quickly. Their motivation will come from some other factor, like creativity or the exercise of power. We are now in a world where to be second is to achieve little reward, but to be first is to receive a reward that is disproportionate; or where to be adequate is to receive a reasonable salary, but to be superb is to receive one that is twenty times as great. We can see this by looking at the rewards received by sports champions, top solicitors and business people compared with the majority who are, relatively speaking, merely capable.

The motivation is in helping them realize their particular skills, whether by providing the technical training and resources that enable them to improve or counselling them through the human feelings and dramas that will occupy them as they develop their abilities. Their effort is probably best concentrated on skills development. The money they receive is important to them but is almost a residual. It depends on the demands of the market-place, in our example, for sport or legal services. The 'take' can be improved by skilful negotiation, but it is against a background of high demand.

Factor 1, factor 8 (power and influence)

Power is achieving things through other people. The measure of achievement in modern industry and commerce is through such indicators as profit and return on capital. Those who have ability and rise to the top can exercise power and achieve material reward, not only through salary and perks, but also through incentives like share option schemes. More generally, if the drives for power and money are sufficiently intense, given the ability, the drives are mutually reinforcing and the rewards can be exceptional. People with high power and money drives are likely to lead lives of intense activity, to live dangerously, to face the ever-present possibility of failure, and to be tempted to go that one step too far. They will probably inspire, in equal measure, love and hatred. Given the ability, the place for those who have a high need for power and a high money drive is undoubtedly industry and commerce. Government and the public service can satisfy the power drive, but usually fail to satisfy the need for money.

How do we motivate these people? Firstly, as far as possible we provide the technical and financial skills necessary. We say 'as far as possible' because our people may well be operating at the frontiers of technical and financial knowledge and the skills they require may not easily be taught. We should also be prepared to train them in leadership and the basics of employment law. Secondly, we explicitly recognize that the motivation to power is different from most of the other motivating factors in that power acts on other people who may want to resist it. As a consequence, those exercising power need both skill and a thick skin. The only way we can see if these are present is through practice. Our problem is that the exercise of power, as opposed to routine supervision, involves risk. We need to limit the disadvantages by ensuring that the risks at the start of the process can be contained, that is, the business can support any consequences of failure.

We motivate by regular review of the exercise of power. We review both what has been successful and what has not and draw lessons. We make ourselves available for consultation if required. Ideally, we appoint a senior manager in the same field as a mentor, specifically to discuss power issues and organizational politics. As with other factors, the need for money and power must be focused on the requirements of the business as well as on personal needs. We can help this process by clearly stating what the business wants and any incentives to help secure this. For example, if we have a share option scheme, it cannot be manipulated against the interests of the business.

Our study suggests that most of those low on factor 1, are high on the need for influence. For such people, power and money do not work in tandem. The exercise of influence is more compelling and the absence of a strong money drive probably means its exercise takes place in the public and charitable sectors. Such a profile is probably the foundation of the 'voluntary' culture of the UK and the USA.

Factor 1, factor 9 (variety and change)

Those with a high need for variety and for money will want to try and satisfy their money needs by indulging their need for variety. There are a number of ways in which they can do this. Firstly, if the need is not too strong, they can work in an area in which there is variety but within the same overall framework. For example, if they are so trained, they can work at the end of the consumer interface which demands novelty but within a defined product class. They could thus find themselves in the less exciting areas of marketing or new product development. Obviously, they are more likely to be successful if they have a strong creative drive as well. There needs to be close scrutiny of the business benefits of the ideas generated, but in the consumer areas at least, ideas can be tested at relatively low cost without committing the organization.

Where the need for variety is rather more pronounced, we might have problems with people who will want plenty of variety but will not always have the wish to follow things through. We motivate these people by having them work in a fast moving, unstable environment so that they do not have the chance to feel stale. The greater the need for variety, the more unstable the environment in which they will be happy to operate.

The precise mode of motivation depends on the backup factors. For example, somebody with an achievement drive would need targets; somebody with a strong influence drive would require a variety of situations in which to exercise power, and so on. Those with high structure needs as well, an apparent contradiction in terms, will want to move from one area where they know what is required of them, to another area where the same applies. Our research shows that about 30 per cent of those with an above average change need have an above average structure need.

The potentially key weakness of people with this drive is that they will wish to move on as soon as they become bored. In business terms this could be a problem; we need to make sure that either an important part of the financial incentive focuses on completion, or that they are able to hand over to another who will complete what they have started and still achieve their financial reward. Motivation, then, involves recognizing strengths and compensating for weaknesses.

For those with exceptionally high needs for variety and money, say 55 plus for each, we may have serious problems. They may be tempted to satisfy their personal needs by speculation on the stock market, or if they want real thrills, on the futures and options markets where there are enormous opportunities to make money but also to lose it. Companies should be careful about allowing people with this profile to put the company's money at risk. It should be made clear that they themselves must carry any personal losses, on their own account and that the company will not bail them out. Financial controls need to be watertight with immediate feedback. The problem is not so much motivation but ensuring that the company keeps control over where it is being taken. The company can be marginally happier if the need for variety is being satisfied outside work, by activities like paragliding on Everest! These people may be best working in some financial market on their own account, or in a high risk, high return, sales market.

If the need for variety is low, then people with this profile can get on with the business of making money. No matter how routine or boring the task, no matter how many times they start with the same opening gambit, there is no problem. They will have their eye on the pay-off and that is sufficient reward. Unlike those with a high need for variety who may be prepared to risk their money, they are more likely to guard it. It does not mean we can relax the financial controls, but it will be easier to track what is happening.

Factor 1, factor 10 (creativity)

Those with a high need for money and for creativity are probably – unless they are exceptionally talented – in an unfortunate position. Rewards for creativity, for the successful, are enormous, but standards are phenomenally high and the competition intense. We can see this most easily in the fields of sport and the arts. It is also true in business.

Managing those of exceptional creativity is not easy. They do not particularly want to be managed. However, if creativity and money needs go hand in hand, they will accept a brief. It is important to establish that the brief is correct and that any client knows what he or she wants. That may, of course, mean considerable effort because the clients may not know what they want and have to be helped to define their requirements. If the creative party is involved in helping define the brief, there may well be friction between his or her creativity and what the client needs. Bringing the monetary reward back into the discussion will help provide the necessary focus.

In general, people with these drives are best motivated by working in a permissive environment, where new ideas are encouraged, where there is usually an environment of low structure and fun, and where the culture is of no blame. In this context, 'low structure' means lax discipline about hours of work, standards of dress and hierarchy. Usually, the hours worked in this type of organization will be at least as long as elsewhere, though they will not conform to normal office hours, and dress will turn out to be smart but casual.

For those of lower creativity, the rewards will not usually be so great. There may be a constant tension between their need for money and their ability to create. They also need a relatively permissive environment. If their creativity generates the money they require, they will be relatively easily managed. If not, it may be necessary to look to their other motivators. If they have a high recognition need it may be useful to spend time reinforcing their self-esteem, perhaps encouraging them when they produce work not quite up to standard, and making them feel particularly good when they have done well. If there is a structure need, it might be useful to hold workshops or offer opportunities to work through various creativity techniques, like brainstorming or Synectics, all of which provide a structure within which creativity can take place. It may be necessary, if they do not produce the money they need, to encourage them to move on to some other activity, saving their creativity for their leisure time.

If they have a high need for money but a low need for creativity, they can accept any task, no matter how tedious, and satisfy themselves that the money makes it all worth while. The considerations outlined earlier in this chapter then apply.

Factor 1, factor 11 (self-development)

A high factor 11 need can be an important driving force for a high factor 1 score. Those so endowed are likely to drive themselves to acquire the skills necessary to achieve the high income required, possibly to the exclusion of skills that do not have a monetary value. Motivation involves the provision of time and resources to enable the learning to take place. It involves not only learning off the job, for example, through taking an MBA, but also providing opportunities at work for them to learn from projects and from the work experience by systematic and regular debriefing. It is worth noting, however, that part of the self-development drive may not be money related, and that there could be benefit in informally encouraging that aspect of self-development even if only by ensuring that, as far as possible, their timetables are respected.

If the need for self-development is low, then encourage them to work to make their money. However, there may be an element of compulsion required to ensure they learn what is necessary for them to be successful at work. This research shows that two-thirds of those with an above the norm money drive have a below the norm need for self-development. This research also suggests that most of those who have a low need for money, have a high need for self-development. That is to say, the energy that is spent by high factor 1 people on acquiring money is used by low factor 1 people to pursue self-development. It is probably fair to say that most of those who pursue self-development, for example, teachers, academics, musicians and crafts people, are not very well paid. They are best managed if they are encouraged to feel that their opportunities for self-development compensate for their lack of money.

Factor 1, factor 12 (interest and usefulness)

Those in well-paid and interesting jobs are probably the most fortunate. They will certainly require little in the way of management. The main management task will be to make sure that as they indulge their job interest, they are delivering whatever it is for which they are well paid.

For the motivator, it is worth bearing in mind that what they regard as interesting may not be what you regard as interesting or even worthwhile. For the purposes of motivation we need to appreciate their interest and learn enough about it to meet them on their own ground and reflect back to them what they see as worthwhile. If they start to have doubts about the interest or usefulness of their work, we need to help them through their doubts. If we are unable to do this to their satisfaction, there may be a tension between the two drives which will lead to worsening performance. If we cannot resolve the matter, they are likely to move on in an attempt to reunite the two drives.

Those who have a high drive for job interest but a low drive for money are likely to find themselves interested but not well paid. Managing them involves encouraging them to feel they have enough job interest to compensate for the lack of money.

Factor 2

Physical conditions

Highest score recorded = 83
Lowest score recorded = 0
Mode 17 Median 17

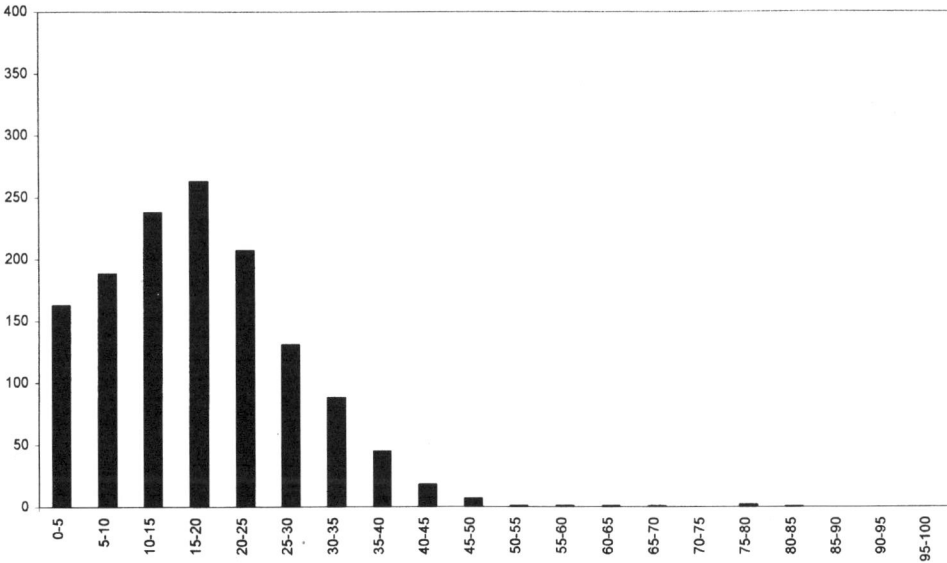

Figure 2   Factor 2: histogram of scores

Factor 2 high

The norm for working conditions is low, in fact the lowest of all factors, with both the mode and median at 17. Relative to other motivators, physical working conditions, on average, are not seen as important. For some they are important. The highest score is 83 and there are several scores of the order of 50 plus. Although there is not enough information to make categorical statements, the compensating lower scores seem to occur in the achievement and influence drives. That is to say, there is a preference for comfort rather than achievement or influence. One can only speculate that low achievers are rewarded by physical accommodation that is so appalling that the need for comfort becomes an overriding consideration!

There is, however, some evidence (mainly from interviews with people who have scored highly on this factor) that, at its higher levels, there is an element of *compensation*. This means that a high need for factor 2 is a displacement for some other need. Perhaps it is a convenient (and socially acceptable) way to register dissatisfaction with a boss or with the faceless 'they' of senior management. It is unlikely that the need will be met by a redecoration of the offices, by better sound reduction measures and by expensive furnishings. A wise manager would look first at the human relationships in the department and at the culture and climate of the organization itself.

The temptation not to do so is strong. Many managers are more willing to alter the physical circumstances of the workplace than they are to try to realign or improve relationships, or to change their own behaviour. This is not surprising when we remember the generally low needs scored on factors 4 and 5 (the 'social' needs). Either managers do not realize that workers' complaints about seemingly trivial matters are important, or they may be unable to even perceive that such things could cause problems. Worse, they might acknowledge others' differing needs, but be unprepared to adapt or to make an effort to meet them.

The lesson is that if staff are complaining vociferously about their physical conditions of work, it might be useful to try to establish if their complaints are a cover for something else. We sit and listen attentively to what they have to say, and provide enough time for other topics to be introduced, if appropriate. If not, then physical conditions are likely to be the problem, the solution to which, if funds are available, is a physical upgrade. If other topics are introduced, we explore and, if possible, provide relevant solutions.

Factor 2 low

For others, physical conditions appear to be totally irrelevant to their working life. The lowest score of zero occurs 22 times in our sample of 1355. We do not know whether the scores are low because the modern offices and factories in which they work are so agreeable that the question of comfort does not arise, or whether their indifference is fundamental. That is to say, they would be indifferent to the physical conditions, or at least not concerned about them, no matter how bad they were.

Interviewing some people with low scores on factor 2 who work in not-so-pleasant conditions shows that they are, indeed, indifferent to their surroundings. Several express surprise that such things should be considered noteworthy at all; for them dust, noise and other physical discomforts are to be expected and are, therefore, hardly noticed unless at a very high level. Others take a relativistic view. One site engineer was of the opinion that he did not mind how bad conditions were on site, but when he was at HQ he did like to have good working conditions. Presumably, he did not want to be seen as having to tolerate worse conditions than the Head Office staff. In those circumstances, there was a clear link between status and physical conditions. The need for good physical conditions was merely a proxy for his need for status. Another engineer, who worked on a Japanese building site, retorted that conditions on his site were excellent, the site was clean and tidy and he would not expect less. He nevertheless felt he would be able to tolerate poor physical conditions if they were the norm for his particular employer.

Where physical conditions are excellent, there are often other important factors at play. A quick glance at the Elysée Palace, for example, soon establishes overt messages about status and power. The White House messages are similar, though 10 Downing Street understates what seems to be the actual power of the incumbent. In a more humble way, the UK Civil Service used to relate status to size of office and area of carpet. In the lower echelons the conditions were probably not particularly salubrious, but any deviation from the expected norm, in either direction, was likely to be accompanied by serious bureaucratic disruption and personal trauma.

The fact that scores are low on factor 2 suggests, in addition to any displacement effects, that the link between physical conditions at work and status may have been partially eroded. There are many examples to back up such a suggestion. Firms like IBM have 'hot desk' policies: you arrive at work and plug in your computer at any desk that happens to be available; you do not have a permanent home. Directors often choose to sit in open plan offices, using the same size of desk as the 'workers'. In so doing, they emphasize that they are part of the team. The situation was set out very clearly by Andrew Grove, the Chief Executive Officer of Intel, the computer chip maker, as early as 1983.

> We at Intel frequently ask junior members of the organisation to participate jointly in a decision-making meeting with senior managers. This only works if everybody at the meeting voices opinions and beliefs as *equals*, forgetting or ignoring status differentials. And it is much easier to achieve this if the organisation doesn't separate its senior and junior people with limousines, plush offices and private dining rooms. (Grove, 1983)

Cynics might argue that the size of their pay packets dispels any notion that they are just one of the lads or lasses. Nevertheless, even that confirms the move away from physical conditions as an indicator of status.

At a different level, the general acceptance of poor quality architecture, as is certainly the case in the UK and often elsewhere, may be a higher level manifestation of indifference to physical conditions. Interestingly, the people interviewed, generally satisfied with their physical working conditions, actually work in a very wide range of conditions. They range from plush City offices with wood panelling and thick carpets to the most basic and functional. However, even those who work in unsatisfactory open plan offices, with noise and lack of privacy, generally do not score high on factor 2. Conditions become part of the way of life. They may not be liked, and they may be complained about but, compared to other motivators, they are not rated as significant.

One of the much-cited Hawthorne experiments at a General Electric (USA) wiring factory in the late 1920s, confirms the situation. As part of their experiment into the impact of working conditions, researchers improved some aspects (heating, lighting and so on). They then reversed the changes, establishing the impact of these changes on productivity. Whatever the researchers did, even when they had the workforce operating in deteriorating conditions, productivity increased! (Roethlisberger and Dickson, 1939.)

The precise conclusion is much argued about, but there is no doubt that factors such as trying to please the researchers, variations in the quality of supervision, the rewards available to the teams and the fact that the workers were now the focus of attention, contributed to the improved productivity. The Hawthorne experiments have led to general agreement that social factors have a strong influence on work behaviour, certainly a stronger impact than physical working conditions.

The Human Relations school which developed after Hawthorne suggested a simplistic model in which workers treated 'properly' would respond by supporting high production goals and would also help one another. Sadly it was not to be, and experience and further studies have shown that unhappy workers can be highly productive, while satisfied workers in cohesive groups can be unproductive. If happiness (which would suggest satisfied needs) and unhappiness cannot be correlated with productivity, what chance is there for physical working conditions to have an impact? The answer, of course, is very little, and this appears to be borne out by our research. People do not, as a rule, rate physical conditions as a motivating factor. Intrinsic or internal motivational factors like reward, achievement and power, attract more points on average than contextual or external drives, like working conditions.

The factors in which the average scores are higher than the norm for physical conditions, that is reward, achievement, power and so on, are intrinsic factors, that is to say, they are internal rather than external motivators. The question of happiness or unhappiness, with internal motivators, can become irrelevant. We believe that if what people have to do fits in with what motivates them, they will be capable of giving that much more, for a longer time, and more effectively at times of stress, than if it does not. In all of this, the need for good physical working conditions does not have a significant part to play and is low on the list of drivers.

Factor 2 high, and other factors

Since physical conditions are relatively unimportant as a motivator, there is no advantage in a detailed comparison with each other factor. However, there are some interesting relationships which are worth noting, with a distinct watershed in the trend and with some implications for motivation.

Thus, half of those with an above average need for physical comfort have an above average need for money. They presumably know what they want to do with their money! For those people, money can motivate. Over half of those with an above average factor 2, have an above average need for structure and 60 per cent an above average need for long-term relationships. In other words, there is an emphasis on the factors creating stability in their lives. In contrast, with this group there is a significantly below average need for the higher level drivers. Thus only one-third have a higher than average need for recognition. For most of them, good physical conditions are important for the comfort they provide and not as a sign of recognition.

Thirty per cent of the group have a higher than average need for achievement. With them, it is possible that good physical conditions help with achievement. The remainder want to be comfortable and have a low drive to achieve. Just over one-third have an above average need for influence. Two-thirds want comfort and have an average or below average need for influence. Forty per cent are above the mode on their need for autonomy and self-development. Thirty per cent have an above average need for interest and significance. Thus most are below the mode on these two factors.

In terms of motivating those high on factor 2, we have to look to the elements that provide stability, structure and long-term relationships. We will find that most are relatively low on those factors that lead people to exert themselves and to contribute to organizational purpose, achievement, influence, creativity, self-development and job interest. If we need to motivate them, we have to find at least one of those drivers, personal to them, which will stimulate effort, because there is no doubt that increasing levels of comfort is unlikely to provide the incentive that is required.

Factor 3

Structure

Highest score recorded = 69
Lowest score recorded = 0
Mode 26 Median 25

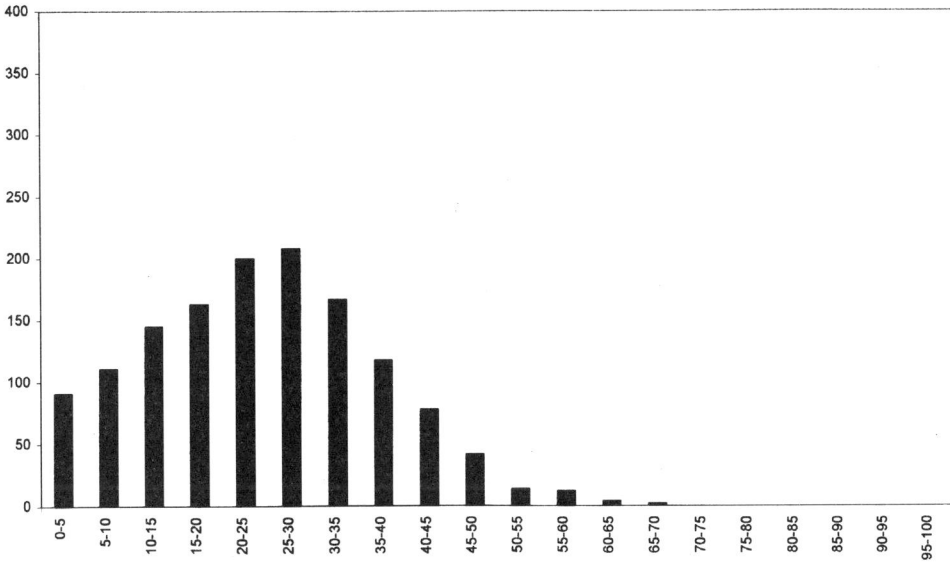

Figure 3   **Factor 3: histogram of scores**

People with differing structure requirements need to be motivated in significantly different ways. The right approach will motivate, the wrong approach seriously de-motivate. At the extreme, if people are wrongly handled, they will be unable to function.

Very highly structured people need to know exactly where they stand. They want to know the rules and need to be reassured that they have followed the correct procedures. Anxiety may be the root cause of their desire for structure and they will find a lack of structure very stressful. They will have problems accepting change. In contrast, people with very low structure needs resent rules and can take strong exception to any attempt to constrain them. They may also be stressed, but for different reasons. However, in compensation, they will be prepared to work in situations of considerable ambiguity and uncertainty. They will want to be managed with a light touch. Both their motivational needs and the needs of the organization should be protected and developed. With such people there should be less difficulty in accepting change.

Factor 3 high, other factors evenly spread

The features of structure, besides the physical (e.g. desks, chairs, working areas), are those that help to limit, organize and control. They include:

- time,
- rules and procedures,
- regularity of events,
- society's norms and expectations,
- religion and ritual,
- repetition,
- predictability,
- planning, and
- good communication (especially written).

All these features serve useful purposes in ordering our lives, but there are important differences in individuals' perceptions of the degree of order needed.

Some people need a great deal of structure. Those who would wish to have the world more orderly, predictable and under control tend to score high on factor 3. To them, rules are good, helping to order the world and to keep chaos at bay. Such people value the apparent certainty and predictability of structure. Rules are seen as limiters, constraints to action and as helping to establish boundaries of permission, all of which reduce uncertainty and its inevitable companion, anxiety. High factor 3s are managed and motivated either with the order they require, or by creating a situation in which they can develop their own order. This immediately creates a problem because we do not live in an ordered world, and the requirements of those with high structure needs may conflict with what we can provide.

Motivation, then, involves finding a balance between these two forces. What considerations should guide us? The first is that we should provide a hard core of order which will present a framework against which all other activities can take place. Consider, for example, the operation of a platform in the harsh environment of the North Sea. Inevitably in such an environment, there will be a need to react quickly to genuinely unpredictable events. There will be a requirement, say, to order some equipment as a matter of extreme urgency. The order will be placed over the satellite link and there will be no paperwork. The buying and accounts departments may be put to a great deal of trouble and anybody in there who happens to have high structure needs will find themselves breaking rules and procedures in a way which makes them unsettled. They will co-operate, of course, because the job has to be done. They will be motivated by an explicit recognition that breaking the rules is wrong and by being encouraged to complete all procedures retrospectively.

If they are unable to demonstrate that degree of flexibility they will need to be relegated to some area of work where such unpredictability never happens, or to work in an area where the needs for compliance are overarching, that is, they become a principal component of the job. Extreme rigidity probably means either working at a very low level or being unemployable. However, we run into problems. When we are looking at significant change rather than temporary dislocation, the best approach is to define as precisely as possible the requirements of the new state and to give people plenty of training in what will now be expected. They thus feel that they are moving from one structured state to another and their resistance is likely to be weakened.

Factor 3 low, other factors evenly spread

Those who feel that enough rules and controls are already in place tend to score low on factor 3. Some need so little structure that they are constrained by its presence, finding any 'givens', rules or parameters irksome and frustrating, as is any attempt to establish their future intentions which will be seen as limiting their options. Any attempt to regulate or control such a person will be resented and can lead to conflict. The fact that there may be perfectly sensible reasons for knowing their future intentions, for example, allowing for the provision of resources, will be disregarded.

Low factor 3 seems to operate as a positive motivator to remove, reduce or escape perceived controls. Those so endowed feel that they would be happier and more productive if there were fewer rules and constraints. They may show a negative attitude to those whom they see as needing rules. These feelings may be reciprocated by the more rule-bound, on the grounds that unstructured behaviour causes problems that they have to clear up. Differing structure needs can be a root cause of personality clashes.

How can such people be managed? The main requirement is that they contribute. They should be targeted by management who need to specify, precisely, the outcomes required from them and to define them at the highest possible level. At senior levels, we can be talking about return on capital, or about the research contribution required, in terms which are as general as possible but still meet the requirements of the organization. We once met a very senior Customs and Excise auditor whose score on factor 3 was zero, and whose behaviour confirmed his score. He would be motivated, for example, by a general requirement to target fraud in a particular area.

The problem then becomes what to do about the low structure need and the need of the organization to have systems and records? If the person is senior enough, it might be possible to provide assistants to take care of that side of the business. This might not be a satisfactory solution if the assistants are treated in a cavalier manner, and left to cope with inadequate information and minimal co-operation; behaviour which is a distinct possibility. The solution in this situation is to make sure that a low structure need colleague understands the extent to which the company values and benefits from their lack of structure, but to explain that, although we have made it as easy as possible for them, the full benefits of their work cannot be enjoyed without their administrative co-operation. It is a message that will probably need to be delivered on a regular basis. Management can supplement it by trying to help them to develop a constructive working relationship with the administrators, so that the administrative side of the business is delivered as a personal favour. But it is an area on which management will need to keep careful watch and might find that motivational efforts are continually required.

If they do not have an assistant and the company is unable to provide one, there may be problems. Once again, we should recognize explicitly their lack of structure and their contribution, and urge them to produce the information or the administration required. The problem that may arise is that of being perceived as naggers. The best approach is to attempt to motivate them with wry humour or sometimes to display anger: 'how can we deal with these important matters when we have to sort out your admin? Let's get it out of the way!' If they will not co-operate and the effort/reward ratio becomes unbalanced – too much effort is required to benefit from their lack of structure – we may need to consider whether they have a future with the company.

In considering people's structure needs, management should also take into account that these needs are likely to fluctuate over time and circumstances, rising in times of insecurity and change and declining when there is stability. Thus, for example, a low structure person undergoing divorce proceedings is quite likely to look for some areas of stability and may seek to find it at work. Their tolerance of uncertainty may decrease for a time. Conversely, we are accumulating limited evidence that some people with very low structure needs score even lower on this factor when they are retested at a time of personal change and instability: this seems to apply in cases where scores are lower than 10 points.

Factor 3, factor 1 (money and tangible rewards)

People with a high structure need and a high need for money are motivated by placing them in a situation where the two needs do not conflict. However, it is probably fair to say that those who live by rules and structure are not usually highly rewarded. The average provincial solicitor will confirm that is the case, and so will people like police officers who, by definition, exist to enforce structure.

Nevertheless, high structure, high earners do exist and they divide into two general classes: those who have to generate business before they can earn and those who do not. Let us first look at those who have to generate business. Such people are found, for example, in the financial services industry. The aim there is to make money and to keep out of trouble by complying with the requirements of the regulators. High structure people comply and are ideal for keeping the industry out of the hands of the regulator.

The problem for managers is that those with high structure and high money needs are less likely to seek out their own customers and to display the sorts of initiatives which create the level of business required. They are more likely to want their leads supplied to them than to generate their own. Thus, although they may be safer in terms of compliance or fulfilment, they will probably need constant supervision in creating business. If managers regard compliance as the priority, then they must try to create a situation where those who comply can earn enough money to satisfy themselves. If this cannot be done, there is likely to be tension between the competing drives. Ultimately the structure need will dominate and the money required will, if possible, be earned elsewhere.

Let us now look at the other general area for those with high structure, high money needs. This is found in those activities where preoccupation with rules is highly rewarded. An example might be the ability to programme in an obscure computer language for which there is high demand and practitioners are in short supply. Motivation in those circumstances is relatively easy: make the reward proportionate to the output and people will motivate themselves. If there is genuine scope for differences in view, there might be a problem in ensuring quality as well as quantity. An important part of motivation will be specifying the quality requirements at the outset. There is then agreement on what needs to be done and problems caused by ambiguity, which are particularly de-motivating, will be avoided. It will probably be helpful to include a review clause, so that if new problems arise, the contract can be revised in a way which is fair to both parties, taking into account any scarcity value in the skills being provided.

In general, the really high rewards tend to go to those with a low need for structure and a high need for money. Such people are able to tolerate ambiguity and risk, and to exploit the areas where rules have not been established. They are most successful when they are fleet of foot, seizing opportunities as they arise. A problem might be their failure to establish or to work with the structures necessary to capitalise on the best results of their effort or to maintain their advantage. If they are not careful, they could crash to earth and indeed have been known to do so.

They do not like to be controlled. They value freedom almost more than money. Motivating them is a delicate business, which involves maintaining contact and giving them the freedom to earn, but staying close to them to ensure that they meet the organization's need for structure. We should try to establish the minimum ground rules and the desired outputs at the beginning. We should try to set up automatic monitoring. Then we should give them as much freedom as we can, commensurate with our need to be informed. Such motivation is time consuming, so it can only be afforded where results are forthcoming. The consequences of failure to maintain such contact can be devastating.

Finally, there are those with a high need for structure and a low need for money. Their high need for structure should not be allowed to create organizational paralysis. We can work with them through their other motivators, such as achievement.

Factor 3, factor 2 (physical conditions)

People with high structure needs like to know where they stand virtually all of the time. This means that they like to know where their desk is situated and that the filing cabinet is reasonably close by. What they will not like is 'hot desking', or having to come into the office fighting for an empty desk. They will also be unduly worried about having to move offices or moving from one building to another. Our research suggests that a significant proportion of those with above average structure needs have above average needs for good physical conditions. Above all, high structure demands order and clarity, and shabby but orderly conditions are likely to be preferred to those that are good but unstable.

The motivational demands are, thus, clear; the provision of stable physical working conditions. Stability is not always on offer. If a move is proposed, as much time as possible should be taken to explain the move and to answer any questions. We should try to to solve all the problems raised before the move takes place. If that is not possible, we should try to offer elements of structure, for example, let them bring in their family photographs and put them wherever they are working. At least they then have something to cling to.

In the worst cases, they will find the situation too unstable and will want to leave.

Factor 3, factor 4 (people contact)

High structure people with high people contact needs may like meeting people, but they will prefer to do so on safe ground and in circumstances where there is a degree of predictability. For example, a VAT inspector will be on safe ground meeting taxpayers with whom he or she has to discuss the VAT regulations. A traffic warden may enjoy the work because the contacts are, by and large, structured. However, very high structure people might find even this degree of contact unacceptable. For example, there might be issues that seem to be beyond the regulations, or the people met might become difficult.

To motivate them, let them meet people on familiar ground and structure the interviews so that they follow a predetermined format. As far as possible, avoid the unexpected. If it occurs, take time to listen to them as they describe the difficulties they have encountered and help them to appreciate the overall structure. Particularly difficult problems should be analysed so that they can be fitted into the most appropriate framework.

Below average structure need people are more relaxed about the circumstances in which they meet and would be happy for contacts to take place in an unstructured, unpredictable environment. They are, therefore, able to manage the contacts, but do not necessarily seek them. In motivational terms we need to check that their level of people contact does not become overwhelmingly high.

Factor 3, factor 5 (relationships)

Those with high factor 3 needs might be expected to have a strong preference for longer- rather than shorter-term relationships, if only on the basis that they might not like who they work with but at least they are always there and predictable! Our research suggests that this might be so.

In motivational terms, we need to indulge this need for stability and to keep high factor 3 people together, as long as this stays consistent with business interests. If this is not possible, we create the situation where, even if they are not working together, at least they have access to each other, or they are brought together from time to time on projects, special exercises or in regular meetings. Groups of like-minded, high structure need people are likely to be resistant to change. If we introduce change, we are in danger of de-motivating them. It may be beneficial, in terms of securing change, if we are able to demonstrate that working with the change will enable the relationships to continue, but resisting the change is likely to lead to a break-up. We should not expect too much from this approach where the need for structure seems to be much stronger than the need for relationships.

In motivational terms, management can probably let factor 5 take care of itself, though, as before, keeping a watching brief in case there are problems, which are likely to involve conflicts between organizational and relationships needs.

Factor 3, factor 6 (recognition)

Taken to the extreme, people with high structure and high recognition needs are vulnerable. If they are fortunate, they will receive fulsome recognition for indulging their need to operate within a structure. The company secretaries who keep their companies on the right side of the law, and who satisfy the shareholders and the regulatory authorities, may receive constant approval and recognition from grateful and sensitive management. They will consequently be well motivated.

If they are unlucky, they may be regarded as the drudges who do what is necessary to enable the real work to continue, not at all the recognition they want. In that case, they are likely to seek some mechanism which will allow them to satisfy both needs. If they cannot do so at work, they might, for example, join some professional association, perhaps sitting on a rules committee, developing rules and procedures. They have found the environment in which they can satisfy their need for recognition and structure. If these needs cannot be satisfied at work, they can be motivated by being encouraged to undertake such activities outside work, perhaps as a representative of their employer. Their new-found prestige will help them to undertake structured activities at work which receive low recognition.

Those who are high structure/low recognition will be prepared to undertake work with a high structure component, away from the limelight, and to just get on with it. In the non-work context, they might, for example, be happy to be an auditor for a charity. People read the accounts. The Chairman thanks them. There is perfunctory applause and they are appointed for another year. The work needs to be done and they are happy to do it with minimum recognition. The problem with the work equivalent is that such people might easily be overlooked. They then carry on with routines which become inappropriate because they are not looked at and they are not developed. They move towards inflexibility and become incapable of change and, when change is required, become seriously de-motivated. They reach a plateau and, in the worst cases, they can do nothing with themselves and nothing can be done for them. From a motivational standpoint it is essential that they receive attention and are preferably involved in incremental change. They must not be allowed to develop the expectation that there will be no change.

Those with low factor 3/high recognition needs may do all the sorts of things that get recognized, but ignore the requirements of structure and, perhaps, even the requirements of the organization. Motivation involves withholding recognition, unless what they do benefits the organization and the structure is in place; but being generous and effusive with recognition when it does. This includes letting them know that senior management have been informed and that what they are doing has full approval. There is an absolute necessity for consistency; recognition is always given when earned and always withheld when not. The lesson will soon be learned.

Factor 3, factor 7 (achievement)

People with high structure and high achievement needs can find that these twin drives work both for and against them. The drives work together when the task to be achieved (and measured) takes place in line with the rules in a rule-driven environment.

Motivation is simple when the person's needs and those of the organization coincide. They are given measurable targets, checked for compliance with the rules and given regular feedback. With support and persistence, they may turn out to be self-starters. Ideally, there should always be congruence between what has to be achieved and the rules.

Motivation is more difficult when the drives work against each other, when what has to be achieved needs to take place against or in spite of the rules. The problem is exacerbated where there is conflict between the imposed rules and the rules that this person thinks 'ought' to be. If the conflict is between those latter rules and the achievement drive, there can be real problems. The drives work in opposition to each other, with the need for structure predominating, and can lead to frustration and stress. The situation can arise, for example, when there is a conflict between safety or quality and output.

In this situation, we need to start with the organization's need. To what extent does the organization demand adherence to the rules? If adherence is vital, the consequences of non-adherence are, possibly, prosecution or unacceptable risk. They need to be built into everyday working. Management should establish an audit trail to verify adherence, and to monitor and report back on non-adherence, very quickly. 'Nods and winks' should be avoided, they are ambiguous to high structure need people. It is better to create an environment in which non-adherence is unthinkable. Motivation in these circumstances is time consuming and there may be some people who find the effort too much. They should perhaps be encouraged to move or to transfer.

If achievement is more important to the organization, then cutting across the rules can be accepted more readily. For example, using incorrect purchasing codes may be inconvenient, causing disruption, but may be tolerated if business needs are met. Motivation will in this case be towards providing measurable objectives and feedback, with more of a plea to use the codes than an insistence. High structure need people should be given 'permission' to break the rules, though they may find this stressful. If their structure need is low they will find it easier to cope and may, indeed, relish breaking the rules.

Motivating people with high structure and low achievement drives may be a problem. Such people simply do not want to achieve, or do not want to achieve more than they have to. If the organization can accept work at little more than a level of routine non-achievement, then the principal motivator will be to try to increase their level of performance by techniques such as benchmarking. This will make clear to them what levels of performance are required and will encourage and help them to achieve them. If they are unable or too inflexible to meet them, management have to decide if the cost of supporting their rigidity or low performance outweighs the benefits received.

In general, low structure/high achievers will do whatever is necessary to achieve. They are usually best kept away from areas requiring strict compliance. Outside such areas, they can be very productive.

Factor 3, factor 8 (power and influence)

Motivating those with high structure and high influence needs requires care. We need to have real knowledge of where they wish to exercise their influence. If their drive is to impose order and structure on people who like order and structure, they have the chance to be successful and to be liked. We can motivate them by requiring them to impose structure where structure is required. There may be problems if they try to impose their requirements on others, outside their part of the organization, who may not have high structure needs or who feel that the demands made are too inconvenient to meet. For example, the logistics and supply departments may well have procedures, but they are too demanding for the engineers in the field.

Motivation of these people will involve encouraging them to use structure appropriately but to understand that not everybody shares their fondness for order and predictability. We should remind them that experience suggests it is not possible to make the unstructured more structured and we should steer them to develop systems which are easy for those with low structure needs to use. Those with high structure and low influence needs should be allowed to get on with whatever structured activities they are engaged in.

Those with low structure and high influence needs are probably more effective in those situations where there is ambiguity and considerable change. Those with low structure needs will probably do whatever is necessary to get things done, regardless of the rules. If there are no rules, so much the better. If there is no required output, that also is acceptable. Our problem is to harness their energies to the organization's objectives. When they are focused there, we can start to encourage them to use their influence. Their additional problem might be that, if they feel no need for structure and make no attempt to provide it, or to have somebody else impose it, the organization could dissolve in chaos. Motivation will involve encouraging people to use their influence drive to best advantage and to help them to understand that structure is required and is a test of the acceptable use of influence. We remind them that organizations falling apart for lack of structure are bad for morale!

Factor 3, factor 9 (variety and change)

Those with a high need for structure and a high need for variety have their work cut out. Structure requires stability and predictability, variety suggests lack of predictability. High structure people may suffer considerable stress and an inability to cope if they are put into situations of flux and change; this applies even if they seek variety. Their ability to cope with change, however, will be enhanced if the change has been thought through, so that the end state and the new sets of rules are known. They will be helped even more if they are given assistance with learning the new rules in advance of implementation. Since, in practice, change does not seem to be thought through with the attention to detail required, people with high structure and high variety needs tend to be considerably stressed. They may expect that managers spend a considerable amount of their time providing reassurance. It is probably a more productive use of that management time to help them to understand and, perhaps, to help to create the new rules that will be required. Such a proactive approach will be much more likely to motivate them.

Those with a high need for structure and a low need for variety will want to work in a predictable way, undertaking the tasks and routines which are an essential part of an efficient and reliable organization. They will be reliable and predictable. So that structure does not become an end in itself, we should take care to relate their need for structure to that which the organization requires and no more. For additional motivation, we will probably need to look at their other basic needs, like achievement and recognition, and to work with those.

Factor 3, factor 10 (creativity)

People can, though perhaps we might not expect this, live comfortably with high structure and high creativity needs. The reason is simply that in industry and commerce they need to know the rules before they can be creative. They will also be used to working within the constraints imposed by clients. An example is an architect or an advertising copywriter. There is a high element of creativity, but an architect has to know both the building regulations and the client's brief and the copywriter must know both the brief and the requirements of the advertising authorities. Consequently the two factors can coexist.

How do we motivate? We need the correct brief, standards and protocols and be confident that these have been thoroughly and carefully established and are not going to change continually. If they do, the creator becomes demoralized and indifferent. Establishing the correct brief is a considerable problem in industry and commerce. In some industries, it is almost routine to give inadequate briefs, with the consequence that unnecessary re-work is common. We can motivate by making obvious and visible efforts to establish complete briefs and by acknowledging the distress that may be caused when work has to be done yet again. Overhanging our efforts will be a specific acknowledgement that the rules of our particular activity, the building regulations or whatever, must be adhered to. Then, within these defined limits, we give the maximum creative freedom: space within clear boundaries.

Those with high structure and low creativity needs will be motivated through their other drives. We should do that or there is a danger that they will create structure for its own sake and not for the good of the organization.

Factor 3, factor 11 (self-development)

People with high structure and high self-development needs are most likely to develop themselves in rule-based topics, like law or accountancy, or perhaps to immerse themselves in subjects based on ritual. Their approach to learning is likely to be structured. They will prefer lectures and organized learning with defined outcomes. They will like a syllabus and are probably happier with an authoritative approach to learning; the teacher will be seen as an expert advising the students on what is received wisdom. They will welcome the opportunity to go on courses. They will be motivated by being given structured learning opportunities. If they have high recognition needs, they will want some sort of qualification at the end, and will be happy to take exams if these are considered necessary. We motivate by listening to their preferences and taking them into account.

People with low structure and high self-development needs are more likely to look towards 'fuzzier' topics, where intuition and experience have a role to play, or where there is possibly a more open-ended element. They will not necessarily look to a prescribed body of knowledge and will be prepared to work in more ambiguous areas, learning by exploration and experience. They will be relaxed about an absence of defined outcomes and probably about not receiving qualifications. They will be motivated by being put into work situations where they can gain experience and learn on the job. Their recognition will be partly internal – they will feel they have learned – and partly external – they will be given work which demands the experience and skills they have now acquired. In motivating them, we need to monitor regularly with them what they have learned. Some of the outcomes will be difficult to measure. That does not make them less valuable. But we will need careful joint evaluation to discern where further development should take place.

Factor 3, factor 12 (interest and usefulness)

People with high structure needs and high job interest will be unable to perform until their structure needs have been attended to. When that has been done, they will be able to pay attention to the interest in the job. Our prime motivational task is to address their need for rules and procedures. We can then consider the extent to which the interest in the job is congruent with their own need. If the structure is right, there will be considerable tolerance of jobs which are not quite so interesting. In the long term, however, we should endeavour to match personal and organizational needs.

Our research suggests that there is a slight inverse correlation between structure needs and job interest. People with structure needs above the norm have a job interest need below the norm. They may be seriously de-motivated or unable to cope with an 'interesting' but unstructured job. Likewise, those with low structure needs tend to have a higher need for job interest. Motivation of those with lower structure needs involves keeping the rules to a minimum, and trying to establish congruence between personal and organizational interests. De-motivation occurs if the 'interesting' or 'useful' job is structured. Management motivate by either lowering the structure needs of the job, or by counselling staff as they try to cope with the stress induced, if such reduction is not possible.

Factor 4

People contact

Highest score recorded = 81
Lowest score recorded = 0
Mode 27 Median 25

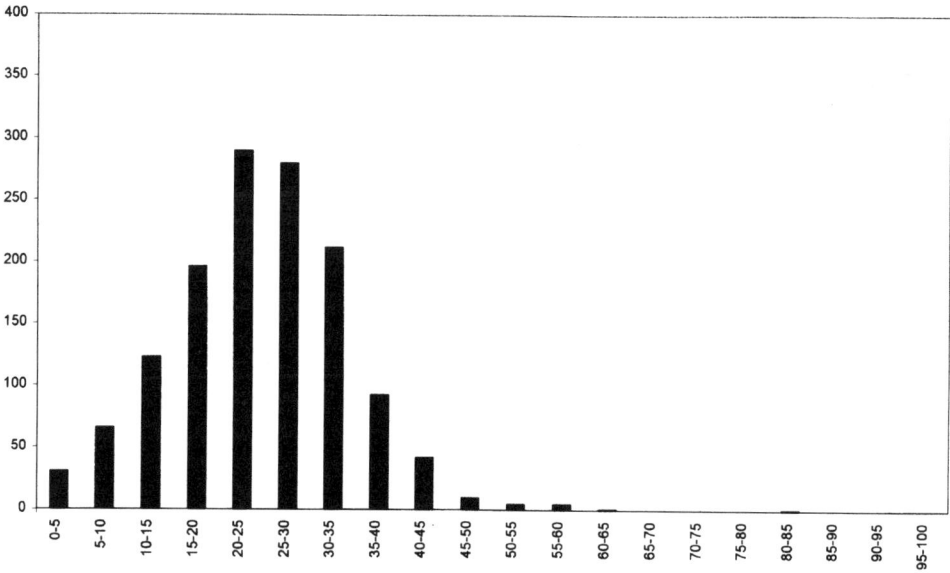

Figure 4   Factor 4: histogram of scores

Humans share a tendency with many animals: the need to get together with others. Dogs, for example, hunt in packs, many bird species flock to migrate or to forage for food and sheep crowd together in bad weather to share warmth and to gain reassurance and comfort. The extent to which individuals differ in their need for such social contact is measured by factor 4.

Factor 4, other factors evenly spread

People with a high score on factor 4 enjoy dealing with other people and derive comfort and satisfaction from having a number of others around. They would like to come across a wide range of 'interesting' people in the course of their work. Given a choice, such people will choose to work with other people nearby, rather than on their own. Most are likely to be highly tolerant of the bustle and noise that working with others entails. They probably even like the buzz that a group of people generates and, of great importance to anyone who manages them, they will perform better in such conditions.

This need is like the herding instinct exhibited by animals who crowd together as a defence against predators. They may well feel their stress levels abate when they are with others and they are likely to be the kind of person who talks over their problems with friends and family; believing in the adage that a problem shared is a problem halved.

People who exhibit high factor 4 needs may, in their management role, find that they have to ask people to do things which those people do not want to do. There may be a conflict here between the need to 'cuddle up', as it were, and the need to send an unwelcome message. The typical approach is to deliver the message and then to move on to another set of people, always keeping the option open to move back to the 'offended' person at a later date. Interestingly, we meet a surprising number of people who work in financial markets and in service industries who seem to communicate with only a computer or a telephone. Their scores are still probably around the average.

For those with a very low score, there is no suspicion that they are unable to deal with others, only that they do not need that contact, at least not frequently or in large doses. They may feel an aversion to others, a preference for their own company, a delight in being locked in the basement with the computer and a resentment of the time that has to be taken in talking to others.

One respondent who scored only three points remarked that, although he gets on well with other people (and it was clear on the seminar that he did), he sometimes resents the attention they seek: he regards his staff as rather fractious children who interrupt his work more than they should, seeking guidance and reassurance. His behaviour is not affected by his low score, he does not rebuff someone who appeals to him, but his attitudes to them are certainly negative.

Factor 4, factor 1 (money and tangible rewards)

Those who have a high factor 4 score can manage with or without money, depending on the sort of people they want to associate with and on what they have to offer their would-be companions. If their need for money is low, they will want to associate with people with a similar low money need. Those with a high money need will want to associate with those who are like-minded.

The motivational implications are straightforward. Those with low money need will like to work in a convivial environment where there is the opportunity to talk to others. Even short periods alone may create problems. As far as possible they will want to work in groups, either as part of their working day, or in problem-solving working parties. The culture will need to be open, so that people are not separated by organizational barriers. That is to say, an autocratic style of management, where people are isolated and kept working in water-tight compartments, will be unsuitable and will create stress. Objective setting will be best on a group and not an individual basis. People should be encouraged to network, to have the opportunity to reach across functions and levels. Where the technology is available, their skills and experience should be listed on the company intranet, accessible to all. Company events, ranging from training sessions to away-days, should be designed to bring such people together. The house magazine should be full of gossip. There should be opportunities for client contact. Getting together with others, the social side of work, should be recognized as paramount.

For those who have a high need for money, there still needs to be an emphasis on the social side of work. But the social currency is now money and there will be a wish for the contact to be financially productive. We are now looking at like-minded people working together with their colleagues to make money. We will want incentive schemes, if we have them, which should be designed to bring people together and not to drive them apart. The focus here should be on group schemes, but if we use individual schemes, we have to be absolutely sure, and this can sometimes be difficult, that they do not create the potential for division. This means that there should be no opportunities to contest who has actually earned the incentive from a particular transaction. If there is, there will be two outcomes. The first is that the overriding need for social contact will mean that the parties will agree to split the incentive between them, thus undermining the incentive effect it is supposed to produce; or they will fall out and social harmony will decline to social division.

Factor 4, factor 3 (structure)

There is no incompatibility between the need for short-term relationships and structure. Those with high factor 4 and structure needs will be happiest working in some large bureaucratic office, polished with routine and ritual, everybody knowing their place and with not too much change, but honest tiredness after a hard day's work. The routine will be leavened with gossip and the small change of office politics.

Where the whole of the organization or department is high on factor 4, motivation will be fairly straightforward. As much as possible, it should be done on a collective basis. The output of all discussions will be either developing a structure, or explaining it. Taken to extremes, conversation will be about rules and regulations and 'how it should be done'. There may be some grumbling about the bureaucracy but, ultimately, it will be seen as a safeguard, providing comfort in an uncomfortable world, and the grumbles need not be taken too seriously. Meetings will be regarded as ends in themselves; chances for getting together, for reassurance and ritual. Any outcomes will not be seen as important. This is the start of a talking shop where the social event is the end product.

If the department has a mixture of high and low factor 4 people, it will be necessary to maintain a balance between those who like to work as part of a group and those who like to work alone. There may not be full-blooded participation and decision making will probably be collective and made in the name of the manager.

Motivating those with high social but low structure needs will be a more subtle affair. They are likely to enjoy company for its own sake and will probably be more inclined to relate to those with similar low structure needs. We can have no expectations of their behaviour. They will certainly not be discussing rules and regulations, except perhaps to dismiss them. Conviviality may become an end in itself and the organization's needs, whatever they might be, may receive little attention. We will need to motivate them, firstly by providing scope for interaction and short-term contacts, secondly, by concentrating on their other motivational drives, such as achievement and influence. It will be in our interest to specify the outputs required and to use group activity to gain commitment to them.

Factor 4, factor 5 (relationships)

The comparison between the need for long- and short-term relationships is, at its most extreme, that between the person who likes company but is unwilling to commit him or herself to forming deeper ties, and the person who lives solely with the familiar group, perhaps grumbling but gaining a sense of satisfaction and stability, and feeling no need to make the effort to get to know others.

Our research suggests that more of those with factor 4 (sociability) above the norm have a need above the norm for long-term relationships (factor 5). In a sense, this is to be expected. It means that most of those who are sociable like to develop more lasting relationships. The correlation, though, is weak. As a rule, they will try to maintain trust and stability in the long term, but seek out opportunities to work with as many others as possible. The long-term relationships will form the basis on which they launch themselves for other endeavours.

Those who are high 4/high 5 will be very people centred. In general, people with these drives who are in management, are more likely to be at the people end of the people–task continuum. At the very best, they will work with others to help them to achieve both their own goals and those of the organization. In the Blake and Mouton (1964) terminology, they will be team players. They will be thoroughly effective. At worst, they will give their personal needs preference over those of the organization. In the same terminology, their management style will be 'Country Club'. Which of these extremes will prevail depends on other drivers. Thus, for example, a high need for influence is more likely to mean a team approach, a low need, 'Country Club'.

Where the members of the department are all high 4, motivation should offer opportunities for contact and the development of long-term relationships. More subtly, we could try to create a culture in which 'bonding' can take place. The characteristics of a culture will include team working, a no-blame environment in which teams can be strengthened rather than weakened by reviewing their mistakes and regular celebration of 'us' as a team. As far as possible, we heed people's team and colleague preferences, and where we cannot meet them because of the demands of the business, we openly mourn our inability to do so.

Where there is a mixture of high and low 4 people, we can expect that the low factor 4s will not take up the opportunities for contact. We have to keep them fully informed of events and decisions so that they do not become isolated as a result of their preferences.

For high 4 people who are low 5, sociability is enough. They will feel the need for constant company. They will probably enjoy the buzz of the open-plan office and even look forward to the company outing! They will move office location without difficulty and probably not worry too much about moving jobs. They might even be happy in an internal consultancy role, where they can meet many people and then move on. However, this combination is in some ways curious. High 4 likes people, but only up to a point, in the short term. Why should this liking change in the longer term? Is it because establishing long-term relationships requires that we open out to people, perhaps even creating a little vulnerability? It certainly involves creating trust; if there is no trust, long-term relationships cannot be satisfactory and are probably better terminated.

This is something we need to consider when we motivate those with high 4/low 5. Is there a problem of trust? We can never be completely sure. An inability to open up to others might be due to a feeling of personal insecurity. In this case our motivational task is to try to bolster their self-esteem. Alternatively, they may not take the trouble to create trust because they have an expectation that they will subsequently break it. As managers, we can only hope to learn the answer by listening and observation. Obviously, it is in our interests to create an expectation of all-round trust. Training in interpersonal skills might help to achieve that. If, however, we expect that the trust might be broken, we should be careful not to build up an expectation that it might be sustained. That will be very damaging and we would be better not to raise the matter.

Factor 4, factor 6 (recognition)

Those who are high 4/high 6 have an interesting combination. Taken to the extreme, they will like to rub shoulders with lots of people. They will prefer people who give them full recognition. It may turn out to be an unending quest, and as each group fails to give recognition to the extent required, so there is the necessity to move on to others who in their turn will disappoint. If one group does give recognition, however, there will be an incentive to continue the acquaintanceship and we have the beginnings of a long-term relationship. But the need for people is greater for this group than the need for recognition. They would rather have company even if it is not very satisfactory company, though they might try to improve their standing by adopting the norms of the people with whom they are currently relating.

What are the implications for motivation? Most important is the opportunity to make contact. Ideally, we would like those contacted to give recognition, but that is unlikely to happen. It is more likely that those who are contacted will themselves be looking for their own share of recognition. We can help to oil progress by going out of our way to provide what recognition we can. Within work, we try to create a positive working environment. We can aim, in the words of Blanchard and Johnson (1983), for everybody in the organization to 'catch people doing something good' as opposed to the more common 'attempt to catch people doing something bad and then let them have it'. Recognition and the need for sociability thus reinforce each other.

We do want to discourage people from attempting to gain their recognition by flouting the norms of the group. People can do this by staying just within the bounds, being seen as eccentric or maybe being seen as the resident figure of fun, a butt for unkind jokes. It means they are acknowledged, which is what they want, but it can lead to a deterioration in group working and is to be avoided.

Those who are high 4/low 6 can enjoy people for their own sake. They will not be permanently in a lather as to whether or not they are gaining approval. They are in a better position to enjoy company and will not value people in terms of the degree of recognition they accord. Their colleagues will not feel the strain of having to give frequent acknowledgement with the feeling that the relationship is demanding and sometimes a little one-sided. The relationship is essentially healthier. In motivational terms they are easier to handle than those with high recognition needs. We may need to look to other motivators like achievement as a way of focusing their effort on the objectives of the organization.

Factor 4, factor 7 (achievement)

Those who are high 4/high 7 are more likely to relate to their colleagues and perhaps even be friendly while competitive with them. They will at least enjoy the warmth of sociability which, if it gets in the way, can be discarded to be picked up later when the achievement urge is not so insistent. Given the right conditions, that is role clarity and trust between team members, they can take part in, or at least tolerate, teams. With this particular combination, if there is a clash between relationships and achievement, relationships are likely to dominate. This is facilitated because, in general, those with a high achievement drive prefer to work by themselves. Their achievement is for them and they feel it is diminished if it is shared with others. Rather than create problems with the relationship they may try to avoid the loneliness of achievement. With a high relationship drive, they will be easily encouraged to do that.

Factor 4, factor 8 (power and influence)

High factor 4 and high factor 8 seem to go together naturally. The need is to be in constant contact with a variety of people. When contact is made, there will be an effort to influence. People with this profile who are successful can be expected to possess some sort of charisma, or at least personal presence. They may not attain formal rank, authority or status. If they do, they are likely to wear it lightly. They seem to like and need people and in their contacts they naturally exercise influence. However, their principal driver is relationships. If the influence drive clashes with this they are either likely to withdraw their attempts at influence, or to move on. We do not see the exercise of power as the dominant force, it is more 'fair weather' and likely to be used to build relationships rather than to focus on organizational needs.

What are the motivational consequences? Those who are high factor 4/high factor 8 will want the opportunity for short-term contacts. They will have the ability to influence, but we will need to be sure that their influence is exercised in the interests of the organization. We help them by spending time with them establishing our expectations and defining outputs so that they understand what we need. We may have to stiffen their resolve when they see a clash between their need to maintain or build relationships and the organization's need for results. We will want to build in a formal review at agreed intervals, so that we can both be sure that their energies are productive in organizational terms.

The owner of a profile with high 4/low 8 will seek the company of people, but will not want to influence them. We motivate them using their other needs.

Factor 4, factor 9 (variety and change)

High factor 4/high factor 9 people will be happy to rub shoulders with many sorts of people, in many sorts of situations. Just meeting different people may be all the change that they require. In terms of different activities, there may be a tendency to see change as a vehicle for increasing contacts or to enjoy change for its own sake and for very little, if anything, to be taken to fruition. We may find them delightful companions, perhaps even the life and soul of the party, and in that sense good for general morale. In motivational terms, though, we obviously want to maintain the opportunity to make contacts but may have to look to their other drivers, such as achievement, to get things done.

Those with high factor 4/low factor 9 will like contact with people. They are more likely to take things to completion. Motivation will require the opportunity to work with a range of people on reasonably stable tasks.

Factor 4, factor 10 (creativity)

Creativity in business needs to be focused on business requirements, and is likely to take place in teams. Generally speaking, it is different from the traditional stereotype of the lone creator driven by only his or her creative needs and totally unfocused. Those who have high factor 4/high factor 10 will enjoy using their creative drive to enhance the buzz of working in teams. Their need is for the team to be an enjoyable experience. Our need is for a productive team and we encourage this by accurate problem definition and team understanding of what is required.

Motivation will involve providing contact opportunities, right across the organization and trying to ensure that the best people experiences, the most fun and enjoyment, are associated with creativity. The way to do this is to ensure that all the attention and any celebration relate to creative achievement.

Those who are high factor 4/low factor 10 probably enjoy company, but creativity will not be part of the deal. They will probably need to be motivated through the need for variety or achievement, or some other factor.

Factor 4, factor 11 (self-development)

Those with a high need for contact with others will obviously be happiest relating to others. That will be their primary interest. If the people to whom they relate have a high need for self-development they will like working in groups for that purpose. In business, this will find its most obvious expression in the evaluation of completed joint projects, with the clear agenda of establishing 'what can we learn from this?' and 'what can we do better?' If those to whom they relate do not have this interest in self-development, they are likely to adopt the group norms, whatever they may be. In this case their self-development may take less priority than they would really prefer, or may take place on a solo basis. We may be able to help them with shared learning by steering them in the direction of those with a similar motivation.

Team learning requires that the organization has an open atmosphere so that people can learn from mistakes and not fear that admitting to mistakes, even those made in good faith, could land them in trouble. Those with such a profile will need to be confident that the organizations they are going to work for are open minded enough to permit such learning to take place. If not, they will question whether they want to work in such an environment and their commitment is likely to be reduced. The motivational requirements are obvious.

High factor 4/ low factor 11 will enjoy company for its own sake. There will be a low personal need to learn, but probably a willingness to learn when the group learns. Motivation requires that we take the trouble to increase the learning of the group as a whole. We cannot expect the same level of soul searching that will take place with those who have a high need for self-development. The questions are more likely to be along the lines of 'How can we as a group do things better?' rather than the high factor 11 question 'What could I have done differently to achieve better results?'

Factor 4, factor 12 (interest and usefulness)

High factor 4/high factor 12 people will find job interest in working with others. Part of the pleasure will be the people at work, and all their comings and goings. They will want to work with people who share their view of job interest. If they do not, the group norms may distract their attention from job interest, which will become less of a motivator.

Our research suggests that there is a significant number of people with high factor 4 who are low on factor 12. This means that people who are above average in sociability are at or below average in needing interesting or significant work. One compensates for the other, perhaps?

What are the motivational implications? For those who are high factor 4, we do not have to explain in such detail why we want them to do things. They do not have the same need for job interest, provided they have contact with others and can work as part of a group or in teams. This does not mean that we should take the opportunity to give them insignificant or uninteresting work. The fact that the median for factor 12 is 43 against that of 25 for factor 4 shows that we cannot ignore job interest. What it does mean is that there is less likely to be this incipient breakdown of commitment which occurs with those who have difficulty in maintaining interest if the work fails to match up to their expectations.

Factor 5

Relationships

Highest score recorded = 45
Lowest score recorded = 0
Mode 18 Median 19

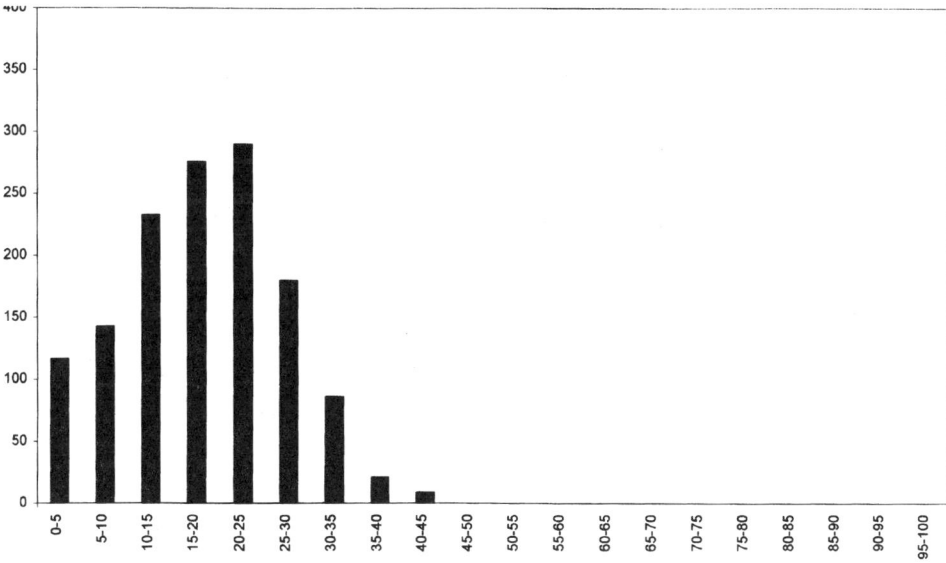

Figure 5   **Factor 5: histogram of scores**

Factor 5, other factors evenly spread

Before we explore the motivator of long-term relationships, we should note that our research shows that the mode and median are low, at 18 and 19. In other words, whatever the requirement at work for good relationships, people do not regard the need to establish them as an important driving force. Conversely, the low average means the need is more easily satisfied. If the mode is so low, does the topic merit any consideration? Since organizations are made up of relationships, it should matter. The question probably most worth considering is, in which organizational structure does it matter most? This question gives us a useful way of exploring the subject.

We can instantly see that there are some sorts of organization where relationships of any kind are relatively insignificant. We can think of burger bars, some of them significant businesses in their own right, where the staff are interchangeable. They work in shifts, turnover is high, the tasks they do are standardized, the level of skill low. People working in that sort of organization are probably disadvantaged by having a need for long-term relationships. If the need is overwhelming, they will have to satisfy it elsewhere.

In a complex economy, however, people are not always interchangeable. They are not interchangeable in a university, or in a complex de-layered business, one in which people are empowered and direct management is kept to a minimum. The resulting structure can only work if the staff who now have all these responsibilities know what they have to do; are trained to do it; are given clear areas of discretion, responsibility and information about their performance; and can form effective teams, one of whose prime functions is to support each other. The absence of a command structure means such an organization can only function on trust.

This also applies to organizations which are characterized by continuous change, usually brought about by the dynamic nature of the environment in which they operate. The organization is effective to the extent that managers think through its objectives and assign roles. It can only be effective if those within it are committed and work to keep it on track. Inevitably, as with de-layered organizations, those who work there will be interdependent. They can only function if there is trust. Although, in theory, it is possible to replace trust by good procedures, in practice, procedures are rarely flexible enough to maintain full effectiveness, particularly under conditions of continuous change. Commitment and trust help us to run an effective organization.

Since we are concerned here with the need to form long-term relationships, we ask if there is any connection between that need and the creation of commitment and trust. Common sense suggests there is, and this is backed by our research. The components of commitment were described by Martin and Nicholls (1987) as a sense of belonging, a sense of excitement in the job, and confidence in management. The first of these, almost by definition, requires more than superficial relationships and indeed must require longer-term relationships.

We come now to an apparent paradox. We have a myriad of organizations which can only function effectively if there is trust and long-term relationships, and yet, as we have seen, the need for long-term relationships is low. How can these contradictory requirements coexist? There is a range of possible explanations:

- Organizations are not functioning as effectively as they might.
- Organizations can, in fact, function effectively without the establishment of trust.
- People underestimate, or suppress, their need for long-term relationships.
- People can establish and maintain long-term relationships although they do not feel the need; or the organization can help them to do so.

Looking at these, it is easy to accept that organizations are not as effective as they might be. It is difficult to accept that complex organizations can function without trust and it is more likely that any under-performance is partly a result of a trust deficit.

On the third point, it is possible that people underestimate their need for long-term relationships. These needs may be met outside work; or, on the other hand, they might feel that long-term relationships have little to offer them and so do not see the need as important. Under the present conditions, there is one additional matter to consider. There has been a move to a more flexible market economy and organizations are now less likely to offer a job for life. People may not regard it as sensible to develop long-term relationships at work.

The competitive nature of life in so many firms reduces even further the incentive to establish long-term relationships at work. Even if the need is there, its exercise may be suppressed and denied and regarded as subsidiary to the other motivating drives. Such is the dynamic nature of change, or the dynamic instability built into some organizations, that there is no time to form relationships before the next reorganization has moved on. Once again, the need is suppressed. In effect, there is little point in expressing the need if its achievement is unlikely. Vroom utilizes this point in developing his expectancy theory of motivation. (Vroom, 1964; Vroom and Deci, 1970)

From an organization's point of view, there can also be an obverse side to the need to form relationships. If the organizational environment is perceived as sufficiently hostile, the formation of established relationships could be seen as an attempt to subvert the organizational purpose, or at best an attempt to provide a mutual aid and comfort club whose rationale is to protect the perceived interests of individuals against the perceived predatory instincts and practices of the organization. Some organizations, therefore, will think they have an interest in discouraging the formation of long-term relationships.

We should note that many modern slim-line organizations are regarded unfavourably by those working in them. For example, two-thirds of those polled in a Roffey Park Survey (Roffey Park Management Institute, 1994) on de-layering reported a drop in morale. There is so much that can, and reportedly often does, go wrong; from failure to provide role clarity and information, to a failure to define organizational purpose. Those failures alone may cause much of the damage. Another part of the failure is, however, likely to lie in the field of relationships. On this point, we believe that organizational pressures and the sheer business of working together are enough to hold together workable relationships, even though the relative need is low. This, we think, provides the basis for motivation.

Our approach is threefold. First, in motivating people, we need to pay more attention to people's need for achievement and recognition than to their need to form long-term relationships. We have the freedom to change working relationships and need not, in the main, expect motivational problems if we do so. Since trust is more likely to grow out of the formation of closer relationships, we need to establish a culture which requires trust, one in which people's word is their bond, so people can expect that if somebody has promised to do something and subsequently cannot do it, they immediately advise those affected so they can make alternative arrangements. More subtly, we need an assertive culture, in which people do not feel the need to say 'Yes, I will do something' when more realistically they should say 'No, I cannot'; or 'I cannot do it now'. People say 'yes' when they should say 'no' because they are frightened of seeming to be unco-operative. They do not trust the response they will get.

We can develop an assertive culture by training and by example and, indeed, by discipline. The motivational benefits are considerable. The organization begins to exert some control over one of its main problems which is that people are interdependent and, increasingly in modern organizations, dependent on others over whom they have no control. We compensate for the relatively low need to form long-term relationships and the growth of trust that would naturally follow.

Secondly, we can also compensate by developing and propagating a sense of organizational purpose. Given an agreed sense of purpose, there is the beginning of an effective working relationship. People then have to work through how this purpose will be discharged. They relate to each other in terms of what the organization has to achieve. Purpose forms a framework for effective working relationships. As part of it, we should try to make explicit each participant's personal needs and establish congruence with organizational needs. Thus, when managed well, people relate to organizational goals and to each other.

Finally, we recognize the breach of trust that has taken place between organizations and those who work for them. Since we cannot offer lifetime employment, or any commitment to employment beyond the organization's requirements, we must put something in their place. Current thinking, which we commend, is centred on the concept of 'employability'; the organization and employee will together build his or her skill base and experience so that they are more employable, either inside or outside the organization. They will consequently be in a better position to take advantage of employment opportunities. The organization has thus provided a substitute for the commitment which would normally result from the development of long-term relationships.

In summary, motivation entails developing a culture which compensates for the relatively low perceived need for long-term personal relationships.

Factor 5, factor 1 (money and tangible rewards)

High factor 5/high factor 1 can be effective if a team needs to work together to achieve the desired financial results. The modern example would be the high value football and rugby teams. Effective teams need trust, role clarity and good working relationships. Now we can add a hunger for money. The team members depend not only on their own efforts but also on those of their colleagues for financial success. They are likely, at the very least, to be honest with each other. The situation is quite different from that of the relative loner making large sums of money but not allowing others to interfere. Our research shows that a significant minority of high factor 5 people are money focused.

What are the motivational implications? Money has to be explicitly recognized as a purpose. The team will enjoy working together and making money. If there is a point where problems could arise, it is to do with the differing requirements for money within the team. While some may require enormous sums, others might aspire to more modest amounts and their motivation may tail off when they have reached their goals. This is the point at which tensions might arise and the team starts to falter, though since relationships are the prime need, there will be a serious effort to keep people together. We can contribute to commitment if we can work, at the same time, on other motivational needs, such as the need for achievement. We do best if we can match money needs at the beginning, keeping like with like.

High factor 5/low factor 1 can also go well together. The relationship is all important and the money does not matter. However, in business terms it can go wrong. For example, neither party will worry about money and will enjoy the relationship, perhaps pursuing some common interest. We need to motivate them by concentrating on some other factor, such as achievement. We should look out for the situation in which one of the parties has a considerable interest in the money and uses the relationship improperly.

Factor 5, factor 3 (structure)

People with a high factor 5 and a high structure need will do better if they can establish relationships with those who have similar structure needs. If they choose those who have differing needs, there is a possibility of serious problems, especially if each party tries to project their own needs on to the other. (Working with others, pages 247–54, deals with this problem in detail.) The high 3 person tries to organize other people's lives or to impose an unwanted structure which the other person resents, creating tension; and conversely the low structure person is 'disorganized', 'nothing ever gets done' and there is anxiety. On the face of it, such relationships should not establish themselves, but they do. Sometimes there is a high level of tolerance and they work but, on occasions, there is much friction and unhappiness can result. High structure people can enjoy organizing each other, or working within a structure. Low structure people will not feel that same need.

What are the motivational implications? In so far as we can, we should attempt to organize in such a way that similar types of people have the opportunity to form long-term relationships. If this is not possible, we should alert each person to any tendency to impose their need, or lack of need, for structure, on the other. We can at the same time try to establish, or better still, have the participants establish, a division of labour which allows one group to engage its structure needs and the other side not. So, for example, those more tolerant of ambiguity can interpret the outside world to those who are less tolerant and so on.

Factor 5 high, factor 4 (people contact)

Our research shows that there is a slight tendency for those who are above the norm on factor 5 to be above the norm on factor 4. People who form long-term relationships are more likely than not to be sociable. The converse is also true. People who are below the norm in needing to form long-term relationships are below the norm in sociability. Both of these are to be expected.

In motivational terms, if we believe that the organization will develop from the formation of long-term relationships, we will need to try to create an environment which encourages this. We should aim for transparency and trust, so that the burgeoning relationships are not destroyed by the organizational climate. In the end, the organizational culture and the relationships should become self-reinforcing. If this does not happen, the longer-term relationships might form anyway, but be antithetical to the organization's needs.

Factor 5, factor 6 (recognition)

The basis of a good relationship must be mutual recognition. Therefore, it is somewhat puzzling that our research suggests that there is a significant number of people with high relationship needs who have low recognition needs. A possible explanation is that their recognition needs are satisfied within their relationships and this is no longer seen as so important, consequently scoring low. Conversely there appears to be a number with high factor 5 who are high on recognition needs. Despite the relationship, the need is still there. Possibly we are talking of unrequited love, or simply that the need is so high that not even good long-term relationships are able to satisfy it? It could also be that while their need for relationships is there, for some reason, it has not been satisfied and so the recognition need also remains unsatisfied.

What does this mean in motivational terms? The research suggests, and common sense supports, that long-term relationships can help towards the satisfaction of recognition needs. The research does not say, though it is a defensible conclusion, that a lack of long-term relationships means a deficit of recognition. Again, common sense would suggest that this is a possibility and it is a good working hypothesis. The implication is that, in the observed absence of long-term relationships, there is great benefit in making extra effort to give people recognition, or making organizational arrangements to put recognition high on the agenda.

Factor 5, factor 7 (achievement)

People who score highly on relationships and achievement clearly benefit from being able to achieve in an environment where relationships are possible. They are likely to benefit where there are fellow achievers who can stimulate each other, inspiration will come with the realization that they can achieve more than they ever felt was possible when they were working alone, and where the conversation and the culture favour achievement. The relationships are probably friendly and competitive with insiders, and possibly less friendly and competitive with outsiders. Such people tend to be in the minority. Our results suggest a significant number of those who are high on long-term relationships tend to be low on the need for achievement.

What does this mean for motivation? We recognize that for those who are high factor 5/high factor 7, there is a possible tension between these two factors. The principal drive is for long-term relationships, the secondary drive for achievement. Those high on achievement can be loners. They want to achieve and the need to co-operate with others (as opposed to have others co-operate with them) can blunt their sense of personal achievement. They are more likely to maintain long-term relationships on the basis that there is no interdependence, at least in the areas in which they achieve; though there may be mutual respect and even admiration for each other's achievements. Where appropriate, there can be friendly rivalry.

Motivation requires a recognition of the need to maintain the relationships but to have personal space in matters relating to achievement. Where there is a need for people to work together, the manager should define roles thoroughly and clearly, with clear team and personal objectives, which are mutually reinforcing. If management fail to maintain the required space, there may be a failure to achieve. The relationship will not easily be sacrificed to the organization's needs.

If factor 5 is high and factor 7 low, we should motivate, in terms of organizational results, through some other need such as recognition.

Factor 5, factor 8 (power and influence)

Those who are high factor 5, high factor 8 are in an interesting position. Their need is to establish long-term relationships and to exercise influence. The question for those who motivate them is, over whom do they wish to exercise influence? If it is those with whom they have a long-term relationship, then they may find life easier if they relate to people who are happier to be continuously influenced, or, if they are subordinates, are happy to accept it. They might try to create dependent relationships. If they are unable to do so, they may be unable to form a long-term relationship. Alternatively, they might do so but, unless they have extraordinary leadership characteristics, the relationship could be stormy.

At the same time, if the long-term relationship is with those over whom power is being exercised, it is a serious problem and not very pleasant if power has to be exercised in a way which is unpalatable to the recipients. In that situation considerable motivational effort is required. At one extreme, there can be a refusal to exercise influence. For example, in one case known to the authors, a manager refused to make his colleagues redundant as required and resigned himself. In a case like that, motivation may not be possible, but in less extreme cases, motivation involves trying to help people through the pain and difficulty of doing what is required and providing support afterwards. Even where the task is discharged successfully, from an organizational point of view, the manager should be helped not to feel de-sensitized by the duties that he or she has had to discharge.

If their need to influence is not necessarily related to those with whom they are building a relationship, those considerations need not apply. The relationship is not dependent and its defining characteristic is not the exercise of influence which takes place outside the relationships.

Are there any motivational implications for the dependent relationship? A long-term relationship might be enjoyable for those creating dependency but will be disastrous in development terms for those made dependent. Where this happens, we need to be aware of what is happening and to provide training and counselling in delegation to try to reverse the situation. For a healthy organization, we want staff to be empowered. The long-term relationship becomes one in which power is used to enable people. Training is given and people are encouraged to take decisions up to the limits of their increasing capabilities. The organization has clearly defined outputs so that people know what is expected of them. The relationship becomes based on mutual respect and can be described as a voluntary association. Those who have enjoyed creating dependency need to be counselled and pointed towards the advantages of creating empowerment.

Those who are high factor 5/low factor 8 should not have any problem. The relationship is unencumbered. Any motivation will take place through other factors such as achievement.

Factor 5, factor 9 (variety and change)

Those with a high need for relationships and a high need for variety (high 5/high 9) can only hope that the need for variety refers to challenges or tasks and not people, otherwise the tensions could be tremendous! In fact, our research suggests that only a minority of people who are high on factor 5 are high on factor 9 so potential tensions are avoided. For those who are high on factor 9, there can be a change of scenery as far as personnel are concerned, but there is probably a core group of people with whom there can be a continuous relationship.

If their relationships occur at work and are positive in work terms, we want, as far as possible, to help to maintain them. This does not mean, of course, that we cannot have them working with people with whom the relationships are not close. It means that we help them to maintain contact with their core people. After that, we manage them the way we manage all people who have a strong drive for variety and change.

In terms of motivation, there is one form in which such a need can be satisfied: the matrix form of organization. In that form, people have two bosses. One is responsible for their career development, their appraisal and their pay and has as permanent a relationship as it is possible to have in a modern organization. The other is more transitory, in that he or she is in charge of a current project and manages people's efforts for the life of that project. People in a matrix organization have factor 5 stability with their permanent boss, and factor 9 variety with their current project boss. Organizations like Manpower, which keep staff on their books as employees, but offer their services to a wide range of organizations, fulfil the same sort of function.

People who are high factor 5/low factor 9 should find no motivational tensions. In fact the two drives should work in tandem. We motivate them through their other drivers like achievement, but again keeping open access to their core contacts.

Factor 5, factor 10 (creativity)

People with a high need for relationships and for creativity (high 5/high 10) are more likely to be successful at working in groups. One thinks of orchestras, pop groups and advertising teams. The fact that people can be creative in groups does not mean, of course, that they cannot be creative outside them. The Beatles immediately spring to mind. They were successful together and they have been successful as soloists. But the drive to form relationships will introduce the opportunity for mutual creative stimulation. People with such a profile would probably benefit, if they have not done so already, by finding opportunities to work with groups of like-minded, creative people.

In practice, much creation in business takes place in groups, if only because of the enormous resources that are required for the act of creativity to take place. One only has to think of the resources spent on research and development in the pharmaceutical and software and electronic industries. True, much of it is development, but even within that, there will be continuous acts of creativity.

Concerning motivation, we want to create open, transparent groups, with clear definition of outputs and plenty of personal space. The relationships may have an intensity which we need to respect. We need a lack of organizational rigidity, and have to be prepared to let the groups become self-regulating and even unconventional in the way they go about their business. We also need to be careful about recognition. Even though those concerned may want to build long-term relationships, they still have career aspirations which will depend on recognition of their personal contribution. If the group can manage its own internal recognition needs, and assign significance in a way which is acceptable to all, so much the better. If not, we need to try to establish objective fairness, otherwise we face the possibility of a loss of commitment.

High factor 5/low factor 10 can result in a stress-free environment. Any motivation, in organization terms, will need to take place through other needs such as achievement.

Factor 5, factor 11 (self-development)

High factor 5/high factor 11 encourages self-development to take place as part of a group and it is possible that some forms of development can only take place as part of a group. The most obvious examples are in arts and sport. Development as a chamber orchestra player can only take place in a chamber orchestra. Development as a rugby fullback can only take place in a rugby team. But similar considerations apply in large areas of work. Designing a power station requires that personal skills are integrated with the skills of other people. An important part of self-development is learning how to work with others to realize the overall plan. Similarly, marketing managers will develop to the extent that they join their efforts to those of sales, advertising, distribution and production.

For motivation purposes, we have to present the opportunities for group working and learning. For organizational and individual review, management should stop the group at regular intervals and discuss the lessons that have been learned. Such a review should not only discuss what the group as a whole has learned, but also include individual presentations to display what individuals have learned. In that way we increase inter-group understanding and help people to realize that there were lessons learned of which they were unaware.

If the need for working with people is not satisfied at work, it is likely to be satisfied outside work. That is beneficial except that the energy and commitment required out of work could detract from that required inside work. If this happens, we need to review with them the possibility of satisfying both needs, at least partially, at work.

High factor 5/low factor 11 indicates that relationships are taking place in a development-free zone. Indeed, the relationship might substitute for self-development. We motivate by considering the other factors.

Factor 5, factor 12 (interest and usefulness)

Those who have high factor 5/high factor 12, have an interesting job and are able to build good relationships at the same time, are well situated. Our motivational task will not be difficult because we will be working with self-starters. The most we will have to do is to maintain a watching brief. We will assure ourselves, both formally and informally, that the work continues to be seen as interesting and significant. We will help maintain and develop good relationships, including opportunities for all to participate in setting targets and will meet individual needs through the suitable distribution of work.

There is a problem with those who have the profile outlined in the last paragraph but who find that they are either unable to form long-term relationships and/or have uninteresting work. Management can motivate by either trying to create a situation where it is possible to form longer-term relationships at work, or facilitating their formation in work-related activities like professional bodies, perhaps by allowing time off work or allocating resources. If this is not possible, management might be able to encourage, or at least not destabilize (for example, by requiring long hours) the formation of such relationships outside work.

If the work is not perceived as interesting, even with good relationships, management should spend time explaining the larger picture and trying to relate the job to the perceived interests of those involved. This might include changing the job to suit the person and perhaps moving them to different sorts of work. If management can satisfy both factors, there is likely to be a high level of motivation. If the relationships need cannot be satisfied, there will be a severe loss of motivation, followed probably by the departure of staff. If the relationship is good, some lack of interest will be tolerated if it is necessary to sustain relationships.

Our research suggests that a large proportion of people who are high on factor 5 are low on factor 12. We can tentatively conclude, therefore, that most people like either good relationships or an interesting job. Nevertheless, in motivational terms we need to be aware of this trade-off. The opportunity to build relationships can be a good substitute for job interest or usefulness. If we know the job is lacking in those terms, we can motivate by giving attention to relationships. The work must be done, but by celebrating the relationships, we will facilitate a social and convivial environment which can be beneficial. Having said that, we need to remind ourselves that the median for factor 12, at 43, is nearly two and a half times that of factor 5, at 18. An interesting job tends to be a more important driving force than good relationships.

Factor 6

Recognition

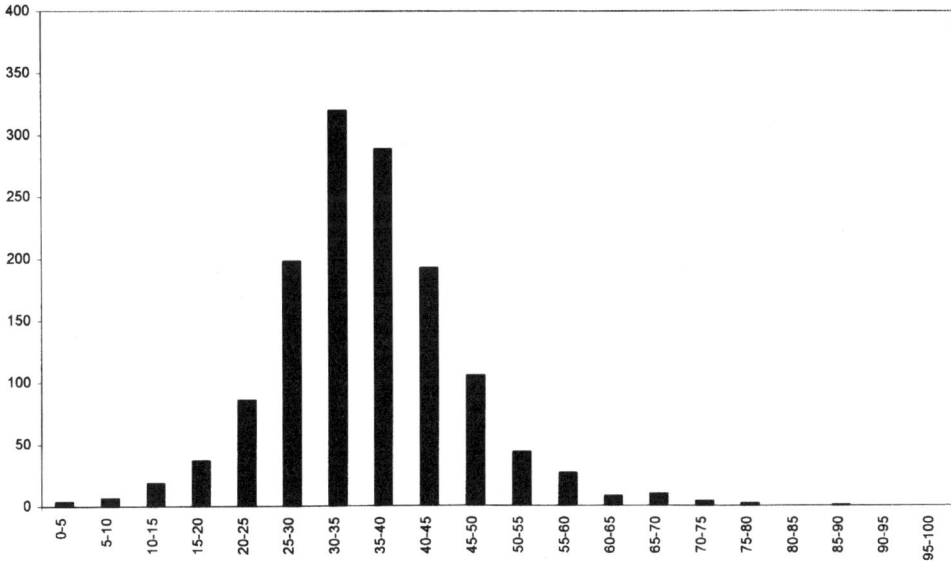

Figure 6   **Factor 6: histogram of scores**

Factor 6 high, other factors evenly spread

In one sense, the motivational needs for those with high recognition are straightforward. They require attention. However, this is not straightforward. There is not only the sense in which they require recognition, but how often? how fulsome? from whom? Furthermore, it is possible that high recognition need can make people so dependent on others for approval that, on those occasions where it is necessary, they become unable to act independently or to exercise judgement. Weaning people from this dependency and maintaining their morale is an important part of motivation. There is also the danger that those with high recognition become blind to other people's recognition needs. They want all the recognition themselves. This is an area that also requires significant management attention.

First of all, let us look at why recognition is important. It is a significant indicator of people's standing in life. People who are well thought of and who have a high recognition need will be comfortable with life. They can expect people to take their opinions seriously. They will take care that what they do meets people's expectations. They will have problems when they have to do or say things that might be contrary to what people expect, or want to hear. That is the point at which attention needs to be paid to their motivation.

Let us consider motivation and recognition by starting with the simplest situations, where there is dependency between the parties involved, that is, between a manager and an employee. The manager wants the employee to improve a skill or take a particular action and the employee is capable of doing what is required. Motivation comes from the prospect of praise, once the task is completed. Alternatively, what the manager wants requires some effort and recognition then comes in the form of continuous support. Even when something has been done incorrectly, recognition and, thus, motivation can come from explaining what specifically has been done wrong and what needs to be done to rectify the situation.

Dependency, however, as a continuing part of a relationship is probably undesirable. Highly dependent people are unable to make their own decisions and find difficulty making decisions in situations even marginally out of the ordinary. They can fail to develop as people. In motivational terms, weaning them away from dependency means developing the knack of criticizing their actions, but reassuring them that they are still valued. Where recognition needs are particularly high, both acts need to take place simultaneously and motivation becomes more complex. The difficulty we are dealing with is that very high recognition needs indicate serious insecurity. Those who strive to assuage insecurity by demanding continuous attention create a particular management problem. Apart from what might turn out to be the tedium of having to provide continuous attention, there is the difficulty of having to provide reassurance and criticism when things go wrong. Additional problems occur when people try to increase their chances of recognition by improving their performance. If they can continue to do so, providing the required attention may not be too difficult. If, though, they reach a performance plateau, the attention needs turn from their performance to themselves. Offering the degree of support required can, in these circumstances, be a challenge.

If a manager is unable to meet it, the people concerned start to direct all their energies to ensuring that they receive attention. To take a simple example, if they are invited to give a talk to trainees they will talk about themselves and not about the topic required. In the end, people will tend to avoid them, which is an uncomfortable situation for those who like recognition, and they are likely to become demoralized. We have here the classic situation where those who are most in need of recognition do not get it, because their continuous demands are resisted by those with whom they come into contact.

The worst situation arises when people start to act, not only against the interests of the organization, but against their own interests as well. (This happens when the short-term benefit of recognition is greater than the damage caused to them by the activities in which they engage.) They allow other people's judgement to substitute for their own. They become beholden to others. An example is an organization where, although the company pays a person's salary, that individual's loyalties have been displaced by their client's recognition and they represent their client's interests without taking full account of their employer's needs.

We are suggesting that in motivating people with high recognition needs we should be aware of their sources of satisfaction. From the point of view of our own organization, we want to be sure that it is we who satisfy their needs, at least as far as work is concerned. Outside work there will be other focuses of attention, including the family and social activities. An employer need not expect to satisfy all of a person's recognition needs at work; out-of-work activities can and should take off some of the pressure. Although it is true that such activities take some energy away from work, they are beneficial in that they reduce the darker side of recognition, all of which we have just discussed.

How do we deal with extreme cases? Eventually, we have to counsel people. We have to bring them face to face with the consequences of their needs; that their actions may be designed to reflect on themselves and may not always be in the best interests of their organization; and that they may find it difficult to take objective decisions. The organization will benefit if we can relate to them the consequences of some of the decisions they have taken and the impact their approach will have on their career development. We need to try to establish with them a protocol for future action. This will be based on the assertion that they have their senior management's full support; that, although errors of judgement and mistakes are not sought, they will be understood and personal support will not be withdrawn; that it is expected that lessons will be learned; and that they consider the recognition needs of those who work for them and provide a framework for ensuring that they receive the recognition due to them. We would aim to review the situation at appraisal time.

We may find that there is little we can do to satisfy those who have an overwhelming need for recognition. For example, if the need is such that everybody must give recognition all the time, we are not going to be able to help. We can perhaps encourage those whose need for recognition is insatiable to recognize their situation. We try to give enough recognition at work so that people do not become discouraged; and we could also encourage people to add to their stock by obtaining recognition outside work.

Leaving aside the cataclysmic side of recognition, how do we go about giving it? The first point is that recognition depends on sincerity for effectiveness. If it appears insincere, it can be de-motivating and is best not done at all. The second consideration is that people want to receive recognition in different ways. For some, it needs to be fulsome and almost overdone. For others, anything more than a brief nod will be seen as patronizing. We have to learn by observation which form is the most appropriate. Thirdly, we give it as closely to the event as possible and are specific in stating why we are giving recognition.

In general, recognition need not involve substantial material reward. This is not, of course, to disparage material reward, but usually people are satisfied with a glass of wine, a certificate, a word in front of their colleagues, or a letter of thanks copied to the Managing Director. Recognition, in whatever form, given with integrity, is sufficient.

Finally, we need to consider the effects of pressure on those with high recognition needs. A pressured job could be devastating. If recognition is not provided, people are likely to become particularly dispirited and are likely to perform to the minimum standard. Their work will seem uninteresting and pointless and they may not want to co-operate. People working under such pressure need careful attention. We find that the merest gesture of recognition will cause their spirits to soar, and we neglect them at our peril.

Factor 6 low, other factors evenly spread

Those with low recognition needs are at an advantage. They can take unpopular decisions without worrying about what those affected think about the decision. That is to say, they have the potential to be objective. They can, in the right circumstances, be a good motivator of others. They will be happy to let them have recognition and be happy to give recognition. They might have the knack of exercising their independent judgement and persuading people to accept it willingly. We discuss this more fully later. Those same people are also at a disadvantage in that they may be insensitive to the legitimate needs of others. They may also tend to be unreliable in the sense that, being unconcerned about others' opinions, they may be tempted to do what suits them regardless of the impact on their team.

How do we motivate those with low recognition? We put them in a position where they can take objective decisions. We also protect them against any tendency to insensitivity. Sometimes there is no problem. There are many who have low recognition needs who can be socially adept and agreeable. However, where there might be a problem we discuss with them how their work might be more acceptably presented. We can also help them to think about such issues by making them part of a project before it is undertaken. That is, we can ask them to predict the repercussions of their work and how adverse reaction might be handled.

If they themselves appreciate that their attitude might create potential problems we can suggest they receive interpersonal skills training. If not, we can have them trained on the grounds that such training is standard in the organization. By debriefing them we may encourage them to learn. If they cannot or will not learn and we wish to retain their expertise, we should try to have them work with minimum contact with people, so that the results of their work are handled by others. That will be a personal loss for them, in that inability to work with others will inevitably hinder their progress, but it will at least keep them employed and the organization will benefit from their skills.

Factor 6, factor 1 (money and tangible rewards)

In business, it can be asserted reasonably that those who are paid large sums of money have been sufficiently recognized and should require no more. In practice, this is not so. Our research suggests that there are many who have an above average need for money together with an above average need for recognition.

The implications for motivation are obvious. For those with high factor 1, we need to use money as a motivator. The topic has been covered fully in Money and tangible rewards, pages 15–19 but the principal requirements are that their need for money should coincide with the needs of the business and that there should be a logical relationship between the contribution made and the reward received. At the same time, we need to provide recognition for what they have achieved. We can do this by publication of results, by league tables or whatever way is deemed appropriate to the environment. We can even use status symbols like cars and fine offices, though these can be divisive and need to be used with care. If we fail to give recognition, we will find that money still works as a motivator, but there may be a loss of goodwill, which could result in the minimum contribution being made to achieve the business results required, together with a loss of informal and invaluable feedback.

Recognition in a group setting offers an additional advantage in that those who are self-starters and not team players are brought into contact with their peers, with possible advantages for team work. We can try to use the recognition drive to help to create a team dimension. If the team setting is not appropriate, we still give the recognition and publicize the fact that it has been given.

We also need to consider the extent to which the money earned is used to buy recognition outside work. This is frequently demonstrated by buying property, yachts, fast cars, exotic holidays and so on. We can motivate by sharing the obvious pleasure they will demonstrate in whatever they have bought. Strictly speaking, such matters are no concern of the employer. In practice, staff will be only too pleased to discuss them and they should be discussed. The organization is then clearly party to their external recognition. Sometimes the money earned will be used to take the opportunity to leave work and to devote time to achieving recognition elsewhere. There is not much that can be done about that and it is not likely to be disclosed. We simply need to be aware that this is a possible outlet for those whose recognition drive is more important to them than their money drive. We encourage the move if we fail to provide recognition at work.

Our research also shows that a sizeable proportion of people with an above average need for recognition have a below average need for money. What this means is that those people will want to be well paid, to achieve 'felt fairness' in pay, but their motivation is such that other motivators than money are likely to be more important to them. For them, recognition is important and should be given as a regular part of their motivation. In some parts of the public sector, where pay levels are relatively low, recognition of their 'public service' ethos may be an effective motivator and should be generously given.

Factor 6, factor 3 (structure)

People with a combination of high recognition and high structure needs require jobs with clear rules and guidelines. The range of jobs available is considerable, both in commercial and technical fields. Some of these jobs carry recognition in their own right, for example law and accountancy, through to pharmacy and technical specialisms in a range of areas. However, most people in these jobs soon discover that the external recognition is not enough, that they need satisfaction from the work itself.

From the point of view of motivation, the combination can be difficult. High structure needs require regularity and routine, valuable in the right circumstances. But the routines become so established that they no longer become noteworthy. To make them a matter for recognition we need to establish published standards and celebrate their attainment, or review their non-attainment. We can, additionally, set productivity standards. For example, we take the routine tasks and try to do them faster or more cheaply. To motivate fully, we need to make the standards a matter of importance and to have them written about, discussed and publicized. Seen as important, they become a significant vehicle for recognition.

People with high recognition and low structure needs are in a different position. They do not feel constrained by any system and will, of course, be happy to work in areas of ambiguity and change. Given the chance, they will do what is necessary to achieve the recognition required. Motivation involves matching their needs with what is good for the organization. We need to spend more time with them, working with them to define the requirements of the organization and making it clear to them that when those needs are met they will receive recognition. We need to give what was promised. If we do not, we will quickly create cynicism and will lose a valuable motivational tool.

Those who are low on recognition and low on structure will need to be motivated through their other drivers. If they relied on those two drivers only, they are likely to be happy to work in areas of ambiguity without regard to what people think or want. Such a profile suggests that from a business point of view they require close supervision. Unhappily, that is exactly the opposite of what they want. They work best with a clear statement of what the business wants and then being allowed to get on with it, with review at agreed intervals to make certain that they are delivering in a business sense.

Factor 6, factors 4 and 5 (people contact and relationships)

It is a curious paradox that those with a high need for recognition can have a low need for long- and short-term relationships (high 6/low 4 and 5). Our research shows that there is a significant number of people with an above average need for recognition and a below average need both for sociability and for long-term relationships. On the face of it, high recognition needs demand a high need for relationships. How else can people gain recognition except from others? It seems that such people do not need or, maybe even like, others much, but want to receive from them attention and recognition: this is a dependent stance similar to that of a fractious child to a parent.

An alternative view is that there is not a high need for people in general, for all their human qualities, but only for the recognition they offer. People are thought of as mirrors, reflecting back valued qualities. At the extreme, we are talking of narcissism; self-love. People need others to the extent that they reinforce the image they wish to project. If they do not do so, after they have been given the opportunity, there are two choices. They can either be ignored so that they do not matter; or there can be a serious attempt to win their approval, at least to the point where it becomes apparent that the effort will not be successful, and then there is a need to move on, hence the high factor 4. Lack of recognition reinforces the need to engage more people.

We know from research and observation that people feel they do not get sufficient recognition. They can feel alone, even abandoned. At worst they are mired in a sea of indifference. In terms of this deep need, other people are felt to be irrelevant.

What is the motivational lesson? It is that a more generous supply of recognition at all levels could foster a more positive attitude to people and help to create more commitment in organizations. Recognition is cheap to give, valuable to receive, can improve relationships and is worth its weight in motivational gold. Giving more of it often leads to a multiplier effect where people bask in the glow of receiving it and then pass on the warmth to others. Specifically, we as managers should be seen as a principal source of recognition and should practise giving recognition. If we do not, somebody else will, and work will, in motivational terms, be devalued.

We should note that people with a high need for recognition are likely to find difficulty in those situations where they have to take action which makes them unpopular. They are more likely to keep their ear tuned to prevailing sentiment and can make good team players. They may try to avoid conflict and will tend to 'go with the flow'. We help them in these difficult situations by bringing problems out into the open to be dealt with in as objective a manner as possible. This means that the team should work as a team on the problems, suspending decision making until all the options have been explored and, as far as practicable, reaching consensus. In other words, motivation will maintain relationships within the team and will direct the team to achieve business objectives. The same considerations apply when we look at people with high 6/high 5 (long-term relationships). In this situation we have to be very careful to build on these existing relationships. To disturb them could be particularly de-motivating.

Those who are very low on recognition and very low on relationships may be loners. At extremes they could upset their colleagues by their refusal to join in. They may also be unreliable and unlikely to be upset by letting their colleagues down. They are best motivated, and others are more likely to remain motivated, if they are allowed to work on their own and the scope for interaction with others is reduced to a minimum. This is particularly so if they combine their motivational profile with poor social skills.

Factor 6, factor 7 (achievement)

Those with a high recognition drive backed by a strong achievement drive are easy to motivate. They want recognition and they achieve measurable targets to get it. They require recognition at the point at which they achieve and they are likely to draw attention to themselves when this happens. All that the manager has to do is to impart the recognition. Before the point of achievement, they may well want to be left alone, perhaps to receive no more than the odd enquiry as to progress. Anything more than that may detract from what they regard as *their* achievement.

When targets are being set they may require encouragement. This is where there is a conflict between their need for recognition which will encourage them to aim for high targets, and their need for achievement, which may limit how high they aim; aiming too high creates the possibility of failure. The motivational effort will be put into helping them to reach an acceptable balance.

All those who have a high achievement drive have a tendency to see the world in black and white terms (that is, targets can either be measured or they cannot). Taken to the extreme, that which cannot be measured does not merit attention. In truly measurable situations this might not matter. In more subtle situations, it may matter very much. We can help high achievers to at least consider this area by working with their recognition drive, drawing attention to the softer areas and being lavish in our praise where they make progress. They thus achieve an additional source of recognition.

Those who have a high recognition need with a low need for achievement may be more difficult to motivate. We can use their recognition need to centre them on the need for achievement. However, we are unlikely to be able to take them to the point at which achievement becomes a significant motivator. We are more likely to be successful by concentrating on their other motivators such as creativity. If they are weak elsewhere, they are likely to try to obtain recognition either by disruptive behaviour or by developing eccentricities, or by having themselves transferred to a part of the organization, if it exists, where there is no expectation of achievement or contribution. They will not want to be motivated and the organization may not want to retain their services except perhaps at a very low level.

Factor 6, factor 8 (power and influence)

A high need for recognition and a high need for influence can be a heady cocktail. If both reinforce each other, that is, the person exercising influence does so in a manner or on a topic which meets the approval of those being influenced, we have congruence between the wishes of both leader and led. For example, political leaders who both capture and express the national mood, will not only lead people in the direction in which they want to go but will receive high approval ratings. If there is some overarching goal whose attainment is difficult, both leader and led may be prepared to make sacrifices to achieve it.

If recognition is not given to those leaders who have a high need for recognition, there can be problems. Leadership not based on consent, or at least tacit acceptance, is hard to exercise for those who have a need for wholehearted recognition. They will not like the disapprobation they are receiving. There is a second group of leaders who are in a better position in that they do not require total approval, but are content with approval from a limited but important group of people, their senior managers or whoever else constitutes their business reference group.

Recognition needed from everybody, influence drive

In motivational terms, there may be little to do beyond confirming that the goals of leaders and led coincide with the goals of the organization. We will want to monitor to make sure that decisions are taken in the interests of the organization and not to bolster the ego of the leader. Beyond that, however, there is a danger that with their recognition need apparently satisfied, the leader will become insensitive to what is happening on the ground. For example, some people may not be comfortable with what is happening and may start to lose their commitment.

They will not go out of their way to raise doubts, but will continue to give the appearance of being co-operative.

Influence is being exercised and people are giving the appearance of compliance. The leader starts to hear only what he or she wants to hear; apparently achieving recognition. People are not then giving of their best and the organization is probably being deprived of their energies. This can induce the growth of dependency and increase the burden of leadership. Decision making falls more and more on the shoulders of the leader; everybody else withholds commitment. The way around this is to motivate the leader from the very beginning to encourage a climate in which issues can be discussed and full answers can be expected. It is ideally one in which people are genuinely valued and they are helped to establish congruence between their own objectives and those of the organization. What happens is that the leader is valued because the followers are valued.

If their recognition needs are not satisfied, they may use their influence needs to ensure that they are, but what they do may not be in the interests of the organization. We motivate by encouraging the leader to persuade people as to the new direction, or if that fails, to steel him or her to lead in a different direction to that wanted by those who are led. There are thus two motivational approaches open to us.

Firstly, we can encourage them to try to recapture wholehearted support. Sometimes this happens when it is made clear that the top group in the organization supports what is being done. In those circumstances people will sometimes be prepared to suspend judgement and co-operate. Or we can encourage them to persuade people that the new circumstances are in fact desirable and coincide with their own interests. When they can do that, they have effectively restored their preferred situation, that is the exercise of influence combined with recognition. We can help them to do this not only by giving training in the formal sense, for example in topics like persuasive speaking and the management of change, but by personal coaching, which involves helping them to explore different scenarios and ways of handling the situation.

When the leader with a need for recognition is unable to persuade the larger group, then he finds that his need for recognition is unsatisfied. We can try to motivate them by reinforcing our recognition of what they are doing; they have lost or are losing the recognition of the larger group, but receive intense support from the managers. We are trying to teach them to accept the separation of recognition and influence. We may not be successful. The drive for recognition may be too strong, in which case the motivational effort required may be too much to sustain. We will know that they are unable to stand 'the heat of the kitchen'.

Recognition needed from a select group, influence drive

Those leaders who can be satisfied with recognition from their managers or peers are more able to take decisions which are unpalatable to those who are led. We want to encourage them to remain as sensitive as possible to the impact of their decisions, but not to expect recognition in the form of approbation from those affected.

Finally, those with a high recognition need accompanied by a low influence need have to be kept away from positions of influence. They will probably make good team players, following the direction of the team but not leading it. People will not feel threatened by them, and they will not threaten. We motivate them by giving them recognition, particularly recognition for the part they take in maintaining and developing teams.

Factor 6, factor 9 (variety and change)

People with a high need for recognition and a high need for variety are, on the face of it, easy to motivate. When they do something new or different, they like recognition. Attending to variety and change is, they learn, the way to be recognized. The problem, as always with those who like variety, is that they frequently like to move on to something else before they have completed the last task. We need to consider in detail the possible sources of their recognition, because the consequences and the motivational response can be different.

For example, if recognition is seen as coming from colleagues, we have a potentially manageable problem. Their approval and co-operation is generally required for change to work satisfactorily. The strong recognition drive will create a tendency to work closely with them so that their recognition will be conditional on the change being satisfactory from their point of view. There is always the problem, of course, that what their colleagues see as satisfactory will not objectively be satisfactory. The twin drives of recognition and variety/change will, in this case, create as far as possible the conditions for a satisfactory resolution of differences. Every effort should be made by colleagues to give recognition.

There might be a problem if, in craving recognition from their own department, they do what they think will bring it even though in so doing they damage the interests of other interdependent departments whose recognition is unimportant to them. An awareness of the sources of their recognition need will help us assess what they are doing. In this case it will help us predict possible problems and to motivate them without the need to cause damage.

If they are managers and if it is from their staff they crave recognition, there can be a problem. They may not like change, particularly if they do not see the need for it and if they have no control over it, something which is quite possible when, say, their high 9 boss is in the driving seat. We immediately have a potential conflict, with the change taking place speared on the twin pincers of opposing needs and agony, for the boss, of withheld approval, but the drive for change making it happen anyway. We need to coach them as to the dangers, for bosses, of requiring approval from subordinates. Bosses are paid to represent the interests of their organizations. Making them aware of possible conflict and helping them to manage it is the most satisfactory way of motivating them.

Motivation is thus to give recognition when they have completed a task and to withhold it when they have not. It is also to demonstrate that incomplete tasks do not benefit the organization and to get them to think positively about completion. If they cannot complete, we have the opportunity either of withholding the opportunity for variety, or of giving opportunities for more variety, provided completion takes place. The first approach may start to demoralize, but fulsome recognition when what is required is done can restore morale immediately and positively. Their recognition drive will help them to learn very quickly that the organization requires completion and being generous with recognition will help them to resist the temptation to move on too quickly.

Those who have a high need for recognition and a low need for variety will seek recognition in the more predictable environment they will try to establish for themselves. They will want recognition for their creativity, or achievement.

Factor 6, factor 10 (creativity)

Creativity can clearly be an important source of recognition. Those who have high recognition needs and are successfully creative will feel they are in an ideal position. To a considerable extent they will be self-motivated. Their recognition needs will also help them to concentrate on the needs of those from whom they like to accept recognition. That might sometimes create a problem in that they will try to produce creative ideas that please, which may not actually be the best ideas for the business in hand. In that situation, the need for recognition will restrict their creative autonomy. They will also suffer some pain when the ideas they think ought to be given recognition are not. Their energy may then be expended on demanding recognition and not on further creativity.

How do we manage it? We do so by trying to stop the situation arising. Firstly, we try to give a full briefing so that they have a chance of producing what is required. If we are not able to produce an accurate brief, we warn them in advance that there will be changes and that these will not reflect on their creativity but rather on the failure of the client to provide accurate guidance. Then we remind them that in business terms there is what is called 'creative waste'. That is, what has been created does not do the immediately required job. We have to tolerate it and to give it recognition as something creative in its own right. It is part of the process and might in due course lead to other 'useful' creative ideas. We explicitly acknowledge that creative people need space and that this need sometimes conflicts with the pressure to deliver.

If the creator thinks the idea meets the needs of the business and appropriate people do not, there can be a problem. There may be intense lobbying, but the creator will have to accept that the ideas are not 'right'. Motivation then requires that the creator either truly understands what is unacceptable and has a brief which will help in developing other ideas, or must try again. Doing that, inadequately briefed, will be difficult and the creator will need to be humoured to produce other ideas. We reserve our highest recognition for the creativity that is truly business-oriented and we also encourage others to give recognition.

Factor 6, factor 11 (self-development)

Those with a high need for recognition and high self-development will be motivated to develop in the direction indicated by management. Provided that what management requires is not too far distant from what is congenial or possible, there will be a tendency to take the lead from management. Development can be enhanced by including it as part of planned delegation, agreeing what types of work can be developed as they become available and always fully reviewing work completed and drawing lessons.

If recognition is not given, when, for example, management just forget, this can be de-motivating. Recognition will usually be solicited, and if management miss the cue, that also will de-motivate. If the development is not work related, or not immediately work related, recognition cannot reasonably be expected, but sufficient time, out of working hours, should be allowed. Better still, if time can be made available during working hours, for example, occasionally attending some special function, this will be very motivating.

Those who are low on recognition but high on self-development will be motivated, likewise, if time is made available on occasion for non-work related activities, for example, giving the opportunity to attend conferences.

Those who are high on recognition but low on self-development will need attention for the work they are doing; although the recognition drive can be used to encourage self-development, it will be externally driven and not as self-absorbing or self-starting as for those with a high development need. The initiative for putting self-development on the agenda will come from the management and not from the employee.

Factor 6, factor 12 (interest and usefulness)

Interesting and useful work is again likely to go well with recognition. If the work is useful, people feel they deserve recognition and it needs to be given. If the work is not interesting or useful, high recognition of what is being done will be essential, or de-motivation will take place. As a general rule, people with high factor 6/ high factor 12 need full explanations of everything they are asked to do, including all the circumstances and the reasons surrounding the work. The less interesting or useful they feel the work to be, the more explanation they require as to why it actually is worth while.

There is a possibility of conflict between the source of recognition and the organizational goals. A typical example would be the goal of a government department to save money at the expense of some outside client group. It is then vital to know where the recognition comes from. If it is internal to the organization, say from higher management, then the cost cutting and morale can be maintained. If recognition comes from the client group, then the cost cutting may proceed, but at the expense of morale. This would be a particular problem if job significance comes from satisfying the clients. Another example would be that of the account executive who starts to identify with his or her client and not with the organization who pays their salary. This problem can occur if the supplying organization starts to provide poor service which the executive has to defend.

For long-term motivation, the organization should consider people's recognition. That may not be so easy when the organization is regarded as a vehicle for fulfilling personal views of significance. Again that is something we need to establish at recruitment, but it does not help us if the organizational direction has changed. Nevertheless, the overwhelming motivational need is to make sure that the organization is looked to for recognition. For that we need to use all available means to provide recognition, from praise close to the point of achievement, to formal noting on personal records, to events which celebrate when appropriate, and so on.

When we ask people to move in a direction contrary to that which they regard as significant, we have to give them the opportunity to explain their thinking, to accept it and to try to establish that they will be happy to work with and be motivated in the new direction. We take the opportunity to place what we are doing in the larger context. If, after this, they are not happy, we have to recognize their point of view and consider if they should continue in work which they now regard as insignificant. If they feel inhibited in talking to us, we are likely to detect a falling off in commitment, probably followed by a move to another job.

Those who have high recognition needs but a low need for interesting and useful work will often repay the time taken to motivate them by offering recognition for doing the less interesting work.

Factor 7

Achievement

Highest score recorded = 81
Lowest score recorded = 2
Mode 36 Median 36

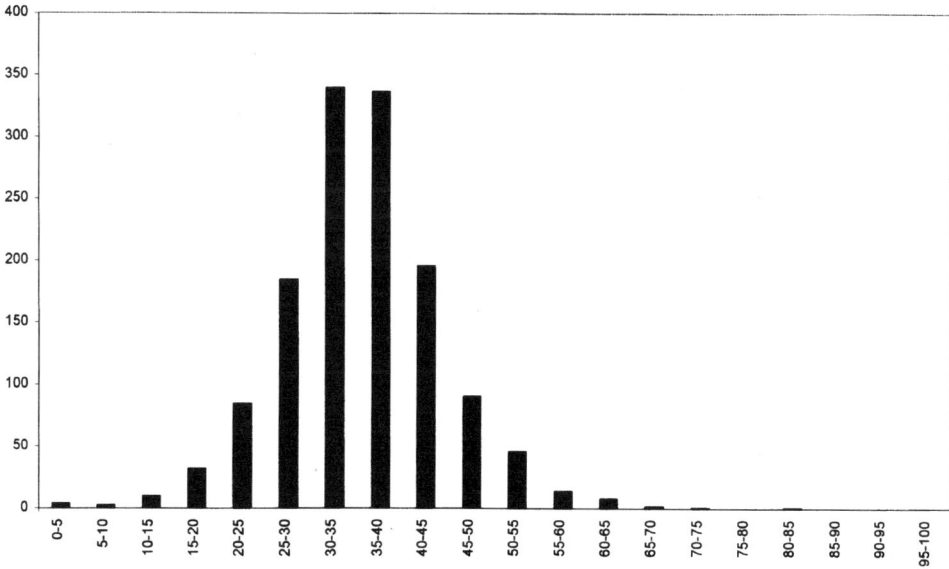

Figure 7   **Factor 7: histogram of scores**

Factor 7 high, other factors evenly spread

A strong characteristic of those with a high achievement drive is that they wish to do things themselves. It can mean that they do not wish to co-operate with others. The drive is an exacting taskmaster. People in the grip of the achievement need can find themselves voluntarily working long hours and driving themselves hard. There are aspects of the drive which, however, constrain them. Before they can start to achieve, they have to be satisfied that the targets they are aiming for are measurable. If they are not measurable, it is not clear if they are being achieved. This constraint is important because not everything is measurable. Taken to extremes, if something cannot be measured it will not be attempted. This means that high achievers are more likely to be attracted to areas like sales, accounting and engineering where measurement is possible. They will want to avoid areas where measurement is not possible or is difficult. In extreme cases they might exclude themselves from the more subtle, less measurable aspects of business.

There is another constraint: they will not want to risk failure. The point of an achievement drive is that people want to achieve. Failure will de-motivate. What that means is that achievers will try to avoid failure by working towards targets that are within their capability. They will be prepared to be stretched, indeed may even demand to be stretched, but only up to the point where success is more likely than failure. If failure is the more likely outcome, they may be tempted to find an excuse not to try. Horner specifically studied women in management in this regard (Horner, 1968). An important part of motivation is to establish their perceived boundary between success and failure. We may be able to move the boundaries by training.

High achievers are likely to be 'driven'. If they are not achieving they can feel worthless. Life may seem pointless. It is only when they have something to do that they come alive. They then feel a sense of purpose and will set themselves or have others set or agree targets for them. Once they have achieved, they will feel a few moments of glory and then the old restlessness will set in and, without something fresh to do, they will feel demoralized. The implications for motivation are obvious. The motivator should provide purpose and be sensitive to lack of purpose and its consequences.

In terms of setting and agreeing targets, achievers can be manageable. Given defined targets, or even fuzzy targets that they can define, they will get on with the job. They may ignore those parts of the job which are not quite susceptible to measurement, or not immediately and obviously relevant to the job, but which might benefit from attention. Part of motivation will be ensuring that those aspects are taken into account without distracting attention from achieving the target. Further than that, if we are developing achievers, we are attempting to increase their tolerance of ambiguities. We want to move them away both from a view of work as a series of 'black and white' challenges and from sidestepping the complexities that cannot be dealt with on a project basis. How we go about doing this will be discussed in the course of the chapter.

The problem is most severe with the really high achievers (55 plus). Such people are ultra-competitive, self-directed and self-starting; willing to accept pain and discomfort in the pursuit of defined and sometimes unchanging objectives; unwilling to let people stand in their way and even aggressive to those who hinder them. They may do whatever is necessary to realize their goals; and they will be happy to work towards a few narrow goals. Their goal achievement is likely to be of considerable benefit to the organization. On a personal basis, they will like working with other high achievers, and may form a closed fraternity, differentiating and trying to remove themselves from others who do not share their aspirations. Their conversation will tend to be single minded. They are unlikely to be team players.

Motivating such people has to start with the definition of the target. High achievers do not like to start working towards an objective to find that it suddenly changes. There is a fundamental requirement to work with them at the beginning of a project to ensure that there is full project definition and that they are committed to it. Their commitment is important. If they are not committed to a target they may be tempted to abandon it. Given full discussion, their commitment or otherwise can be readily established at the beginning.

The importance of project definition is that the objective, once defined, will be pursued with an intensity and energy that, on the one hand, simply must not be wasted and on the other hand, if the target turns out to be incorrect, may lead to a collapse of energy which will be difficult to repair. In establishing the target, full account must be taken of the business objectives. Challenging targets may be exhilarating for the achiever, but the organization wants to share in the rewards for all the energy that is going to be expended. From both a motivational and an organizational point of view there is benefit in a generous provision of time at project inception. Part of that time needs to be spent on considering what can go wrong. What we wish to avoid is precipitous de-motivation because of some insuperable difficulty which, if it had been predicted, would have led to the project being either abandoned or modified. High achievers will be more than happy to overcome difficulties where they have a degree of control. If they feel they have no control, or that there is no way of exercising control, they are likely to suffer a significant reduction in their considerable energy levels.

Motivation entails preparing the ground for the energy that will be released when the project is tackled; letting the achiever tackle what he or she can; and being prepared to remove organizational and resource road-blocks which are beyond their own capacity.

We should take a view on what to do about any neglect of routine administrative work, overlooked while the target receives attention. Do we remove this work from those engaged in projects, or do we insist it is done? We might be able to keep it in sight by having it packaged in the form of a project. Or we might arrange for it to be done in project downtime. We may maintain morale by emphasizing the primacy of the project, and talking with them about the importance of the non-project work. Ideally we do this at inception. Part of the project will be keeping routine matters afloat, discussing with them how and when this will be done.

As the project progresses, we will find it useful to keep in touch, partly for formal monitoring of progress and objectives. We probably help morale if we establish, at the beginning, the expectation of regular review. But informal contact is important so that we know what our achievers are thinking. Otherwise, they may be tempted to think their way through some difficulties and, in a great burst of energy, move off towards the objective in a way we had not expected, leading to unintended consequences. It may be useful for us to know about them in advance.

We find that those who are medium achievers, five or ten above the norm, are not as competitive as the high achievers. They will not have quite the intense interest in the pursuit of excellence and not be so prepared to make that extra effort that will take them to the limit in pursuit of their objectives. Their range of goals may be wider than that of the very high achievers and they may be pursued to a lower standard. That is, they are better able to work in a multi-dimensional environment, able to handle a wider range of measurable targets. They are probably better able to work with others, more likely to be a team player, but still not completely comfortable in teams.

They will be manageable. There will not be quite the same bursts of intense energy, nor the same wish to keep management at arm's length. Agreeing targets with them is a relatively relaxed affair. The targets must still be correct and will repay time spent at inception. The achievers will still want to go off and achieve, but they will be more willing to report back to base, more willing to disclose information. Motivation involves correct project definition, keeping in contact and being prepared to discuss progress in a supportive way.

Low achievers, those with a score significantly below the norm, may be difficult to motivate. They may find targets interesting, but not feel inclined to do much about achieving them. Some of them may, interestingly enough, be delightful company. They will have diverse interests, which they will pick up and drop as they feel inclined. Their conversation will probably be more discursive and rounded, tinged with shades of grey unlike the black and white, measurable and non-measurable, conversation of the high achievers. They may be willing to accept group norms but not contribute to their development. Some may be different from this, with low self-esteem and an inability to think positively about themselves.

The low achievers will be happy to let the world pass them by. They will be difficult to motivate to achieve targets. There will rarely be the bursts of energy that push them to the limits. If there are difficulties, they are likely to retreat or wait to be told what to do. They are probably best used in a not-too-demanding routine environment with closer supervision than would be acceptable to the higher achievers. In today's competitive world, they may not find their services too much in demand.

So far in this chapter we have talked about motivating people with different levels of achievement. There is another aspect to the high achiever which requires attention: the high achiever has difficulty in managing others. In a nutshell, managing others means giving them the opportunity to help others to achieve, which they see as losing an opportunity for their own personal achievement. High achievers have difficulty in letting go or in delegating. However, these same high achievers are quite likely to be promoted to management. Their qualifications for promotion seem excellent. They are capable and get things done. But, not only is there the temperamental difficulty in letting go, there is the added problem that they will consider that the reason they were promoted was that they were achievers and that what is required is more of the same. As managers, of course, what is required is less personal achievement and more encouragement of other people's achievement; managers need to be high on factor 8, the need to influence.

This does not mean that high achievers cannot be effective managers. They can, but it is a precondition that they learn to separate their achievement drive from their management role. Thus, for example, they could keep some high achievement activities for themselves, not involving their staff. One instance would be a sales manager who might keep some personal clients. With those clients, they are, in role terms, a salesperson as opposed to a sales manager. Alternatively, they could aim to satisfy their achievement drive outside work, by climbing mountains or running marathons, for example. To keep the high achievement drive in its place, of course, requires self-knowledge and self-discipline, particularly at times of stress.

We can see the implications for motivation. High achievers need to be managed in a way which keeps their attention on what is required and gives them space to achieve. If they are managed by high achievers, there is a danger that they might be denied that space. High achieving managers, in giving others space, might have problems with their own motivation. There may be little team support in a department of high achievers. They – and that would include the high achieving boss – are more likely to be competing with each other.

Motivation thus requires a deep understanding of the underlying dynamics of the high achiever. Those who manage them have to understand and practise delegation. The successful motivational style is 'loose–tight', that is tight on objectives but loose in giving breathing space to those who do the achieving.

Factor 7, factor 1 (money and tangible rewards)

Those with a high achievement drive and a high money drive are, in the right environment, relatively easy to motivate. They obviously want to be targeted and measured, and they would like a simple relationship between their personal measured achievement and their reward. Provided their work is susceptible to that sort of approach as, for example, in some forms of selling, they will be self-motivating. If there is a problem, it is that they will be resistant to any form of intervention that they see as undermining their earnings. We try to overcome this potential difficulty by noting that the point of maximum management influence and acceptability is at inception, when targets and payment incentives are being established. Changes thereafter will be more difficult, particularly if they are seen as disadvantaging the achiever. We maintain morale by trying to give people as clear a run as possible after agreeing objectives and payments.

Of course, we recognize that, in practice, a clear run is not always possible. Nevertheless, there is a contrast between the two approaches. The first is doing very little and hoping we can adjust as we go along, a form of management which is extremely common and which can be de-motivating to achievers whose earnings are tied up with their achievement. This approach also creates considerable internal conflict as people argue about what money they have or have not earned. The second is spending time and effort to establish objectives, anticipate problems and provide necessary resources, building consensus as to what has to be done. Such an approach is less likely to be deflected at the first sign of difficulties and will, at the very least, have established a means for dealing with those difficulties. This second approach has a better chance of sustaining morale.

If the work situation is not susceptible to measured targets and incentives, we might do better to try to separate achievement and payment. That is to say, we expect achievement but pay a basic, non-incentivized salary. This means the need for money can be met (assuming that value for money is being delivered!) but we are now managing target achievement, uncomplicated by issues of payment as well. We remove day-to-day money as an issue that can undermine morale.

Managing those who have a high achievement drive but a lower relative need for money can be less painful. It is possible to motivate them to achieve without constantly having to worry about the impact on earnings. They will be prepared to achieve targets other than those which bring immediate monetary reward. This does not mean that they are prepared to be financially exploited. It does mean that they are prepared to take a broader view of what needs to be done and to tackle a broader range of projects. They still need to be managed in the sense that objectives must be carefully considered and established. There will still be a wish to go off and to achieve on their own; they will still want their own space; they will still be de-motivated if they lack a sense of purpose; but it will be possible to concentrate on work without perennial negotiation about the impact on pay.

There is one longer-term danger that if the money need is low and the achievement need high, a sense of not achieving at work will either cause them to leave, or perhaps to move out of work altogether, or into a less demanding work environment so that they can achieve at sport or at whatever else interests them.

Factor 7, factor 3 (structure)

High achievement and high structure drives represent a very demanding combination. Given the right circumstances, we are looking at successful and relaxed people. Given the wrong circumstances, we can be looking at under-achievement and a permanent state of tension.

Where is the potential source of tension between these two drives? Essentially it is that the achiever is looking for measurement and those who are structure-driven are looking for clear guidelines. In the right circumstances, targets and the rules will be congruent, that is, they will reinforce each other. An example might be a sales person who finds the reporting structures sensible and helpful in that they present useful information which helps selling. Another example is a clear and uncomplicated incentive scheme where the path to rewards offered can be mapped without ambiguity. Vroom recognized the need for transparent routes to success in his expectancy theory of motivation (Vroom and Deci, 1970). The tension will occur when the rules are not helpful, and indeed hinder the job. A good example might be of a police officer with a high structure need whose pursuit of criminals appears to be hindered by excessive bureaucracy and paperwork. The officer's high need for structure means not only that all the procedures are followed religiously, but also that he or she feels less successful than might otherwise have been the case. In extreme cases it might seem that the system is paralysing them.

How do we motivate in such circumstances? Clearly, our first step is to try to create congruence between targets and rules. Where there is an absolute need for rules to be followed, as for example where there is a need for compliance with the requirements of regulators, there is a clear benefit in working with people who find such compliance natural and even agreeable. They know what they are expected to do, nobody can overrule them in doing it, and they have the satisfaction of knowing that they have done what has been demanded.

The problems arise when the needs for compliance are so demanding that they make achievement difficult. Then there is tension, but there is the possibility of overcoming or at least reducing it by providing training and technical support. Morale can be sustained by involving people in trying to find better ways of meeting the compliance needs, something which will inherently appeal to the achiever. Properly managed, using the achievement drive to manage the structure drive can be energizing and morale boosting. Real morale problems occur when there is an incompatibility between achievement and structure. That is to say, that the rules seriously undermine the possibility of achievement and external factors make resolution of the conflict impossible. People have the option of trying to work in this difficult situation, but morale will tend to be low and turnover and sickness probably high.

We motivate people with high achievement and low structure needs by working with them to establish and agree targets and then by giving them space. Their lack of structure means that the principal method of managing them will be through their targets. We give the maximum amount of space by agreeing a feedback process at the beginning. The more competent and committed they are, the less feedback required. The lower the structure need, the less stress caused by any incompatibility between the needs of the job and the structure in which it is embedded. There will be a strong temptation to do whatever is necessary to achieve. However, any necessary structure might be ignored, with disastrous consequences. Some pensions salespeople will understand the point. We protect ourselves by giving space and insisting on feedback and we maintain motivation by explaining the need for feedback.

Factor 7, factors 4 and 5 (people contact and relationships)

There is an incipient tension between the need for achievement and the need for short-term relationships. The achievement drive can be lonely. It is a person pitting him or herself against some target. Other people's contribution can be seen as diminishing a person's effort, an effect magnified if there is a high recognition need as well. At the time the achievement is taking place, people may feel a need to distance themselves from others, may even become prickly with them. The preferred profile will be high 7/low 4.

However, people do always have the opportunity to work in such a fashion. Much of business is about interdependence, and increasingly, with the de-layering that is taking place, working in teams. This poses the question of whether a high achiever can ever work in a team. The answer is that they can work successfully, but the situation has to be handled with care. We can see this by examining how teams develop.

Teams go through various stages of development. To be successful they need to have purpose and their goals have to be accepted by the team members. The first stage is one of goal definition, followed by a level of conflict the intensity of which depends on the magnitude of the issues at stake, the range of options available for the achievement of success, and the personalities and needs of the team members, but which is concerned with how the team should go about its business. People of all profiles who are members of teams have to work their way through these stages. If the members are unable to commit themselves to the team objectives, or if there is no resolution of how the team purpose is to be achieved, the teams will perform poorly and even fail. If they are able to commit themselves, to agree how the team will organize itself and appoint members to roles, then the team has the chance to move on to the next stage and become effective.

High achievers may have problems with the first two stages. They are happiest when they know what they are doing. The ambiguities of indecision as the team gropes its way forward can cause real, personal stress. How they react depends on the circumstance of the group; if the boss is present they are likely to sit there drumming their fingers, waiting for the team to decide the way forward; if the boss is absent, they tend to do something, anything, to resolve their anxiety over non-action. They rarely sit still, but nearly always burn off their energies by finding something to do. If the tension in the group is high, they will leave the room, go and negotiate, even take a walk. Once they know what they have to achieve, all their energy and sense of purpose will flood back. This is the point at which their achievement drive could benefit the group.

The operative word is 'could'. Teams perform well because the members have defined their purpose and the roles they will play. They are successful to the extent that team members allow their colleagues to get on with whatever it has been agreed they should do. In other words there is a high level of trust. The usual sporting metaphors apply. In the successful team, the striker does not attempt the defender's job. They each rely on the other to play their respective roles. If there is no trust, and the members check each other's work, perhaps duplicate it, the teams will not perform so well and may fail.

Those who are high achievers can operate in an environment of trust. They will know what they have to do and will be given the freedom to get on with it. They may prefer, at times of uncertainty, that somebody else redefine their measurable targets, or that they at least are given reasonable space to do it themselves. The prerequisite for their success is that the team trusts them. When that happens they will be able to deliver. If the other team members interfere, they may lose interest. Given that degree of autonomy within the team, they will be able to operate successfully with high factor 4, the need for people contact. The need will be for animal warmth and they will enjoy it, provided it is accepting and does not crowd them. If it does crowd them, it will cramp their style, the tension between factors 4 and 7 may become intolerable and they may want to opt for the animal warmth without the achievement, or vice versa. The tension will be reduced, the greater the role definition achieved and the autonomy allowed.

The motivational lesson is obvious. High achievers need clarity, measurement and low ambiguity. The team needs to be encouraged to define roles. There should be enough training so that people can discharge their roles without others feeling the need to interfere. As far as possible, we need to create an atmosphere of trust and tolerance.

Finally, what about those who resist working as part of a team? Our motivational task is not to enforce sociability, but to maintain contact with those who, in work terms, are potential loners. This is not only for our benefit, but for their benefit also. To the extent that they are not 'plugged in' to the organizational network, they risk cutting across the organization's concerns. Contact helps maintain long-term morale. We maintain contact by helping them to define their objectives, giving them space to perform and then recognizing their achievements.

Factor 7, factor 6 (recognition)

High achievement and recognition drives can go well together. Motivation is, at first sight, easy. People achieve and we make sure we catch them at the moment of achievement to give fulsome recognition, informing all interested parties so that the achiever knows this is the case. At times of failure, recognition is also required. Those concerned will not be so anxious for everybody else to be informed. They will want the matter to be discussed explicitly, lessons learned and the necessary steps taken to ensure there will be no recurrence.

As always with recognition, it is important to note that if we do not give recognition, it will be sought elsewhere. It may be sought outside the organization, or from those inside the organization who are not committed to its concerns. The message is that giving recognition is an imperative. If it is not given, there will be a reduction in commitment and a dissipation of effort.

The higher somebody's relative recognition drive, the more they will consider other people's opinions on whether or not to undertake something. For example, they will worry about the risk of failure. If the risk is too high, they might lower their targets to make sure that they do not risk losing recognition. Motivation involves encouraging them to think about risk and how they might reduce it. Where taking the risk is in the organization's interests, they should be reassured about the consequences of failure which will not be too serious, and there will be generous recognition for success.

The lower the relative recognition need, the smaller the problem and the greater willingness to take risk. Indeed there might be willingness to attempt to achieve even if nobody else knows of the results, and in the face of hostility. However, we need to remember that high achievers do not like failure, whether they are demanding recognition or not. Part of motivation is to ensure that, given fair effort, there is a greater chance of success than failure.

Factor 7, factor 8 (power and influence)

There is tension between a high achievement drive and a high influence drive. One wants to do it all, the other wants those they have influenced to act upon their ideas. Motivation entails trying to help achieve a proper division of labour between that which it is appropriate to do and that which others should do.

Before looking at delegation we should consider the possibility that high 7/high 8 will use their influence drive to bolster their achievement, using people merely as a resource, but not motivating them or empowering them in any way. In an extreme case, people will be used and cast off when not required. Motivation finds the balance of what is required. Are we looking for achievement? In that case, there should be opportunities to achieve which are separate from the need to exercise influence. We can facilitate this by reserving some activities and, if it is necessary to involve other people in their achievements, by providing training in delegation, so that those who participate have the opportunity to attain some sense of contribution and development.

Are we looking for the use of influence? In that case, we will want to move them further from achievement and encourage them to derive their satisfaction from the achievements of others. This proper delegation is essential for the two drives to work in harness and not undermine each other. Interference creates a vicious circle. People will stop doing things because they know the manager will do it for them, or undo what they have done so that they will begin to wonder if any effort is worth while. They will become dependent and the manager will have to make more and more decisions and start to do more and more him or herself. In a sense, the achievement and influence drives start to work overtime, but the effort usually becomes too great, leaving a dispirited manager and a dispirited team.

Maintaining a proper balance between the two drives will help the team to develop confidence and the ability to work on their own without constant reference to authority, releasing time and energy to use the influence drive where it is appropriate. Motivation is thus a subtle affair. It helps people to think through the requirements of the job and about the optimum use of their time; what they should do and what their team should do. It can encourage them to work with their team to resolve these issues. It might involve holding their hands as they are tempted to interfere; perhaps holding them back so that they learn to gain confidence in their team. The influence drive can then predominate and not be undermined by the achievement drive.

A high achievement drive and a low influence drive creates a different motivation problem. People with this combination are probably happier outside management. They prefer to do things themselves. They might regard influence as a chore distracting them from their 'real' work and find management stressful. If they are outside management, they are motivated by concentrating on their achievement drive. If they are inside management, they will particularly benefit from training in management; an understanding of the process will help reduce the stress of exercising influence. If they are, for example, working in a flat organization where successful operation requires influence skills, that is, there is insufficient management resource to provide day-to-day or even medium-term direction, they will similarly benefit from training ineffective influencing skills.

Factor 7, factor 9 (variety and change)

People with a high need for achievement and a high need for variety and change will want to work on a great variety of projects. They will not concentrate their efforts on one area of achievement. They will probably become bored once a project has been completed and want to move on. There may be a great reluctance to tie up loose ends. In extreme cases, they will have great difficulty in repeating a project.

Motivating such people is, in principle, simple. They need to be fed new projects and be provided with opportunities for the enormous release of energy that accompanies them. We will need to specify, at inception, the definition of project success, so that they are clear about what they are aiming to do, and know when they have done it. They will derive satisfaction from project completion. They will then want to move on very quickly and they will see the completed project as history, not to be revisited. They may be reluctant to review why projects succeed or fail; perceiving the necessary process of 'examining the bones' as a mystifying irrelevance.

Those who have a low need for variety will have different motivational requirements. They will be prepared to put in time and effort to achieve perfection in a limited area of activity. They may be prepared to work to standards which are unnecessarily high. It is important to choose with care which projects they are going to work on. There should be a business benefit in the use of their time and they must be committed. If we want to move them on and create too much variety, as they see it, we are likely to have motivation problems. However, the benefit to the organization from this combination of drives can be considerable. We will have people who will stay the course, often for years.

Because the time spans can be considerable, in motivational terms, we should keep close and make sure that there are no developing problems, or issues which can distract attention and effort. We should take the time to work with them to review progress, not allowing them to become isolated and possibly springing an unwelcome surprise on us which we could have dealt with earlier.

Factor 7, factor 10 (creativity)

There is an apparent incompatibility between a high need for achievement and a high need for creativity. Achievement needs measurement. Creativity, to the extent that it concerns exploration of new ideas, is immeasurable. We do not know the end product of the creative process. Indeed, there is risk in creativity. We do not fully know where we are going and might produce nothing.

However, if the achievement drive is predominant, the creative drive is likely to be used to help achievement. The usual measurable targets will apply, but the creativity will be called in aid, something which can be useful for the more complex projects. If creativity is seen to hinder achievement, it will probably be relegated. Where this is the case, there are, in motivation terms, no particular requirements beyond providing space to allow creativity and achievement full scope. As always, project definition is important and is the basis of successful motivation. If there is a conflict between the two drives it will be expressed in tension between the exploratory and divergent characteristics of creativity and the hard-edged search for measurable objectives which characterize achievement. Motivation is fulsome in its recognition of both but works to encourage the balance between creativity and achievement which best serves the interests of the organization.

Those who have a strong achievement drive with low creativity will tend to achieve by going along the straight and narrow. Unlike their more creative colleagues, they will not feel the need to take creative risks or creative short cuts. They may lack a certain flair but will be safe, reliable and productive. We may find it in their interests to keep them away from those aspects of achievement which, for success, require subtle creative insights.

Factor 7, factor 11 (self-development)

The drives for achievement and autonomy go well together. Achievement means doing it ourselves, autonomy means being in control. The achievement drive helps people develop and learn in a way which enables them to increase control. But people with high achievement/high development needs will tend to be selective in what they set out to achieve. The question they will ask themselves is 'Can I learn from this activity?' If not, they may not want to do it.

At work, we may have to motivate them by showing how a particular project or activity will help their self-development. If we cannot do so, they may be reluctant to proceed and we may have to demonstrate that the organization needs the work and that there will be future opportunities for work leading to self-development, in other words, a trade-off.

Projects are best structured to offer learning opportunities which the achiever sees as relevant. In motivational terms, most benefit will be realized by debriefing projects after completion to see what lessons have been learned. If these lessons can be formally noted in a record of achievement, so much the better. Sometimes there is an additional benefit in that work-based projects can be tied into educational projects, contributing to the acquisition of qualifications, something very acceptable to high achievers. There is a whole system available to help with this. There are examinations, courses and libraries. The educational system is designed to give people the opportunity to develop, and to exploit their need for achievement. After education, similar opportunities are available for professional development. People then have the satisfaction of both achieving at work and adding to their relevant stock of knowledge, skills and experience. The drives work together to the benefit of both the organization and the individual. At best, motivation becomes an intrinsic part of the work experience.

For those who have a high need for achievement and a low need for self-development the achievement drive will be directed to non-developmental purposes. Outside work, such people might, for example, aim to beat their record on computer games. Inside work, they might aim, say, to exceed the laid-down standards of performance. There is no sense in which they use the drive to develop themselves, or to make development a major plank of their working life. We motivate them by harnessing their achievement drive, helping them become better at what they do. We perhaps draw their attention to development opportunities. We do not de-motivate them by letting them think that we regard their failure to grasp development opportunities as a weakness.

Factor 7, factor 12 (interest and usefulness)

Those with a high need for achievement and a high need for jobs which *they* see as interesting and useful will be at their best in jobs which meet both those requirements. Motivating them requires setting challenging targets and presenting the opportunity to achieve. If the achievement drive is strong, we may overlook their need for interest; but it is there. We should take time to explain the background to our requests and how they relate to the larger picture; and how it links to their view of what is interesting.

The challenge of achievement will keep them motivated in the short term, whether there is intrinsic interest or not. In the longer term commitment will reduce. If we are unable to establish or restore their interest, or unable to convince them that what we want is worth while, we will probably find a joyless attitude to work, possibly followed by a move elsewhere.

Those with a lower need for interest and usefulness are more likely to be motivated by achievement for its own sake. This does not mean we should ignore larger considerations, but that our motivation should concentrate on the mechanisms of achievement which will provide most of the motivation they require.

Factor 8

Power and influence

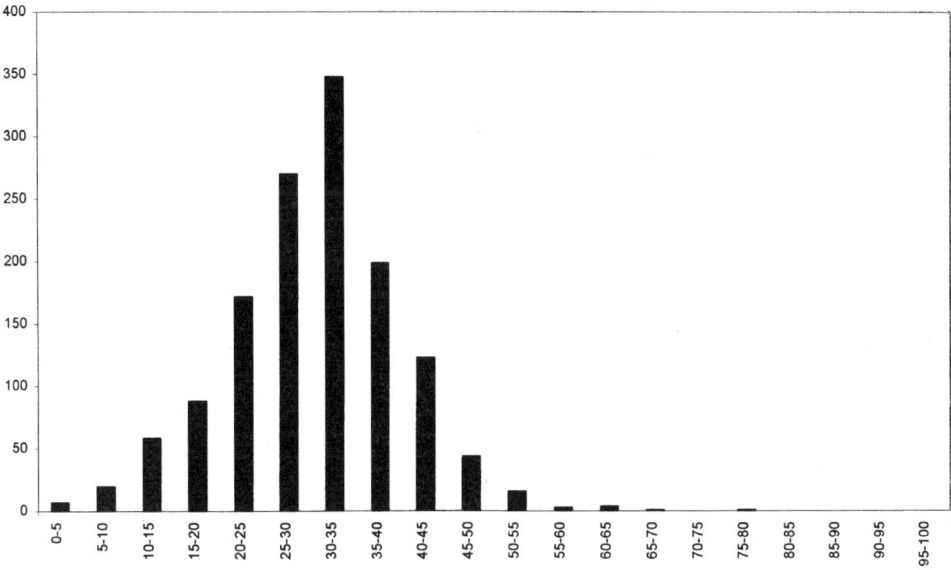

Figure 8   Factor 8: histogram of scores

Factor 8 high, other factors evenly spread

The ability to lead and influence others, used properly, is clearly one of the most desirable human qualities. It can release human energies, empower people and focus all their efforts in the same direction. Its successful exercise requires good intent, purpose, technical as well as interpersonal skills and a willingness to accept personal exposure and risk. Used improperly, as the history of the twentieth century tells us, it can produce disaster.

Factor 8 is different from the other factors in that the exercise of influence involves people impinging directly on other people. There is a much greater need with factor 8 to consider other people's reactions. There is an element of risk in that other people might not react favourably. There is also the possibility that the exercise of influence might be unsuccessful; things might go wrong. This means that it must not be undertaken lightly. If it is exercised ineptly, there may be damage, so it has to be used with care. That is why we will take some time to consider the various aspects of influence.

Purpose

Some people want to exercise influence without purpose. But this is pointless. If there is no purpose, then influence has to be exercised for its own sake. In fact, today, there are few opportunities to exercise influence without there being some sort of end product, such as increased sales, successful development projects or quality research. In terms of management, which can be defined as 'achieving results through people', it is reasonable to expect that the exercise of purposeless influence would be damaging and the careers of the managers concerned relatively short. The purposeless exercise of influence belongs to another world and is irrelevant in a management context.

Influence with purpose is a different matter. It implies that there is some idea of what should be achieved. Although it is theoretically possible that influence can be exercised through, say, sheer force of personality, its success usually requires commercial or sector specific insight; and possibly technical and functional skills. This immediately puts training high on the agenda, for both technical and motivational reasons.

People

People can be harnessed to achieve goals in different ways. At one extreme, people can be coerced, at the other, they can be empowered. We know coercion creates dependency and leaves behind an enfeebled organization. We also know that empowerment is time consuming and hard to engender, though there is general agreement that the commitment created breeds success, particularly at times of environmental and market turbulence.

The organization thus has an interest in how power is exercised. Its preference in today's more sophisticated and informed world is for empowering and informing leadership; and that is particularly true when the output of the organization is dependent on the quality of the people working for it. This suggests a twofold approach, one based on mentoring, the purpose of which is to inculcate the preferences and culture of the organization. The other is based on training so that there is a technical understanding of interpersonal processes, including delegation, which can help to inform the influence drive. With the influence drive, and this applies more strongly than for any other drive, we need to consider not only the motivation of those who exercise influence, but also its impact on the motivation of the recipients. Throughout this chapter, we look at the motivation of both parties.

Training involves clear motivational objectives. Its purpose is to ensure that the exercise of informed influence produces beneficial outcomes for the organization, its people and for the person exercising influence. To be effective, we need not only an acceptable purpose but a willingness to do something about it, that is, to have a willingness to take risks. And that raises the possibility of failure.

Risk

The question influence brokers have to ask themselves is the extent to which they want to risk failure. It is the same question high achievers have to ask themselves, but there is a difference. If the high achievers fail, they let themselves down, and other people too. Given the opportunity, they can pick themselves up and start again. But if people are overt in the way they exercise influence and what they have suggested fails, they must persuade people to follow them for a second time. Assuming that people have a choice, this time they will be more cautious. In the end, with too much poor performance, the exercise of influence will become extremely difficult, if not impossible. Technical and functional training again becomes an important issue.

The less overt exercise of influence is perhaps not so risky. It can either be done in the capacity of *éminence grise*, the power behind the throne, in which case the person to be satisfied is the person being advised. Or it can be done in the wider arena in a more subtle manner so that blame for failure cannot be so easily attributed. How power is actually exercised by somebody is a matter for both instinct and training. Training, including coaching, is again an important part of motivation.

Ability

The question of technical or functional ability in the field of operation is again crucial. Those who have a strong influence drive and a high propensity for risk, but who are not competent, are likely to have short careers, though that will not stop them trying to exercise influence. However, they may have to be prevented from acting in the organization's name.

The greatest safeguards against failure are ability and training. Those thus equipped will be better aware of the steps to be taken to reduce risk. They will be able to assess, for example, where the risks are so overwhelmingly against movement that the status quo is the only realistic option. Or they can quantify the risk and take steps to reduce the chances of failure. Depending on their personal toleration of risk, they are in a much better position to decide whether to go ahead, or partly ahead, or not to move at all.

Ways of exercising influence

Those who wish to exercise influence are of considerable interest to any organization. Key questions to be considered are not only about ability but also about purpose. Will its exercise be benign, in the interests of the organization and empowering? Or at the other end of the spectrum, will it be in their own interest and exercised in a debilitating manner? Or somewhere in between? Is its exercise high profile, is there any doubt who is in charge, and how is it accepted by those who are being influenced? In contrast, is the exercise through other people? To what extent is the influence exercised personally and to what extent is it dependent on the authority invested by the organization?

Again the question of technical and functional ability requires attention. The organization can harness purpose to itself, provided it takes the trouble to be clear about the outputs it wishes to achieve, and progress is carefully monitored. This does not mean that there has to be detailed surveillance of method which will be de-motivating, but that the results obtained are clearly communicated and available to the organization. The question of how power is exercised, in an empowering or debilitating manner, can be judged by techniques such as 360° assessment, followed by coaching if necessary.

Issues of control

The exercise of influence is ultimately an exercise in control. Sometimes that is obvious, for example, if influence is exercised in a coercive way. Sometimes it is not so obvious, when for example, the use of influence is to empower. In one sense, empowerment means reducing control and releasing energy, so that committed people achieve in their own way. Nevertheless, within business organizations, we require people to deliver business objectives. No matter how agreeable and hands-off the management style, and no matter how indirect we may be, ultimately our requirement is for control.

In motivational terms, there is an important issue in that managers are frequently in favour of the principle of empowerment but concerned about loss of control. The issue is real even at senior management level, and there needs to be detailed explanation that financial and other objectives will still be achieved. We need not ignore the issue but explore it openly and demonstrate how establishing clear outputs makes a loosening of management style possible. We need also to consider, as part of our coaching, what is to happen when outputs are not being achieved and intervention is required, something which is usually handled by pre-arrangement.

Factor 8, factor 1 (money and tangible rewards)

The successful exercise of influence and the acquisition of income and wealth do, of course, go hand in hand. However, accepting as always that it is in the interests of the organization to pay at least the market rate, there is a question as to the balance between a person's influence drive and their need for money.

Those who have an influence drive that is higher than their money drive will prefer occupations that are high on influence but low on material reward. In an extreme case they will be permanent secretaries in the UK Civil Service, with extraordinary budgets and extraordinary influence, rather than captains of industry or commerce. Money will be a less important motivator and, though their salaries are likely to be many times higher than average, these are unlikely to be as much as could be obtained elsewhere in the market-place.

In this situation, we motivate by offering the maximum freedom possible, though again working hard to specify outputs. We should also pay attention to factor 12, their need for intrinsic job interest, which will probably be high and, as far as possible, attempt to meet it. We should note that, if their influence needs are not being met, they are likely to be de-motivated and they will not have a high salary to compensate. To keep them within the organization, it is essential that they find opportunities to exercise influence.

Outside the strict organizational context, the two drives together are likely to lead either to attempts to use money to buy influence (a larger than life case was the late Sir James Goldsmith who financed the Referendum Party in the 1997 UK general election), or to work in the voluntary sector where influence is possible but not material reward. We can, in appropriate cases, retain and motivate people by giving them the opportunity to use organizational time and/or resources to exercise influence outside the organization in areas of relevant public life.

There is an additional group who are high on the need for power but low on the need for money. For such people, power and money do not work in tandem. The exercise of influence is more compelling and the absence of a strong money drive probably means its exercise takes place in the public and charitable sectors. Such a profile is probably the foundation of the 'voluntary'culture of the UK and the USA.

Factor 8, factor 3 (structure)

A high need for influence together with a high need for structure form an explosive combination. Power concerns influence, structure is knowing the rules and needing to be bound by them. The contradiction is obvious. From the motivational point of view, there is a need to be aware of the conflict and of how the two drives might interact in the environment under consideration.

In a very structured environment, those with high power drives will want influence over the rules and to establish that those who work in the organization obey the rules. The development of rules will be one of the tools of influence. The style of influence will tend towards coercion rather than empowerment. There may be difficulties when there is conflict between the influence drive and the rules. Those with a higher influence than rules drive are likely to bend the rules, but at a cost to themselves in terms of personal tension, with possible concerns about setting a bad example and a consequent undermining of authority.

Drafting the rules will require a balance between the needs of the organization for predictability on the one hand, and the retention of flexibility to deal with the many circumstances with which the rules cannot cope. Part of using influence will be retaining discretion to deal with those situations. The problem is that, if the balance is not right, the organization could approach paralysis and the management overload and stress.

To motivate we should identify the inherent tension and educate on the need for balance, trying to develop an acute awareness of the difference between organizational needs for structure and personal needs; then trying to match those personal and organizational needs. If the organization needs to be rule bound – for example, it is public sector and dispensing funds according to rule-driven criteria – there is likely to be a motivational match between those who are both high on structure and influence. There may, however, be a problem with thinking about issues which overstep the rules. Motivational problems may arise at points of change, creating stress. Motivation at those points will involve providing counselling and support and trying to focus attention on the new outputs, so that new rules can be developed. But, in reality, those with high influence and structure needs are likely to find difficulty managing rapid change and in the long run are better off elsewhere.

Those with high influence and low structure needs are in a strong position in that they can use their powers of influence without feeling any need to pay attention to rules or structure. For them, the sky is the limit. A more realistic limit is what people will accept. They will be more acceptable inside the organization if they can create rules for those who need rules and do not create them for those who do not. At a higher level, we talk of those with high influence drives as *pathfinders* and *culture builders* (Leavitt, 1986; Schein, 1985). They create vision, meaning and significance for those they influence. The culture they create is the set of rules and expectations that govern the behaviour of those they influence.

Motivating them entails the training and technical and personal skills required to exercise power usefully, or the opportunity for them to acquire that training. Performance indicators for what the organization requires are useful to show how they should use their energies. We need to offer opportunities to exercise power in a relatively risk free environment, where they can make mistakes without damaging the business; and review what has happened so that they can learn useful lessons. Motivation includes the provision of counselling and mentoring so that they can learn about what is workable and acceptable in the organization. Finally, we need to establish with them that the structure required by the organization is provided either by them or by others on their behalf. Although they may find our efforts de-motivating, in that they would rather not have to think about structure, the organization requires it and it must be provided.

Factor 8, factors 4 and 5 (people contact and relationships)

Those who are high on the need for influence and high on the need for short-term relationships will find their drives well matched. The power drive requires people to influence so the two needs work in tandem. There may be a problem if there is a need to exercise power in a way which people find unacceptable. The relationships can then become disagreeable, particularly problematic if the person exercising power lacks political skill. Given that the influence drive is higher than the relationship drive, the problem is surmountable. In motivation terms, we are probably looking at no more than recognition that the dilemma is painful, perhaps talking through any difficulties involved.

With a high need for long-term relationships there might be a more serious problem. Long-term relationships take time to build. If they are used to bolster the influence drive, that is, power by association with the powerful, as can happen with wives of presidents of the USA, the problem occurs if the influence has not been exercised successfully. The damage is done both to whatever cause is being pursued and to the person attempting to influence. There is very little that can be done in motivational terms except try to pick up the pieces afterwards. Before the fall, those associating with the influential are usually beyond reach and do not seek motivational help.

If the long-term relationship is with those over whom power is being exercised, there may be a serious and unpleasant problem if power has to be exercised in a way which is unpalatable to the recipients. In that situation a considerable motivational effort may be required.

Those with high 8/low 4 are in a different situation. Thus although it is a truism that influence needs people to influence, the people being influenced do not have to be physically present. The role of the *éminence grise* has, through the ages, been well attested. Talk of 'faceless bureaucrats' suggests a common belief that there is much impersonal exercise of power. This is the lonely exercise of power. Assuming good intent, it is beneficial to the extent that issues can be considered on their merits, undistorted by the consequences of personal loyalties. It is dangerous to the extent that it is insensitive to, or even out of touch with, human needs. If we assume bad intent, the consequences can be disastrous. As managers, we may need to mediate someone's use of influence. We can do this directly, by using them in a staff role in which they give (powerful) advice but the power is exercised by others. Or we can impose checks on their use of influence, so that what they want is filtered by others. In their motivational terms, this may not be very satisfactory, but in the motivational terms of everybody affected it might be the only sensible way forward.

If people with this profile have direct influence, our motivation concerns watching staff as much as supporting managers. We should also encourage the manager to explore staff feelings so that they can be taken into account in the decisions made; these decisions should not be more damaging to staff interests than necessary. It might be worthwhile to establish a formal process for decision making wherein other people's interests are fully considered.

Factor 8, factor 6 (recognition)

Exercising influence and needing recognition from 'everybody'

High need to exercise influence and a high need for recognition can work both ways. Let us first look at the need for recognition from 'everybody'. On the one hand, there might be the temptation to exercise influence in a way which increases recognition, to 'play to the gods'. People who behave like this are looking for short-term gain. This need for recognition can flaw their judgement, so that they fail to make optimum decisions. Whatever goes wrong then occurs in the full blaze of courted publicity. On the other hand, a high need for recognition can make people very careful about how they use their influence. They will take a longer-term view. Even if they have to do things that are unpopular, they will prepare the ground so that they will be seen to have made a reasonable decision in the circumstances.

Clearly, those in the first category are living dangerously, possibly having to spend more time recovering from adverse decisions, while those in the second category are more likely to be in a position to increase their influence. The morale of the second group is probably higher than that of the first. Motivation involves increasing the sensitivity of people in the first group to the likely impact of their impetuosity, encouraging them to pause before deciding and perhaps introducing them to formal processes which encourage them to think about the impact of wrong decisions on their own situation.

A formal process can be used to establish the likely impact of an important decision before it is taken, including the effect on people involved.

Exercising influence and needing recognition from particular people or groups

If the need for recognition comes from a particular body of people or a particular person, we have a different situation. If the person or body is legitimate, in organizational terms, the exercise of influence is likely to be supportive to the organization. If the persons or body are not legitimate, there may be a conflict of loyalties.

In motivational terms, we need to identify the source of the recognition and to consider any implications for performance. Once the issue has been brought into the open, it is more capable of management. The objective, then, is to make the organization the focus for recognition, bearing in mind that it is more likely to happen if the organization takes the trouble to give recognition, both formally and informally. We can help the process by trying, through observation and questioning, to establish the form in which recognition should be given. But we can start by applying a few basic rules, like giving recognition at the point at which it has been earned and by being specific about why the recognition is being given.

Exercising influence and not needing recognition

Those who are high on influence but low on recognition can be good decision makers, though there may be a tendency to disregard the opinions of others. They will be in a good position to make objective decisions, but may be excessively insensitive to their impact. If they possess good social and political skills, quite possible in somebody with high influence needs, they may be able to drive through their decisions without too much disruption.

They are motivated by being given the opportunity to exercise their power, but are coached to understand that disregard of the legitimate concerns of others, a direct consequence of their low need for recognition, can harm them. They need to be taught that the sensitivity dimension of their work requires as much attention as the more objective part of what they are doing. We may have to suggest a formal process to ensure that, in decision taking, the interests of those affected are at least considered.

Factor 8, factor 7 (achievement)

Those with a high influence drive want to get results through other people; those with a high achievement drive want to achieve the results themselves. Those with both drives may find them in conflict. They are in the best position if the influence need is greater than that of achievement. They can then probably manage to allow people to do things without continuous interference, though they may have difficulty in so doing at times of rapid change and stress.

Two problems may arise. The first is that staff are not allowed to develop, and the second is that those who exercise influence may not develop themselves. Staff will not be allowed to develop if their managers constantly involve themselves in the details of their work. That will be de-motivating for the staff and will eventually lead to an increase in dependency. Before they do anything difficult, they will feel a need to refer upwards. The corollary is that the manager will become more and more involved in the details of the work, finding himself with less time to exercise, or even think about exercising, influence at a level higher than the day-to-day. Finally, a de-motivated manager will lead de-motivated staff.

We motivate the manager (and indirectly the staff) by making him or her aware of the potential conflict. We reinforce the power drive by giving opportunities to exercise influence, framing them in such a way that they are simply unable to attend to detail. Thus we rewrite the theory that a manager should have no more than 6 or 7 reports. The right number is 10–15. That way you have no choice but to let people grow and mature. With 10 or 15 reports, a leader can focus only on the big issues, not on minutiae.

We train in delegation, so that there is a deep and eventually intuitive understanding of how to achieve the outputs required without constant interference. We look to see if there are areas where it is possible for the manager to indulge his or her need for achievement without impinging on the needs of the staff to achieve. For example, we might give a sales manager their own personal clients so that he or she can go some way to satisfy the personal need to make sales. For a university head of department, we would look for personal research in addition to team research.

We might encourage achievement outside work, for example, in sport or crafts where it is the personal element that is important. These approaches attempt to relieve the temptation to gain personal achievement at the expense of the staff. The benefit that arises from encouraging good practice, that is, an end to unnecessary interference, is that it allows the manager to develop. The problem of interference is simply that it creates enormous time management pressures. So much time is involved in working through details with people, there is never enough time for working at a higher level, or indeed even for beginning to think at the higher level. Failure to work at that level means failure to develop. The problem can be partially tackled through good training in time management and discussions with senior management about time usage, in particular time available for working at a higher strategic level. The process can be encouraged by senior management pressure for work to be undertaken at the higher level, so that there is simply no time to work at the lower level. This will be good for the morale of the staff and, given good initial training and support in delegation, good for the morale of the manager.

There is a final point to consider. There is often the temptation for influential people to reserve the nice jobs for themselves. In extreme cases, the staff have all the low grade jobs and the manager has all the fun. This is best tackled by helping the manager to create an environment where there is a trade-off between interesting jobs and necessary but uninteresting jobs. People then feel they are being given a reasonable balance of work, beneficial for morale.

Those who have a high influence drive and a low achievement drive are in an excellent position to focus their energies and input on influencing people. The priority is now to ensure that they are technically and functionally competent. As they progress, they move away from personal achievement and enjoy it. They will not feel the temptation to interfere. Motivating them entails giving them opportunities but not putting them into such a position that they can make mistakes which damage their career. If they have a high factor 11, a need for self-development, we can attempt to make sure that this works in tandem with their influence drive.

Factor 8, factor 9 (variety and change)

The drives for influence and variety are dynamic. Even if influence is focused, the drive for variety can either help or hinder performance. It helps if it allows response to a fast changing situation. It hinders if it creates a continuous urge to move on, or to be bored at the first hint of repetition, so that tasks are never completed. The effect on staff can be traumatic as they find themselves continuously changing, possibly feeling an ongoing loss of control. Even worse, they may find themselves in a constant state of reorganization.

How do we retain motivation in this situation? As always, we need to make managers aware of the impact of the two drives. Secondly, we need to encourage their ability to use influence in situations of continuous change and ambiguity. High influence/high variety people will have the energy and will enjoy the juggling and manoeuvring that needs to take place. People with these twin drives are probably the *only* people who can make an effective impact in that sort of environment; and deregulation and increased competition means that turbulent environments are going to be more common. People with such skills need to be nurtured, even if they can be difficult to manage and even more difficult to work for. As always, we need a high level of technical and functional skills. These will improve the likelihood of good decision making.

How can we tackle the problem that the high need for variety often means that tasks are left unfinished? We can either do it by getting somebody else to finish the unfinished, or by making sure that those who start also finish. The problem with bringing in somebody else to finish work off is that it encourages more of the wrong sort of behaviour; it gives permission to start something new before completing something old. At times of turbulence, that might be acceptable behaviour, otherwise it is probably undesirable.

How do we manage the follow through without undermining morale? The answer is that we relate all our arguments back to their need for influence. Every argument we use implies the question: 'Will what you are doing increase or reduce your influence in the organization?' or 'What would the senior manager think if he or she knew?' The role is that of mentor, attempting to develop a conscience, or certainly an in-built mechanism so that the key question about completion raises itself automatically whenever there is temptation to move on to the next project.

Moreover, if payment is involved, we do not pay until the work has been completed. If the pay is not directly dependent on the work, we have to bring lack of completion to the fore continuously. That can be demoralizing. We can improve the situation by making it a matter of humour rather than a matter of nagging. We can make completion conditional on their personal assurance that members of their staff complete the task and that they are personally responsible for managing it. We can train them to think in terms of objectives which, by definition, have completion built in, though when there is turbulence, completion and objectives are not always so clear cut.

If there is no response, we can, if the business situation allows it, refuse to allow them to move on to the next task until the previous one has been completed. That will have a negative impact on morale, but if we work through it with them, being generous with our praise at the right time, we can reflect that the message is getting through and that we are doing the right thing.

In working to resolve the problem caused by these two drives, we will undoubtedly be encouraged by the need to maintain staff morale. Continuously changing direction can seriously undermine morale, especially where the staff do not have the information available to the manager and are not aware of the reasons for change. We can help to improve morale where there is turbulence by encouraging transparency and availability of information. The staff will then be in a better position to know why things are changing and are more likely to be supportive.

What we want to avoid is the manager becoming coercive and imposing change. When that happens, staff, particularly where the reasons are not clear, are likely to become less supportive, less willing, and in the end less able, to work with change. This becomes a particular problem when the change imposed involves continual reorganization. We can try to avoid unnecessary internal change by focusing energies on external matters.

People whose need for change is low are going to be happier exercising influence in the steady state. The problem is that there are many more people who are capable of managing the steady state and there is not usually the same need for influence to be exercised. A low change need probably means that influence can only be exercised on minor issues of low complexity. They are probably not going to enjoy what is described as the 'heat of the kitchen'. The lower the drive for change, the less chance there will be failure to deal with each matter fully, but the more chance that there will be failure to deal with the range of matters requiring attention. Motivating high influence/low change people will be easier, but they themselves will be less useful.

Factor 8, factor 10 (creativity)

Managing those with strong power and creativity drives can be most demanding. Both drives demand freedom and minimal control. Properly harnessed, they can make excellent bedfellows. In managing, we need to be aware that the drive to influence is buttressed by a kind of creative scanning of the horizon to see how influence is best obtained. At its best, the creative drive allows for experimentation, to see what is most likely to produce the influence required. It is the opposite of the approach that tries and re-tries the same approach, like the caricature of the Englishman abroad who shouts louder and louder in English to make the uncomprehending foreigner understand what he is saying. The more creative person learns the language, or uses a phrase book or gestures. So it is with creativity: those who seek to influence ring the changes to find what works.

The combination works at a higher level too. One only has to read an account of battles fought and won by people like Alexander the Great, against overwhelming odds, using imagination, applying pressure where least expected, to see how creativity can work at a strategic level.

Of course, the creativity has to be focused. When called in aid to the influence drive it is probably stimulated by the flow of adrenaline. It is at its most useful when it is grounded in reality. Not being grounded in reality is probably the point at which the two drives stop being supportive and become mutually destructive. The successful use of power depends not only on an assessment of its limitations and an awareness of where it should and should not be used, but it also requires a wary eye on its accompanying creativity. We should question not only its brilliance but also its practicability. Hitler's invasion of Russia may have seen the two drives working in tandem but, of course, their use was insane and ultimately unproductive.

Influence and creative drives are the two wild cards of motivation. They have no structure and no limitations, they can pay only cursory attention to rules. The two strong drives, used well together, will move mountains. Used carelessly, they can destroy.

Managing in these circumstances requires us to empower and give the maximum possible scope. At the same time, we need to be very clear about our objectives, which must be communicated and understood. That means taking time; having them fed back to us to ensure understanding; agreeing the circumstances and the time for review; ensuring that the areas of influence are not beyond the scope of the persons empowered; and that any mistakes made are unlikely to disable the organization. To emphasize, managing and motivating this combination requires us to be firm on objectives. That is a precondition of empowerment. Without it we are in danger of seeing a misapplication of energy and effort.

Factor 8, factor 11 (self-development)

High influence and high self-development drives work well together. Those with a high power drive define themselves in terms of their exercise of influence on other people. The more they are able to do that, the more they have a sense of their own autonomy, and the 'better' person they will feel themselves to be. Simultaneously, they will want to develop so that they become more skilled and better able to exercise influence. They will probably be trying to increase their spheres of influence and the areas of complexity they can handle. The two drives feed off each other.

Motivating people like this is relatively easy. They want to be fed with development opportunities. They are probably jealous of their reputation and do not want to use their power in a way which seems to detract from their development. Mentoring will consist of drawing lessons from activities and seeing how the lessons relate to future possibilities.

They are likely to resolve any conflict between the need to exercise influence and the need for self-development in favour of influence. There will not be a permanent need to relate the two, but in the longer term, they will wish to restore the balance in the direction of self-development. In the short term, they can exercise influence on behalf of the organization without worrying that they are not furthering their own development.

If they have a high influence need with a low factor 11, they are apparently facing a contradiction. The more that people exercise influence, the more autonomy they inevitably have. The question must be, what are they doing with that influence? They could be happy to exercise it in a way which they see as achieving the goals of the organization and they are unconcerned that it is not contributing to their own autonomy. Indeed they might be satisfied if, instead of autonomy or self-development, they could meet some other need, for example, money or recognition. Any autonomy they happen to obtain they will see as a by-product of little concern to them.

There might be a problem in that self-development is undertaken in a minimalist way, perhaps hindering the growth of the influence drive. Lessons are perhaps not eagerly sought and there could be more of a tendency to trial and error. Motivation should require that lessons and skills are learned.

Factor 8, factor 12 (interest and usefulness)

Those who have a high need for both influence and interest will clearly be better in a job which satisfies both needs. Their primary motivator is the exercise of influence and they will be able to sustain it, at least in the short term. In the longer term they would like to feel the work is interesting. Motivation involves putting what is required into context and helping to find utility; or demonstrating the way in which the exercise of influence is stimulating. Once the two drives are aligned, we can expect a huge release of energy, with the larger picture being communicated to others.

Those who are high on power but low on interest can easily exercise influence on behalf of the organization for its own sake. They might be tempted not to convey the larger picture to those who are working for them. An important part of motivation will be drawing their attention to the majority need for interest and helping them to convey that to others.

Factor 9

Variety and change

Highest score recorded = 78
Lowest score recorded = 0
Mode 34 Median 35

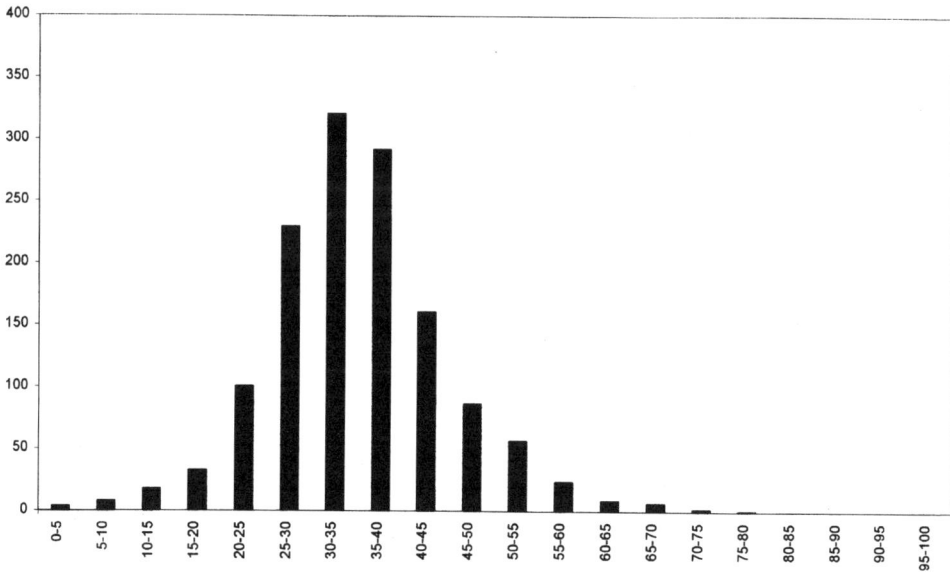

Figure 9   **Factor 9: histogram of scores**

Factor 9 high, other factors evenly spread

Take the need to change to an extreme and you will have somebody who can literally not even sit still. They will need constant stimulation, to move on to something different, with boredom setting in after an initial discharge of energy. For example, somebody who will continuously discharge his or her energy in something like a dealing room. They are likely to leave work and to engage in some frenetic activity which will leave them time enough for perhaps two or three hours' sleep before the next day's work.

In one sense such people are vulnerable. If the job does provide the stimulation they need, they will forever be wanting to move on to the next one. Where there is constant stimulation and change, where fresh energy and new initiatives are in constant demand, they cope brilliantly. However, the problem is that there may be an unwillingness to see things through before wanting to move on. They may be most effective where there is somebody else to pick up the pieces. Since this situation does not always arise, we are likely to find ourselves either with business uncompleted, or a motivation problem.

How do we motivate in these circumstances? There are three problems we have to deal with. The first is the urge to move on to something else. The second is that there may be an unwillingness to set appropriate objectives. The third is that even those most avid for change are not going to be favourably disposed to change that will harm them. Looking at the first, the urge to move on, motivating in this case is difficult because what was done yesterday is now seen as history, with people feeling astonished that they were ever involved. We have to motivate in a way which points in the direction of further stimulation. 'When this is completed, these other new activities will be available', or try to re-present what is left of the task as a new activity. We might try to keep them engaged on the incomplete activity while giving them tasks which will absorb some of that surplus energy, but leave them with enough capacity to complete the task. What we need to be careful about is leaving them without stimulation, because they are quite likely to create it for themselves by engaging in activities which consume energy but produce no organizational benefit. Our management task is thus one of giving considerable opportunity for stimulation, but moving in quickly at the point at which the activity loses its interest, re-stimulating to ensure completion.

If the need for variety is present but not so acute, we are in a better position to aim for completion, but it will involve considerable effort to make sure it happens. Completion will still be externally as opposed to internally driven.

The second motivational problem we have to deal with is an unwillingness to establish formal management objectives. The reason for this is that part of the drive for change is associated with a wish to embrace risk and even danger. If there is no excitement, it is not worth being involved. They very quickly observe that, if they follow the old management formulae, that is to say they set objectives and plan carefully, they are in danger of killing the excitement. There can be an almost subconscious avoidance of planning. Far better to have a go and see how it turns out, and we can always cope with any exigencies that arise. They get things done, but often at an enormous cost in effort and with candles burned at both ends.

This plunging in without clarifying objectives is a serious problem at the highest level as can be seen by looking at, for example, defence project cost overruns, or at projects like the UK Stock Exchange Taurus which had to be aborted after millions of pounds had been spent. All the reports on these projects show the inevitable changes in specifications made, not only early on, but even later when the projects were quite advanced. If the tendency occurs at the highest level, how much greater the chance that it will occur lower down? It is also worth noting that there is a more subtle disadvantage to the drive for change and it can be measured in lost and wasted resources. Indulging the need for change can create a need for even more change so that there is no stability, possibly leading to system overload on the part of those who have to execute the changes, but do not feel the same need for them.

How do we motivate here? What we are trying to do is move away from a culture in which people set the general direction and adjust in the face of the unforeseen. Of course, there will always be a necessity for these adjustments, but with greater planning, more can be foreseen. In a lax culture, it is difficult to persuade those high on the need for change to take their planning seriously. Motivation is easier when the culture is more rigorous.

The first lesson for managing high change people is to operate a more rigorous management culture. The second is to engage fully those high on change in that part of establishing objectives concerned with exploring options: brainstorming. There is plenty of scope for stimulation and activity at that point of the exercise, as there is in the subsequent prioritizing that takes place. Interest will probably start to wane at the point where consideration of resources, priorities and feedback takes place. Nevertheless, interest can be encouraged even here by trying to involve participants in considering all options and making it as enjoyable as possible. Having impaled our high change activists on objectives, we then change the scene and let them handle the variety of results that flows from the action. They will be happiest when things go wrong and they have the chance to put them right. Nevertheless, the process of establishing objectives is likely to help to channel their energies where they are required and not where they gain the most stimulation.

Thirdly, we have to consider how to motivate when those who are high on the need for change see proposed changes as likely to be damaging to them. The answer of course is that we can only keep them on board with great difficulty. There are two extreme situations. One is where the need for change is compelling and they can see there is no other alternative, even if it damages their interests. In that case there is a good chance they will proceed. The other is when there are alternatives, but they do not see that they should have to accept the damage. Like everybody else, they will look for compensation and guarantees. If we cannot offer these, we will probably see reduced commitment.

We conclude by noting that there is a positive side to the high need for change. The obvious point is that if there were not a change drive, there would be no progress. But, perhaps more than with any other factor, the significance of the change drive lies in its association with the other factors. Change for its own sake goes nowhere, but change in association with, say, creativity or achievement, can be highly significant.

Factor 9, factor 1 (money and tangible rewards)

The obvious point is that those who are high 9/high 1 are going to try to make money by managing or being involved in change. For example, if they are creative as well, they will be working in those areas where creating change is rewarded, as in many of the consumer industries. If they are sufficiently talented, what they are doing might become more and more outrageous, but bring greater and greater reward. If the creative spark is lacking, they will be ringing the changes on achievement. An extreme example may be doing something like trying to corner the tin market. If things start to go wrong, and their need for change overrides their sense of risk, they will become involved in more and more difficult trades until, in the end, the whole pack of cards collapses.

The danger point is that they do not persevere long enough to make the money that could have been theirs. That will not be a problem if the market in which they operate thrives on change. The real difficulty they then face is that, whereas getting change right can bring outstanding reward, getting it wrong will leave them flat on their faces. Those with a high drive for change and a need for money may be forced to live dangerously, but there is no other way for them to live.

How do we motivate such people? The first thing is to offer an environment where managing stimulation and change brings financial reward. The opportunity to experience change with reward sometimes must come second to the need to experience change. Secondly, we need a very clear view of what the organization requires, so that only change that benefits the organization and not change for its own sake is rewarded. Motivation requires that those we are motivating have a clear understanding of what is needed. If we do not do this, energy is expended fruitlessly, which is de-motivating. We need to make it clear that financial benefits are only paid on completion, that is to say, that they are rewarded when the organization is rewarded. Thus, those who become bored and move on to something else will not benefit. That will be seen as irksome by those high on change, but they will learn to tolerate it. We might help them by confirming to them that we understand how difficult this is.

Those with high 9/low 1 need are more likely to want change regardless of the financial consequences to them. They will be happy to be stimulated in a way not directly related to personal reward. Motivating them will involve giving them opportunities, but again ensuring that the organization benefits. We will be looking at their other drivers, like the need for creativity or self-development, and giving them the opportunity to ring the changes in these directions. As always, a low need for money does not mean that they should be underpaid; that will be de-motivating. But, money for its own sake will not energize them.

Factor 9, factor 3 (structure)

There are interesting possibilities with this combination of motivators. Our research suggests that most of those with an above average need for change have a below average need for structure (what, in fact, we would expect). High 9/low 3 people would seem to have the greatest opportunities for either extreme success or extreme failure, particularly if allied with high creativity. With such a person we have the potential for anything. Change, with or without creativity, will drive them into unique areas, and the absence of a sense of order means that anything is possible.

In management, they should be watched with extreme care. If they are brilliant, with an empathic feel for the direction of the market, they could move mountains. They will need excellent administrative backup. If their touch is less sure, and they are in a position of influence, they will find themselves sidelined as being much too dangerous to the organization. Successful or not, the likelihood is that they will be excellent company, though perhaps a little wearing, depending on your energy levels.

How can we motivate them? The answer is, with some difficulty, because they will tend to be self-starters and not happy to be directed. They will be at their best where there is ambiguity and a need for movement. Indeed, they may be the only people who are able to work with any effectiveness in such an environment. If they are creative as well, they could develop unique and unexpected solutions. As managers, we need to keep an eye on two aspects of their work. The first is how it relates to known organizational outcomes. The second, are there outcomes which were unpredictable but now require consideration? In giving space, however, we need to inculcate them with a strong sense of organizational direction, reinforced at every opportunity. We can do this by discussion and by creating an organizational culture which is so strong that those who work in it are overwhelmingly aware of what is required. The stronger the culture the less the discussion required and vice versa. We can improve our chances of success by establishing tight deadlines. That will increase the sense of stimulation they want and, at the same time, bring the end closer in sight. Tight, enforceable deadlines can be a powerful motivator.

The high 9/high 3 people are a different proposition. There is a potential conflict between their need for change and their need for order. They will feel driven towards change but will feel tension as the change takes place. They are most likely to resolve it by creating a framework in which change can take place. Change is planned, the new destination marked out and the new rules learned in advance. There will probably be more of an exploration of the options for change and an analysis of the effects of change on the existing order. There will certainly be a tendency to reduce change to the minimum necessary. Our research suggests that an important minority of those with an above average change need have an above average structure need.

We motivate by trying to give as much notice of change as possible and by giving the fullest possible involvement. As far as possible, we allow the status quo to continue while the process and outcomes of the proposed change are considered. If this is not possible, we focus the available time on the proposed final state and encourage movement there as quickly as we can.

Factor 9, factor 4 (people contact)

High 9/high 4 work together. The drive will be for change and, as part of it, much contact with people. We could expect that any change would aim to be positive or neutral in its effect on people. If there is a wish to rub shoulders with a variety of people, it would be more agreeable for the meetings to be pleasant rather than unpleasant.

Motivation will encourage the contacts to take place. One of the problems with change is that many of those involved, particularly those who have change imposed on them, frequently complain that they have not been informed about, or do not understand what is happening. Provided we are satisfied that our high 9/high 4 colleagues are behind the change and understand it, there can only be benefit for the organization and benefit for them in communicating what is happening. The almost certain variety of responses will reinforce their sense of change and their wish for agreeable contact will tend to make them sensitive to people's needs. As managers with a change programme to implement, our only concern will be that they do not become too sensitive and undermine necessary change. We can help ourselves here by maintaining contact and understanding their thinking as their work continues. We will also need to ensure that the 'rubbing shoulders' is not completely casual, but that plans are made to see all those who need to be seen.

In contrast, high 9/low 4 people will aim for change, but might see people as being incidental to the change, perhaps almost as cardboard cut-outs. Change then, could well create casualties to a greater extent than might have been necessary. Preferred change will be task related and not people related. Thus, although we might have good objective thinking about required change, we could have serious problems as people's legitimate concerns are ignored. As resistance builds, we can find de-motivation all around. We need to consider people's concerns systematically in planning for the change and report on them as the process gets underway; corrective action should be reviewed as required. In this way attention to people needs becomes part of the task.

Factor 9, factor 5 (relationships)

High 9/high 5 is problematical. It depends with whom the relationships are being formed. People who are restless for change would seem to be more likely to form relationships with people similarly inclined. If, then, there is a shared need for change, the two drivers could work together and could even be mutually reinforcing. We would not expect any motivational problems, except in the event that the change is seen as likely to damage one of the parties, in which case we may need to be heavily involved to nurture both the change and the relationships.

If long-term relationships have been forged between those with a high and those with a low need for change, we will at the very least have to keep a watching brief. Sometimes those with low change needs absorb and buffer, but do not inhibit, the restlessness of those high on change. We try to let them sort out any tensions themselves. Others with low change needs are an impediment to change and we may need to facilitate transition. Any change could be particularly bumpy and the need for factor 5 may not be enough to prevent damage to the long-term relationship.

High 9/low 5 people again are unlikely to be restrained by consideration of the effect of change on others and are likely to proceed regardless. This is a more likely management profile than that in the previous two paragraphs and is borne out by our experience of the way many organizations are run. 'When the chips are down, people are expendable' is the extreme statement of the position. As with factor 4, we need to consider people's legitimate concerns systematically and the impact of the change on them should be regularly reported and reviewed.

Factor 9, factor 6 (recognition)

People with a high need for change and a high need for recognition are potentially dangerous, to themselves and to their organizations. We have the possibility of a vicious circle. In an effort to achieve recognition, change for its own sake and even extreme change, might be introduced. The problem is one that requires attention. As managers, we need to keep a very close watch on those with this profile. Every time change is proposed, we should be aware of potential tensions between the organizational need for change and the individual's need for recognition. Sometimes they will work together, sometimes the individual's needs will conflict. Part of our motivational task will be to identify the driving force behind the need for recognition. Is it that they are not receiving any recognition at work, even where it is deserved, and so they use their change drive to get attention? In this case, we can help to motivate by providing recognition on a more regular basis.

It may be that the necessary changes they implement are not recognized and they perceive the only way to be noticed is to attempt larger and sometimes unnecessary changes. To prevent this from happening, we need a policy to ensure that recognition is firmly on the agenda and that there is an expectation that it will be given for undertaking change that meets organizational requirements. Every activity undertaken will involve review and feedback as a matter of course.

In contrast, people who are high 9/low 6 will, in creating change, not be deflected by any need to obtain recognition and approval by those affected. This could work for them or against them. It will work against them if they are insensitive to those people's needs and concerns. It will work for them if they can take an objective view of the effect of the change and plan accordingly, and in a way which can be seen as fair. They will also work in those situations where tackling variety is required but there is no limelight. Again there may be the problem of completion and there is no recognition need to be used as a motivator. Motivating them entails offering the opportunity for more variety, provided completion takes place in the tasks already undertaken. To pre-empt possible motivational damage, we have to make sure that the people dimension receives formal consideration and review. This will protect both those causing and those being affected by the change.

Factor 9, factor 7 (achievement)

High 9/high 7 people will have achievement taking place in many different activities. They can best be described as eclectic. They may not achieve excellence in any one of their activities, but they will have fingers in many pies. In many ways they will be easy to manage. They are likely to be self-motivating and active. Their achievement drive will push them to completion. Their change drive will want to move them on. If change is dominant, they may rush completion, or not take the achievement as far as might have been possible. Getting the balance wrong might impinge on their effectiveness.

Motivation concerns helping them to try to maintain the balance. We aim to provide variety and the promise of variety as the principal driving force, but at the same time ensure completion of what is important. We give them the satisfaction of measurement in their achievements and, given the variety of achievements in which they might want to be involved, we may have to spend time making the opportunity for measurement available. If we do not do this, they are likely to be dissatisfied with their achievements and move on. The outcome could be a great deal of activity, but nothing substantial to show for it.

High 9/low 7 can perhaps best be described as dilettante. They will savour this and that, but achieve no particular distinction or expertise in anything. For them that does not matter. They enjoy experiencing new sensations, though some may not experience anything more than a nodding acquaintance with anything. Probably if they are to be of benefit to the organization, they will either have to learn to achieve even if they do not feel the need, or they will have to contribute using some of their other drivers.

Factor 9, factor 8 (power and influence)

The exercise of influence generally needs to be related to purpose. Influence for its own sake, though perhaps gratifying to the person exercising it, has no direction. Influence used consistently, for the same purpose in the same situation, may achieve impressive results. The problem is, for the person with a high need for variety and change, such an exercise of power will become rather tedious. The danger then becomes that influence will start to be exercised not to achieve purpose but just for the hell of it. In the end that can become counter-productive and achieve little, even though people seem to be in a frenzy of activity.

Motivation, and even self-motivation, ensures that there is sufficient purposeful stimulation available. If the requirements of the job are not enough, then we can look to use the drives in a way which is organizationally beneficial. Thus, for example, we can use their energy on special projects, that is, on aspects of the organization that require attention. We can allow them to use their influence in an executive sense, or they can undertake studies in which they have the opportunity to influence the strategic thinking of those at a more senior level. At that level we can allow them to explore areas which are ambiguous and uncertain, but which are important to the organization. It depends, of course, on their capabilities. The golden rule is that association with those who have power, and working in various areas of significance, will go a long way to satisfy the variety and influence drives.

People who are high 9/low 8 will seek their variety in other areas than the exercise of power. They will tend not to want to affect other people. We motivate them through their other drivers.

Factor 9, factor 10 (creativity)

People who are high on the need for variety with high creativity may be personally blessed, but they may represent a problem in the organization. The personal blessing is that they will be restless in their creativity, using it constantly without focus, perhaps following whatever creative impulse strikes them. In many aspects of business, except possibly those parts where continuous creativity is productive, their lack of focus could tell against them, as the organizational purpose is overlooked and they 'butterfly' from one thing to another. At a personal level, the unfocused use of creativity can be very satisfying. In business, it can become very de-motivating, as time pressures mount and work never seems to be finished. Motivation is a delicate balancing act, between giving space for creativity and assuring attention to business goals.

We can approach the problem in a number of ways. We remind ourselves that the main driver is the need for variety, and that variety can militate against completion and continuing focus. We can encourage focus in some areas by giving generous space in others, the one providing a quid pro quo or trade-off for the other. The creative space can be used outside work with the organization making time and resources available, or we can let them use it on areas within work that will benefit from their attention. We stay in contact with them and encourage them to show us, or we spot for ourselves, how we can use the results of their creativity. We do not as a matter of routine, insist on focus and completion, that would cramp their style, though we will do so where we see relevance to organizational needs. The option we probably do not have is to insist, in all aspects of their work, on total work discipline. That will create intense frustration and de-motivation as they feel cramped for space. Motivation requires that there be some outlet, made available with our permission.

Those who are high 9/low 10 will obviously want variety in their work. Creativity is not a large part of it and we need to look at other drivers in our attempt to motivate.

Factor 9, factor 11 (self-development)

Those who are high on variety with high self-development will regard development as one of the ways in which they achieve variety. They will want constant stimulation and the opportunity to experience change. As they move around they will try to extract development opportunities from their current activity. If the activity starts to tire them, they will either move on and fail to maximize development; or, if what they are learning is particularly interesting, they may persevere longer than they might otherwise have done. The need for variety might mean that they will not develop themselves to the full in any one field or as fully as they might have done if the need had been more dominant. Rather, they will move from one thing to another. They may well become 'jacks of all trades and masters of none'. However, they may become masters in one field, provided they are given the opportunity to roam in others; this will require constant motivational effort and refocusing.

Repetitive work should be kept to a minimum, otherwise we are likely to see progressive demoralization and deteriorating performance. Again, if we need some repetitive work, we explicitly recognize its nature and try to arrange a trade-off between it and more varied work. If we want to encourage development, we present work in terms of its opportunities. If we want tasks to be completed, part of our motivational armoury will be drawing their attention to the development opportunities that will be enhanced by completion. If we wish to keep them focused on one specialism we must remember the danger that it will feel stale and uninteresting. We refresh them using new opportunities for learning and experience. There is no reason why much of this cannot be work related. Some of the learning might be relatively trivial, but we should take the opportunity to provide learning which has the potential to be stretching. We should be prepared to accept that sometimes they will lose interest and move on. The learning will be part of their general development and will perhaps be used later.

These twin drivers may be particularly useful in a de-layered organization which, at its best, can empower staff. More self-reliance becomes necessary. By definition, managers are not immediately available to take decisions, which are pushed as far down the organization as possible. The necessity to cope with a wider range of topics and to learn how to manage them can be well served by high 9/high 11 people. In contrast, those with a high need for variety and a low need for self-development are likely to find themselves endlessly re-inventing the wheel. There will be a continuous discharge of energy, but there will be little conceptualization and learning. We help them progress, in the most difficult cases, by doing the learning for them and then perhaps training them; or by presenting a framework for formal review so that eventually we hope they begin to learn the habit of learning. In terms of motivation, they may be quite happy not to learn. Continuous change provides all the stimulus they require. We work with them to encourage learning so that the organization can itself learn the lessons available.

Factor 9, factor 12 (interest and usefulness)

Those with high need for variety and job interest may have their work cut out. If they are lucky, the variety and the interest will coincide. In that case they will probably be self-motivating. At the very most, they may sometimes need to have drawn to their attention how their interests and those of the organization coincide.

Problems may arise when they feel that the job is not interesting or useful, in which case their change drive will quickly divert their attention elsewhere and they are likely to become de-motivated very quickly. They will try to re-establish interest. Motivation is helping them to do this, at the same time working to establish congruence with organizational needs. But, even if we cannot do this, provided the change is sufficiently stimulating, they will be willing to carry on, though they will have a lingering feeling of having lost usefulness. This will not be sustainable in the long term. In the short term, we may have a fair amount of leeway in terms of maintaining their commitment, provided there is enough variety and change to satisfy them.

Those who are high 9/low 12 will take an instrumental view of change. They will like it for its own sake and not according to whether it contributes to job interest or usefulness. The job might even end up being secondary and seen merely as a vehicle which can be used for the enjoyment of variety. They will do what they like and not what the job requires. We have an advantage from an organizational point of view in that they can work with change regardless of considerations of personal significance. There will not be a motivational problem, except that we should monitor them to confirm that they are organizationally on-track.

Factor 10

Creativity

Highest score recorded = 81
Lowest score recorded = 5
Mode 32 Median 33

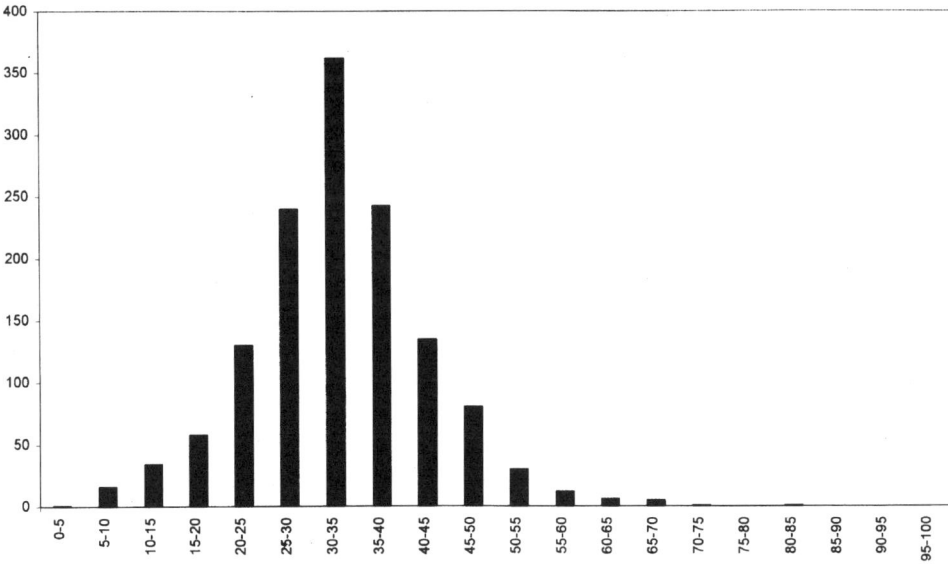

Figure 10   Factor 10: histogram of scores

Factor 10 high, other factors evenly spread

What are we trying to assess here? Is creativity to do with original ideas which come to us like the turning on of a light, out of the blue and without conscious effort, or the systematic search for new connections, for extensions to existing things, to find new perspectives on the old and the familiar?

Factor 10 concerns both these aspects, the original, apparently spontaneous idea and the development of the new out of the old. In either case this should be useful behaviour for people in an organization. Arguably creativity has become even more valuable as our capability, through science and technology, increases, aided and abetted by rising competition and deregulation. We have moved rapidly from a world governed by the cycle of the seasons, through one where invention was introduced over a relatively leisurely time-scale, to one where creativity is *the* way to keep ahead. The rewards can come to those who create, but the time-scale for reaping them is shortening in the relentless global pursuit of innovation.

Creativity now has less emphasis on ideas 'out of the blue'; the 'Eureka effect'. It is complicated by the huge resources that are now the essential backdrop to creative effort. Although Newton might have had his apple and Watts his kettle, NASA has its billions of dollars and a cast of thousands, and pharmaceutical companies merge in a conscious attempt to gather the huge resources required to develop the latest drug. Where does this leave those who have a need for creativity? Potentially in a strong position, but there is a caveat, which for business is, for creativity to be useful it has to be focused and usually it has to be part of a team effort.

Before proceeding, we acknowledge that the end of creativity is not necessarily business. Much of the joy of the world is found in innocent creativity, with never the thought of a dollar or a Euro, and long may it continue to be so. But this book is about motivation and business and so we must explore the constraints of business on creativity. Looking first at the focus required by business; for the creative instinct to be usable, it has to focus on the matter in hand. If it cannot focus, it cannot be used. How it does this is a function of the environment in which it is used. In a more constrained environment it can be to solve the immediate problem. With slightly less constraint, it can be to consider wider problems for which solutions would be desirable.

We are using the word problem here in the sense used by Revans, the man who developed the concept of action learning (Revans, 1983). He distinguished between problems and puzzles. For the latter there is a known and ascertainable solution. Thus two plus two always equals four. For problems there are many possible solutions and it is often difficult to decide which is best. We are operating in the area of informed opinion, of uncertain outcomes and on matters on which even people of good will can reasonably disagree with each other. These are the higher order activities of business. The act of creativity is helpful in devising solutions.

If we remove the constraint altogether and look only at problems, there can be no limits to the operation of creativity. Often this area is relegated to universities, although even they are coming under increasing pressure to produce what has immediate, or near immediate, relevance. However, given the right environment, this activity can also take place in firms. For example, 3M, one of the world's largest manufacturers, has a long history of innovation. The company encourages employees to exercise their initiative and to take risks. This translates directly into financial goals which aim to generate 30 per cent of revenue from products introduced in the last four years. Risk inevitably brings with it some failures and 3M recognizes that mistakes will be made. The trick is in spotting them early enough to reduce the financial and organizational cost.

Inevitably in any company, with the shareholders in the background, there are pressures on results. The balance is between allowing people to get on with it and to create what is required, without wasting too much money; or interfering so that money is saved but the act of creativity is stifled. There are well-understood theories about how the matter should be handled: the stakeholders, including the creators and others such as marketing and production managers who are interested in the outcomes, should together establish objectives, let the creative team get on with it, and then all the stakeholders should, after a pre-agreed period, review and debrief.

Hanging over all of this is an additional feature of corporate culture. Are people allowed, in good faith, to make mistakes? This is important for creative people. They are vulnerable, they may make mistakes, sometimes they may appear exposed and foolish. If the firm is intolerant, if every debriefing is turned into an opportunity for abuse and ridicule, those who are creative will learn to hold their counsel. The successful creative culture has to be tolerant, even fun, so that those who are creative can relax and take a chance. This stricture applies even where creativity is focused on only immediate or not-quite-so immediate problems.

The first limitation on creativity in an organization is the question of focus and that is coupled with culture. The second limitation is the need to work in teams. However, much of the world's creativity has been delivered by individuals. No committee wrote Beethoven's symphonies and Dali was not part of a co-operative. True there have been some significant partnerships, Gilbert and Sullivan with their light operas and Watson and Crick with DNA for example. The point is that, because of the massive resources increasingly required to help in the act of creation, those who create in industry are generally having to work in teams.

We have here a possible source of tension. Who owns the creative idea (not in the legal sense, because in that sense the firm owns the ideas created by its employees), that is who within the firm is credited with the creation? It is an important question, since salary, promotion and standard of living can depend on it. We immediately see the need to encourage an environment which appears to be fair. We need to manage the balance between the needs of the individual and the needs of the team. If we get the balance wrong with the individual, we are in danger of stifling creativity. If the individual is a natural team player, there may be no problem, if not, there will be a need to shape an environment in which creativity will be nurtured.

The creative drive has a very important part to play in the organization. The extreme position is that we are trying to produce creativity to order. Life is not like that, of course, but we fear the creative drive will only be productive if it is focused and nurtured. It is probably fair to say that those who are creative need, above all else, to ensure that the environment in which they are going to operate is sympathetic and conducive. How, in practice, they find that out is difficult to say, but those who choose to live by their creativity, that is those who are operating at the limits of creativity, need to take extra care in deciding where they will be employed and their employer needs to handle them sensitively.

How does creativity relate to the other factors?

Factor 10, factor 1 (money and tangible rewards)

Today it is possible to link creativity and reward. In fact, the world is structured in such a way that those who create what the world wants can be fabulously rewarded, way beyond the dreams of avarice. Usually, those who are so rewarded are seen as being at the top of their particular tree. Those who are just below the top may find themselves scarcely rewarded at all. So the pianist who wins the Leeds International Festival will scoop every jackpot, while the excellent pianist who reached tenth place will be scraping a living as a peripatetic teacher.

The analogy does exist in business. One only has to think of the creative Steve Jobs and Apple Macintosh. The business started in a garage and, driven by creativity, expanded to a turnover of billions of dollars over the course of a few years. The story later on for Apple might not have been so happy, but the creative and successful entrepreneur is the stuff of legend. The risks may be high but so are the rewards. Whereas the Steve Jobses of this world might be independent self-starters, this is not necessarily the case for those who work as employees within companies. Although their needs for creativity and money might be very high, they are either not so high as to tempt them into working on their own, or the nature of what they are doing, for example, the amount of capital required, makes working on their own impracticable.

The need for creativity is greater than the need for money and what is wanted is the opportunity to be creative. Provided this is given in full measure and the rewards are acceptable, we can expect that energy will be directed to creativity rather than creativity being directed to making money. They will want to be rewarded well, of course. They are best paid a basic salary with the possibility of bonuses. These should be related not to particular acts of creativity, but to their creativity in general. They need as much space as possible. They will want to set their own hours of work and their own working patterns. They may have difficulty in accepting or requesting a brief and we may have to accept unfocused creativity. Indeed, we may decide, as part of the price of getting the creativity we want, to provide opportunities for it to occur. There must be an understanding that the large expense requires a return and that should help creativity to be focused when required.

For those whose creative drive is high and whose money drive is low we have a different situation. If they decide to be self-employed, their currency is the act of creativity. They dream dreams and write papers, compose music that nobody wants to listen to, paint for their own pleasure, abandon their job and laboriously make beautiful sailing boats that are so labour intensive that they can never recover their cost. It is a free world and their choice is fair. 'After all' they say to themselves, 'what is the purpose of life if I cannot do what I see is beautiful and what I want to do?'.

Our research suggests that most people with an above average creative drive are below average on money as a motivator. If we employ them, we *have* to provide the opportunity and scope for them to be creative on their terms, not ours. What that means is that they need the opportunity to pursue what interests them. That may mean that we employ them, if they are good enough, in university or research institutes, where a large part of the job is bound up with creativity, for example, research or performance. Or if they are not that good, we recoup our salary costs in that part of their creativity we can exploit commercially, or on some other aspect of their work which is not related to creativity. But if we do not provide them with creative space, they are quite likely to leave us, often moving into a financial situation which those who are less creative regard as disastrous and, as we see it, definitely not in their interests.

Some may finesse their money concerns by finding themselves a job which supports them to a reasonable standard and does not take too much effort, like the novelist Trollope who worked in the post office by day and wrote by night. But for that twin motivational profile – high 10/low 1 – the conditions for creative effectiveness in business, that is (particularly) focus and the ability to work in teams, are unlikely to occur.

Factor 10, factor 3 (structure)

It would seem reasonable that a person scoring high on creativity would value open-mindedness, that is, a capacity to scan his or her surroundings for opportunities (maintaining a state of vigilance in Rycroft's language (1968)). It seems logical then that they should score low on need for structure, avoiding rigidity and predictability. The popular view of the creative person is someone like this: anarchic and unconstrained, worthy of admiration from a distance but probably rather irritating to live with. Is this view correct?

It seems that popular myth, as usual, is partly right. Some people *do* show this link, low structure and high creativity – but many do not. Our research suggests a significant minority who are high on creativity and high on structure.

Low structure need people are often also highly visible and it is probably this that causes distortion in the public mind. There may be one structure-hungry creator to match two Picasso types, for example, but they are far less likely to display the flamboyance which ensures recognition. By definition, their high score for structure implies that they seek order and conformity. Where does this leave the manager trying to encourage creativity? The answer depends on what we want from the creators. If they are competent and the role they are occupying demands only creativity, for example in an advertising agency, and we are happy for the structured part of the work, say, compliance with advertising law, or technical aspects of production, to be handled by others, then we will be happy to work with people who are high on creativity and low on structure. We will require them to be focused on our clients' needs.

To get the best from them, we will have to handle them very lightly. Their time-keeping may be appalling. Their dress may be eccentric or downright unbusinesslike. Their administration may leave much to be desired and their desks a mess. Some of their ideas may strain credulity. We may have to put up also with their moodiness and eccentricity. We will need to develop the capacity to nurture, tolerate, encourage and forgive and to smile at their creative dead ends and irrelevancies. We will suppress our irritation at their resistance to concentration, limitation and endings (narrowing down choices, tying up loose ends, finishing projects, reports and so on). But if we think they have the capacity to deliver, we will discipline ourselves to do all of it. If we think we can manage them by tying them down, we are quite wrong. They will not be tied down and will make alternative arrangements. They certainly will not be creative to order.

Those with high creative needs as well as high structure needs pose a different management challenge. They need a firm foundation or framework of security *before* they will be able to leap into the unknown or feel comfortable enough to let their imagination run free. Alternatively, they will need to operate in a rule-driven environment. For example, they may, as architects, design wonderful buildings but they will need to understand the properties of materials and the building regulations. Complete freedom or lack of rules is not for them: it will raise their anxiety levels, causing their energies to be used up on handling them and leaving little spare for open-mindedness or curiosity. The manager's job is to help maintain the balance between these two opposing drives. On the one hand to allow the tolerant and open environment that will encourage creativity, and on the other hand to make the rules and constraints visible, informing creativity. The approach is to keep a distance in matters of creativity, but enforcement in matters of rules. It will not be too much of a problem. Those who are creating will find it their preferred environment.

If the creators also score low on the need for stimulation and variety (factor 9), we could assume that their creativity is of the more introspective type. Our task here is to build enough security and predictability for these people to liberate their creative drive, which is motivating for them and good for the organization. Leaving such people to work on a task until they feel familiar with it can bear dividends. They will reach a point where they will start to invent easier, cheaper, better ways of doing it. We have to be careful not to write them off as slow, and to lose our willingness to listen. Learning to manage creative people is one of the most challenging jobs facing a manager. The benefits of liberating creativity are so great that a little self-control, a temporary repression of needs to suit those of others, might be seen as a small price to pay. Managers who do this will probably benefit, over the long term, from a happier staff. These will have been offered the best possible climate for working productively and are more likely to deliver.

Factor 10, factor 4 (people contact)

Business probably dictates, as a condition of using creativity, that those who are creative either need to work alongside others, or at least can steel themselves to do so. Those with high factor 4 will not find this a problem. Those with low factor 4 might do so. The lonely creator, like Belbin's (1981) 'plant', probably faces a difficult time in business unless they can be consistently and predictably creative and make an identified contribution to the bottom line. If that is not the case, they probably find difficulty in building a coalition of support. They are unlikely to be tolerated on the grounds that they 'earned a bread ticket for life from the one brilliant idea they had when they first joined'.

Nevertheless, the point must be made. The lonely creator might be able to make significant contributions to the organization. They might be able to present their case. More likely, however, is that they cannot. In which case, the role of the manager may be to act as their champion, to review their ideas and, to the extent that they are relevant, facilitate their presentation and adaptation. It is interesting to speculate on how much lone creativity is not communicated and not recognized, and a reasonable conclusion that the more extreme the creativity the less the recognition. For most organizations, that might not be a problem. They would scarcely know how to market examples of extreme creativity. For those organizatons which actively seek the extremes of creativity, for example in the realms of software development, the problem is a real one. The role of the manager is to identify, encourage and protect. If someone is alone and needs structure, to provide the structure that encourages creative productivity. If they are alone and do not need structure, to give them space and to judge when to give support.

Factor 10, factor 5 (relationships)

Those with a creative drive and a high need for long-term relationships clearly fall into the category of those who are creative and need stability. Their internal drive is to find a comfortable niche for themselves among people who are sympathetic or at least tolerant. A typical environment would be a university, which at its best is a community in which long-term relationships can be fostered. Within those secure relationships, creativity flowers. Long-term relationships allow time for ideas to mature. If there is a problem it is that long-term communities can be tolerant of poor performance and drift towards a lower level. Such communities are slow to take action.

If the long-term relationships formed are generally supportive to the organization's aims, then as managers we would not want to break them. Whatever changes we create, we will benefit by always providing space for those relationships to flourish. If the relationships are not supportive of the organization, we will want to change them. We will want either to replace them or to re-focus them. There will be resistance in doing this. Our best chance of success is for us to be clear about what we require and to leave no doubt about our wish for change. We recognize movement in our direction and withdraw recognition where such movement is absent. We make clear that we are providing the opportunity to re-establish relationships, but that we require change first.

For those who are high on creativity but low on the need for long-term relationships, we engage them in creativity. Their lack of desire to develop those relationships should not inhibit their creativity.

Factor 10, factor 6 (recognition)

There is a positive role for management in working with the creative recognition seeker. But to find it, we have first to consider how creativity and recognition feed on each other. There are many examples, particularly beyond the world of business. Pavarotti springs to mind, but there are many like him in the worlds of music, opera, theatre and the other arts. We also see it in academia where those in universities award doctorates and other degrees to their creative colleagues and parade themselves in brightly coloured gowns.

Creative people share this urge for recognition with those with other motivational drives. Those with power drives express their recognition in more prestigious cars and in the insignia of office. Even if these are not so overt as the red tabs and gold braid on the caps of senior army officers, they are nonetheless there and recognized as such. Those with achievement drives fight for medals. Creative people fight for awards and exhibitions.

The question for management is how to harness the recognition need to encourage creativity. When we look at creativity we detect a problem: the creator is not clear how they do it, or even what they should do. We can see this clearly if we look at other motivational drives. Thus the high achiever is clear about what he or she has to do to achieve recognition. The race has to be run faster, the inaccessible mountain face climbed. The power hungry politician has to be elected. Those with the drive for variety need to do something different. They can expect to be bored if they do something for the second time. In each case, there is something that has to be done. The runner has to train harder, the politician canvass more, those who are bored have to find some new area of stimulation.

But what does the creator do to create more? Creativity is so often like marsh gas: its source is unknown and its timing unpredictable. Those who set out to create can sometimes have no idea as to the possible outcome. They look at what issues forth with the eyes of a stranger. They ask themselves by what process did that creation – idea, design, or whatever – arise and from what input. It is as though the creator is some sort of instrument and what is expressed comes from somewhere outside. Yet we do know that there are some things that the creator can do to help the process. As in the case of marsh gas where we have a fundamental requirement for decaying vegetation, so in creativity, we have already discussed the necessity for a tolerant environment, for a no-blame culture. We know that if the creative spark is there, then hard work will do much to help. As Edison put it, 'genius is one per cent inspiration, 99 per cent perspiration'. Encouraging them to sit down and 'sweat it out' is a serious option for those wishing to encourage creativity.

We also know that there are techniques which aid creativity, like brainstorming, reverse assumptions, word substitution, forced combinations, random words, ideas grids and many others. One doubts if they were used by Debussy or even the more up-to-date Shostakovich, though they probably have a use at Saatchi's. We also know that preparing the soil and letting the ideas germinate at their leisure can sometimes deliver the goods. Recognition will play a part in encouraging people to use those techniques and, in that sense, it is possible to 'manage' creativity.

One is left with the idea that, although those who are creative can use creativity techniques and can work very hard, in terms of output, they can, nevertheless, not respond directly to recognition. The recognition given to the creative, beyond encouragement to work hard at it, is more an act of homage than an incentive. Those who create and wish for recognition are pleased to receive homage, though they may not always be sure how to foster the process which brings them their reward. For business, there is a dilemma. There is supposed to be a measurable link between effort, performance and reward. The business cannot interfere with the creative act. It takes place, or not, outwith its scope. There may be very little effort, or a great deal; the performance depends on whether others recognize the idea and are prepared to invest time and money in it, and the reward depends on how successfully the idea is marketed. One only has to think of the EMI brain scanner. A brilliant idea, but the profit and the business accrued elsewhere.

The lesson for management is to create a tolerant environment where ideas are given recognition and are exploited in whatever way is appropriate. The brilliant idea that is not exploited or is exploited elsewhere leads to remorse and a feeling of recognition denied. In managing the recognition-hungry creative, we want to involve them in our thinking of how the ideas will be exploited, either commercially or through the publication of papers, and so on. We give them generous recognition internally. We explain with care why some of their ideas may not be promoted and we take their protests seriously and let them see that we are trying to accommodate them, even if we do not accede to their requests.

In contrast, those who are creative but with a low recognition need will do what they want. Their creativity might be more outlandish, but it will be unconstrained by the need to have others' approval. In one sense, such people will be ideal in business, but only if their creativity is focused. In practice, this will not be achieved through recognition. There will need to be some other driver such as money or variety. If none of the others work, at least as far as creativity is concerned, there is probably a very limited business future.

Factor 10, factor 7 (achievement)

High creativity and high achievement drives create an internal tension. High achievement requires measurement; creativity is immeasurable, at least in the sense that in producing creative ideas, nobody, in advance, knows how big their impact will be.

There is another potential area of tension in that the achievement drive involves striving against known objectives, knowing how far one is along the way, having a strong sense of direction and recognizing the sort of effort required to attain the goal. Creativity contains none of those elements. The outcome is imprecise, its shape is unknown, how to get there is hidden from view. With achievement, one can always do more, run harder, climb higher. Even if one cannot, in practice, make the grade, the extent of one's failure is known precisely. With creativity, although we might engage in activities to stimulate our creativity, there is really very little idea of what to do to get to our blurred destination. There will probably be long, barren periods of not knowing whether or not one is wasting one's time. And when one is just about to give up, an idea suddenly springs to mind.

The long grind towards achievement can be shortened by the creative insight. Creativity generally works to create discontinuities in the act of achievement. The high achiever will immediately need to re-establish targets and measurement. The tension is between continuing with the need to achieve the set targets, and being flexible enough to change in the light of the new creative insight. Too much creativity and too many insights will generate anguish. In extreme cases it will lead to the 'butterfly syndrome': jumping from one thing to another and finishing nothing.

What can the manager do to manage the tension between creativity and achievement? This is essentially the tension between the measurable and the immeasurable; and between known output versus unknown. That which is measurable and of known output is the most easily managed. Indeed, the high achiever will do most of what is necessary. The role of the manager is usually to point in the right direction and to agree targets. The unknown element of creativity is more difficult to manage, but the manager has considerable advantages. Creativity in business requires focus. Those who are creative achievers naturally focus. They will instinctively use the two drives in tandem. But instead of the predictable progress towards targets, there will be discontinuities as the creative drive interposes. Although the required output may remain the same, how it is achieved will be subject to change. Sometimes, the creative insight might challenge the target itself, and throw up a strong case for it to be changed. The role of the manager will be to stand back to allow the creative process to take place, but to be ready to intervene when targets and paths are challenged. It is in a sense to be a sort of gyrocompass so that despite all the sudden insights and creative challenges, the work remains focused on the requirements of the organization. In addition, the tension can resolve or reduce itself if the achievement and the creativity are separated, perhaps on different time-scales. For example, one is achieving in the present but trying to be creative about the future and resisting the temptation to apply creativity to the present.

Creativity and a low need for achievement are difficult to manage. The creativity will bubble through as and when and there will be no attempt to focus it. The role of the manager will be to encourage focus without inhibiting creativity. The task might be impossible. We may find ourselves working with someone who is delightful and discursive but essentially unproductive. If we are lucky, we might be able to bring some other need into play. If not, unless the creator is very good, we will probably, in business terms, be parting company.

Factor 10, factor 8 (power and influence)

Creativity with influence is a two-edged sword. Its strength is its ability to communicate creative ideas and to have them adopted. Its weakness is its ability to impose unsuitable creative ideas, or the time that people have to waste opposing them.

Influence helps to make sure that all options are considered. Creativity creates solutions and establishes ways of going about things which are not immediately apparent. It allows the consideration of unusual ideas and stops the 'it won't work' or 'we've already tried that' response. It encourages people to consider the unthinkable. It does not allow ideas to be swept under the table. Creativity can be used to help develop teams by ensuring that members are given opportunities to contribute to the process and thus develop ownership. Used this way, it is a significant contributor to morale.

We motivate by helping people to develop ideas which are congruent with the needs of the organization and to use influence only where justified. We are most successful when we work with people so that they internalize the organization's requirements.

Those who have a creativity drive with low influence needs are in a different position. Their ideas may disappear at the first sign of opposition. We motivate them by encouraging them to communicate and to assert their ideas. We may be unsuccessful and we will then need to ensure that, if we think their ideas are worthwhile, they are given consideration. If we are their boss, we may have to do it for them. If not, we need someone else in the organization to take note. Part of our approach will be in creating a culture in which those with low creativity are encouraged to work with and to use those with higher creativity. In this case, the best ideas are brought to bear on decisions and their quality improved.

Factor 10, factor 9 (variety and change)

Creativity and variety would seem, almost by definition, to go together. Yet our research suggests that, although many have creativity and variety above the norm, there are those who have a high need for creativity but a low need for variety. Therefore, there are those who are creative and stimulate themselves by ranging freely in their thinking and those who create in a narrow field. What is meant by this narrow field needs to be explored, since it would seem that people staying in the same field would reach a position in which what started off as creative would become routine.

The manager appears to have two different tasks. In the one case, of those with a high need for variety, the provision of opportunities to work in different areas on different projects would be essential. There would be the old problem of focus: an unwillingness to stay with the problem if the initial creative solutions are not acceptable. In those circumstances, motivation may involve presenting the same problems in a different light, or moving people away to something else, then bringing them back. In principle, the solution is to create the feeling of variety. However, where the creative drive is stronger than the drive for variety, we will be in a position to bring people back to the same problems and they will be more motivated and willing to keep on trying for a creative solution.

For those who have a low need for variety, motivation involves reassuring them that, although they do not need to be moved on to different problems, they *are* continuing to be creative. In essence, the aim is to stimulate so that the creative intelligence is brought to bear on the narrow task, but to find the cut off point at which creativity starts to pall. It involves staying in touch, perhaps offering encouragement in those dark moments when there appears to be no progress.

It should be noted that different organizational environments may have different requirements. In consumer businesses like advertising or retail, where the creativity is directed at satisfying fickle consumer demand and there is the opportunity to work in a variety of markets, a high need for creativity and for variety will be important. Working in a more defined area, perhaps in a laboratory or a specialist field, the need for variety might be a hindrance. In planning motivation strategy, it is worth considering the demands of the organization.

Factor 10, factor 11 (self-development)

Creativity provides the opportunity for self-development. Those who are creative have the ability to look at a wider range of options than the less creative, and to find those that most meet their need for self-development. At the same time, those in whom the two drives are strong will want to use them to reinforce each other. That means creativity will not willingly be used when it does not make a contribution to perceived personal growth. In the other case, those without this drive towards personal development will use their creativity in an instrumental fashion, to achieve organizational as opposed to personal goals.

Motivation should, primarily, grant the freedom to create. For those with the strong self-development drive it should also establish development needs, some of which we will specifically relate to organizational needs, while some will not be relevant. Since the creative drive is dominant, it is likely to be exercised when required, even though there may not be a development spin off, though in the long term creativity without development is probably not sustainable. We aim, therefore, to encourage particularly those needs that are organizationally congruent and to ensure that they are reviewed and debriefed at appropriate times. We recognize the need for other personal development and, if we can, provide the space for it. By doing this we are likely to increase commitment.

For those with low personal development needs, there is again a need to provide space, but there will be a greater willingness to work for long periods in areas where there is little self-development potential.

Factor 10, factor 12 (interest and usefulness)

Where there is high creativity and high need for job interest and that interest is satisfied, we have congruence; all systems can work together. The motivational task is to allow space for creativity but to try to relate it to significance. Creativity will be the driver, but commitment will be greater when there is awareness of how it contributes to the larger picture. We need to provide space, but be prepared to spend a fair amount of time relating organizational to personal goals. Where the need for job interest is not satisfied, we will find that creativity is likely to be focused outside work. This will make the job bearable but it will probably receive minimum attention.

It is possible, with the aid of creativity, to make the less interesting job feel more worthwhile. This will probably work as a short-term motivational strategy though, for the sake of transparency, what is happening should be made clear. There will be considerable tension between the unsatisfied need for job interest and the need for creativity, probably leading to a move from the job at the earliest possible moment.

For those with a low need for job interest, the creative drive can be used where required, though there will possibly not be the same level of commitment as we could expect from those who feel the work is significant. It should be remembered that 'significance' is in the eye of the beholder. What is trivial to some is worthwhile to others. We have to establish from people specifically what they mean by interest or usefulness and accept their view even if it is different from ours. Once we know what they regard as worthwhile, we have a common basis for motivation.

Factor 11

Self-development

Highest score recorded = 84
Lowest score recorded = 7
Mode 35 Median 32

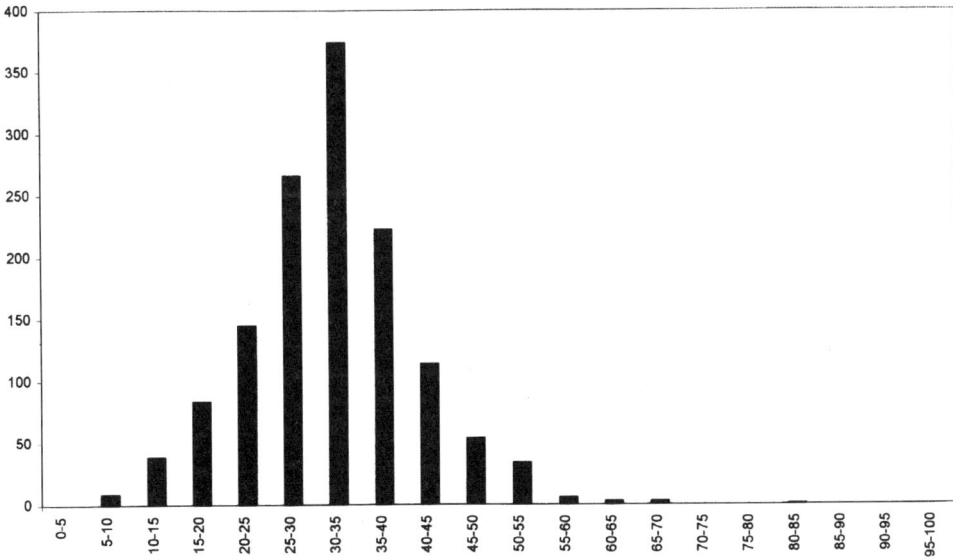

Figure 11   **Factor 11: histogram of scores**

Factor 11 high, other factors evenly spread

People who are high on self-development will judge their work in terms of what it does for them. In extreme cases, if the work does not feed self-development, it will not be done. The view will be taken that if they are not growing, they are declining. In other cases, the work will be done for a limited period, accompanied by a frenzied search for something else to do. Motivating people so driven requires an understanding of what they are looking for and an ability to relate what the organization requires to what they need. If it is not possible to do this, we are likely to lose them. Depending on their abilities and aptitudes, they will move into what they see as a more compatible environment like a university, or even move out of organizational life altogether, possibly to a significantly lower standard of living.

Personal growth links into autonomy, which, at one end of the spectrum, is a wish to be beholden to nobody. From an organizational point of view, management and motivation can be difficult. We are most successful to the extent that we are able to create congruence between personal and organizational needs. Their exercise of autonomy then links in with what the organization requires. If the congruence does not occur, neither will the commitment. If, however, it is possible to create a match we will find an extraordinary release of energy. Whatever the organization requires will be delivered, regardless of personal cost or damage to personal life.

Motivation requires that we take their needs fully into account. The alternative, merely to hope that the work satisfies them, is too risky. It might not, and we may find a sharp diminution in energy and commitment. We have to take time and trouble to establish from them what they see as their self-development needs. In doing this, both sides have to recognize that the work may satisfy a few or none of them. If it satisfies none, we will lose them anyway. If it satisfies some, it might be enough to retain commitment. Bringing the issue into the open is motivational in the sense that we will create an awareness that we value their concerns and will endeavour to satisfy them if possible.

We should ask them questions like 'What do you really like doing? Can it be satisfied at work? What work can we provide that will enable you to satisfy it? What will it mean if you are unable to satisfy it? Will you be able to pay attention to a job which does not feed your need for autonomy? Are there any other drives that we can satisfy at work? What do your other drives tell you about the way you will try and satisfy the need for self-development? Will you still have enough time and energy after work to satisfy your non-work related self-development drive?' And so on.

Once we have established self-development needs, we have to consider how to manage the need for autonomy. Essentially, the staff like control over their work and the organization requires outputs. How we define outputs depends on the organization. In a university, for example, there may be no precise definition of, say, research outputs beyond the requirement that they are academically rigorous and so on. In producing the research, the academic achieves self-development and autonomy and the organization achieves its required output. In commercial organizations, the congruence may not be so easy to achieve. But motivation is obtained by defining outputs and giving as much freedom as is possible, though specifying the circumstances in which matters have to be referred.

For most jobs there will probably not be sufficient congruence. We then try to arrange a situation in which although much of what they do does not afford the self-development they might like, we emphasize the work that does. We may find an additional problem when we try to move people into management. They are removed from their area of expertise, or from its direct practice, into an activity which they think will not fulfil them. They are then tempted to continue to do what they were doing, but not to manage even though they have the trappings of management.

We attempt to refocus their view of their own self-development, drawing their attention to the possibilities which up to then had escaped them. If we are successful, they will start to see management as a vehicle for self-development. If not, we will have a demoralized and probably ineffective manager. To keep them involved as managers we will need to find self-development activities for them, though it is probable that they will never become fully committed to management.

Factor 11, factor 1 (money and tangible rewards)

There are those who are low on the need for money who are high on self-development. That is to say, the energy that is spent by high factor 1 people on the pursuit of money is used by low factor 1 people to acquire self-development. It is probably fair to say that most of those who aspire to self-development, for example, teachers, academics, musicians, crafts people, are not very well paid. They are best managed by encouraging them to feel that their opportunities for self-development compensate for their lack of money.

Our research suggests that most people who are high on self-development have a below average need for money. Of course this does not mean that any organization can pay below what is felt to be fair and maintain morale. It does mean that, once the money need is satisfied, it is regarded as less important than the need for self-development and autonomy.

However, those with a high need for self-development and a high need for money, will probably make a supreme effort to relate their personal aspirations to organizational goals. They will take the view that their development need is important, but that they would think carefully before putting their financial health at risk. If, in their view, the work fails to contribute seriously to their personal development, they are likely to find themselves in a state of considerable tension, possibly feeling unable to contribute. They will not willingly give up the financial advantages of working for the organization, but much of their energy will be spent on either finding other work, or withdrawing.

Motivation will require us to spend time trying to relate organizational and personal goals. We can either do that by changing the sort of work that is on offer, or by trying to relate the work available to personal goals. If we are successful, the organization will reap the benefit. If not, we can expect to see the usual serious diminution of effort, hidden only by the need to remain in the organization as a source of income.

Those with a high need for personal development and a low need for money will undoubtedly turn their attention to the work that interests them. They may, in extreme cases, be prepared to suffer considerable financial deprivation in the pursuit of their interests. All the organization really has to motivate them with is its facilities. If it fails to offer the opportunity and stimulation required, then it will have no further part to play in motivation. We will either see a parting of the ways or a lack of contribution.

Factor 11, factor 2 (physical conditions)

By and large we would not expect any motivational problems provided that the need for self-development is attended to. If there are problems, they are either that the conditions of work are atrocious and inappropriate for the job in hand, or the problems are a surrogate for some other issue. For people with high factor 11, it is obviously polite to attend to their comments on the physical surroundings, but probably more fruitful to enquire into their attitudes to the work and its relationship to their self-development.

Factor 11, factor 3 (structure)

The position with factor 3 is complex. In one sense, factors 3 and 11 can be seen as opposites. People with a high factor 11 are looking for autonomy. Those who are high on factor 3 want structure, rules, guidelines, being clear what is expected, being told what to do and maybe even how to do it. Their factor 11 pushes them towards independence and factor 3 to dependence. The contradiction is more apparent than real. It is possible to have a high degree of autonomy with a strong wish for self-development, but with a need to work within a very structured environment. Judges are an example. All of them have to work within the structure of the law and by precedent. Even where they exercise considerable discretion, they are governed by considerations of equity. Yet the scope for self-development is considerable. There is no limit to how good a judge can be. The scope for autonomy is similarly wide. They are virtually unsackable, though they have to act within well-established guidelines of behaviour.

Judges are a special case and their motivation is not a matter most managers have to attend to. However, they do illustrate a general principle which is that there are people who want autonomy but need to operate within a well-established framework. That is to say, they have defined areas in which they wish to express themselves. For example, professionals talk about clinical or academic freedom. What they mean is that they wish to be autonomous and possibly unchallenged within their area of expertise. They may make no such claims outside that area and, apart from their colleagues, there is usually nobody who wants to challenge them. The exception will be when there are costs involved which other people have to bear, or where what is claimed conflicts with other interests. In the medical world, tensions are shown, for example, in the debate over the use of fertility drugs. The need for professional autonomy may conflict with the community's unwillingness to pay the high costs incurred.

In the commercial world, professionals experience the same tensions. They have loyalties both to their firms and to their professional bodies. They will not expect their organization to require them to infringe their professional code of practice. Sometimes the tension is expressed organizationally through, for example, matrix management. In that arrangement, staff report to both an operational and a professional manager. In cases of conflict over standards with the operational manager, staff refer the matter to the professional manager.

Motivation for those who are high on autonomy/self-development with high structure involves ensuring that professional autonomy is given full recognition and that what is required operationally is done. There may be perceived conflicts between the two requirements from time to time. The higher the structure need, the more painful the conflicts and the more the manager may have to help reconcile them. If no reconciliation is possible, there may have to be a parting of the ways.

Those who are low on structure needs are self-developers in an untrammelled sense. That is, the need for self-development can take them in any direction. They may have a butterfly approach and can work in areas of ambiguity and uncertainty, where the rules may still have to be discovered, or where they are operating at the frontiers. Whatever strikes them as interesting holds their attention. In a fast moving environment, that can be a useful attribute, though they may not develop the depth of knowledge and experience that is characteristic of the professional. If they have professional skills or qualifications, they are probably prepared to observe the protocols, but explore beyond the boundaries. Motivating them will be putting them into a position to explore new areas for self-development, but taking care to relate them to the needs of the organization.

Factor 11, factors 4 and 5 (people contact and relationships)

Those with a need for self-development can exist with or without a need for long- or short-term relationships. If, however, their need for people is low, they are probably self-contained and able to work on their own. Motivation will entail feeding them work which they see adds to their personal development and checking from time to time to make sure that what they are doing meets the organization's requirements.

If the need for people is high, we should arrange for people to develop themselves and at the same time have human contact. We should explore the extent to which they will enjoy working as part of a team, developing themselves as the team develops. In the organizational environment this can be a most desirable state of affairs. At its best, we will have a group of interdependent people working together for a common goal, feeling that they as well as the organization are benefiting. As a side benefit, we see the team members bonding as well as developing.

Motivation here requires clear task definition, and working through the stages of team development, particularly managing the stage two or conflict stage ('storming' in Tuckman's terminology, 1977) ensuring that all issues are explored and there is the maximum scope for self-development. If we are not working in a project environment, there will be benefits in adopting a continuous improvement agenda. Its purpose is twofold: to benefit the organization and to provide scope for self-development. Motivation will be enhanced by encouraging the fullest participation in the establishment of the improvement objectives. If group learning is, for some reason, not possible, the primary need for self-development will mean that it will take place on a solo basis, or in groups outside work where the focus may not necessarily be on work issues.

Factor 11, factor 6 (recognition)

Those with a high need for self-development with a high recognition need will want to choose their own area for development. They will be encouraged if their efforts receive recognition and, perhaps, discouraged if they do not. They will, though, persist in following their own development path, but will seek out ways of receiving recognition. Fortunately, society provides both multiple paths for development and many opportunities for recognition. It provides examinations and certificates and prizes, and people who pass examinations or win prizes normally get praised by someone. Organizations may not be so good at it. They will only want to give recognition when the chosen area for development coincides with what the organization requires. Sometimes they will not be clear what development has taken place, or may not notice it.

The role of the manager in this situation is, firstly, to attempt to define at the beginning the skills and experience required and then to try to relate them to declared self-development preferences. Sometimes that will not be possible and it may be necessary to try to arrange a trade-off. That is to say to acknowledge that the development required is not preferable but that it is necessary for the job and that there will be other preferable development opportunities. If the trade-off is not acceptable, there must be serious consideration of commitment to the job. There is then the need to review achievement at the end and to give due and generous recognition. Debriefing should always occur where development is provided in the form of internal or external courses. There is much anecdotal and other evidence to show that those attending courses are not debriefed and that they return to work with no expectation that they will use the skills that may have been acquired. In other words, there is no recognition.

The general point is that if there is a strong need for recognition and the organization does not meet that need, there will be the temptation to undertake self-development activities, perhaps outside the organization, not to its benefit, but providing the required amount of recognition.

Managers should not operate a 'blame culture': 'Get it wrong and we will bite your head off' or worse. Such organizations, and there are many of them, are hindered by their inability to learn. For example, debriefing will not take place honestly, people will be covering up their mistakes, and the organization is more likely to make the same mistakes again. Self-development requires recognition, but reasonable tolerance of, honest mistakes, so that people can learn from them and improve. Those with strong self-development drives are likely to feel stressed in an intolerant environment and probably will not stay.

If recognition needs are low, there is obviously more likelihood that the development will take place regardless of outside influences. Low recognition needs are clearly more important when the drive for development is in unconventional areas or in less glamorous activities. From the organizational point of view, it is worth regularly reviewing the development that is taking place, otherwise there is a danger that it may bear no relation to organizational needs. It might be de-motivating if effort is expended unnecessarily when, with a brief review, it might still be acceptable but more focused.

Factor 11, factor 7 (achievement)

High factors 11 and 7 should go hand in glove. People can express their need for autonomy via their achievements. They have the additional satisfaction of being able to measure their progress according to their achievements. The combination must be very common with top class sports people. These people excel at mountaineering, golf, tennis and a myriad of other activities where what has been achieved is so clearly measurable.

If the need for achievement is very strong, that might influence the direction of self-development. There would be comfort in aiming for those areas of development which are measurable. They would probably also be areas where there is little ambiguity or doubt as to what has been achieved. There would be a tendency to avoid the soft skills areas. This would not stop people from aiming at non-measurable areas for self-development, but they would not be so comfortable with these.

In motivational terms, we would be helping people to develop in measurable areas. They might want to consider formal, structured courses, possibly assessed by examination. They will want their new skills to be visible and to be recognized. They will like working on projects and would like the self-development aspects to be identified at the beginning of the project. Motivation will be achieved by attending to all those needs, noting also if there is a recognition need that will require attention.

If the need for achievement is weak, then obviously there will be comfort with self-development taking place in softer areas. There are subtleties and intuitions in development. Those who take a 'hard' view of development will not be quite sure what has been achieved, but will sometimes be able to recognize that something good has been developed without quite knowing what it is.

In motivational terms, we will not have the same need to identify in advance and to measure. We are working in a more subjective area and can best handle it by regular review of progress so that we can be sure that staff with this profile feel that development is taking place. If they are not sure, we have to try to establish with them the sort of development opportunities which they think might contribute to their needs and then try to provide it. In the end it is their sense of personal growth which will indicate to them whether or not the organization is fulfilling their needs in the way they want.

Factor 11, factor 8 (power and influence)

The drive for self-development and the drive for influence frequently go hand in hand. The first of the two involves increasing autonomy or independence of others, the second, increasing influence over others. At best, there is no conflict between the two. Self-development increases the ability to exercise influence. Influence can give the freedom needed to continue self-development. This is especially so where the activity in which influence is being exercised includes development opportunities, which is perhaps most likely to happen where both drives can find their outlet at work. One feeds upon the other.

At worst, the two can conflict. The drive for self-development can take us in one direction, the influence drive in another. For example, there might be a wish to develop in a way which is self-absorbing and even not relevant to work, diminishing the effort available for influencing others. Such conflict will cause stress and the need for development is likely to predominate.

What are the motivational implications? There are obvious benefits in having both these strong drives focused on organizational needs. We should pay attention first of all to the drive for self-development, aiming to establish congruence with organizational goals. We can then be reasonably confident that the influence drive will be working in the same direction. Subsequently, we can consider how the drive for self-development can be bolstered by the influence drive. We can discuss this explicitly and counsel accordingly. If we are unable to achieve a match, we are likely to move into a commitment deficit. The urge to exercise influence will be reduced, likewise the energy to attain organizational goals. The manager's job then is to obtain congruence, either by changing the nature of the task, or by successfully relating it to personal needs. If we cannot achieve agreement, we need to spend time showing how there are opportunities for congruence within the organization and that the immediate tasks required should be seen in this context. If that does not work, we must accept that there will be a declining commitment to the exercise of influence.

If the development drive is accompanied by a weak influence drive, we can assume that development takes place for its own sake and might even be personally 'hoarded'. The organization can then expect to benefit from the application of acquired skills, but not their use to influence others. We motivate again by establishing congruence. We have to consider the situation as people move into what could be a position of influence. We will want to discuss with them the necessity to exercise influence, though without much hope that the desire will be there. Influencing will be regarded as a residual activity. Because of this we need to watch carefully any unwillingness to delegate and we should perhaps coach in its mechanics. There might be a temptation to use influence simply to provide self-protection, a continuation of development for its own sake, or a concentration on work that they like doing as opposed to work they should be doing.

Factor 11, factor 9 (variety and change)

Those with a high self-development need with a need for variety may find themselves satisfying their needs in eclectic fashion, absorbing a wide range of knowledge and experience. They might also find that the need for variety militates against self-development in depth. Nothing gets completed before something else is attempted.

In motivational terms, self-development through variety should be made possible. If we require depth in any one area, we can encourage its achievement by ensuring that we have other areas available for development which can be used to relieve the pressure of single-minded concentration. However, the greater relative strength of the self-development drive means that we are in a better position to encourage in depth than where the variety is the greater need.

If there is a low need for variety, then we have the potential to stick to fewer avenues of development and a greater opportunity to obtain depth. Such people are unlikely to be distracted on to other activities. But we need to establish what interests them, so that it is worth the effort to develop in depth. We also need to be sure that development does not continue or take too great an effort in areas which are now of less interest to the organization. If this is the case, we need to spend time to re-establish acceptable self-development goals, matching organizational needs.

Factor 11, factor 10 (creativity)

A high self-development drive with creativity can be a powerful combination. Creativity is a traditional route to self-development. Creativity is, in addition, the truest form of autonomy; nobody does it quite the same way.

People with these drives are, to a considerable extent, self-motivating. They will require space and are not likely to take kindly to close supervision, although they may respond to supportive discussion. There is, though, the usual problem that if the organization is paying a salary, it requires a return. There needs to be extensive, and it can be explicit, discussion about establishing a close fit between personal and organizational goals. By explicit we mean a specific recognition of personal development needs *vis-à-vis* organizational goals. We will want to communicate our understanding that they cannot be fully engaged at the expense of the organization. However, it can be to the organization's advantage to allow some time and resources for strictly personal development, even though there may not be a direct payback. Part of the discussion could be about negotiating personal space.

Factor 11, factor 12 (interest and usefulness)

Those with a high personal development drive and a high need for interesting and rewarding work are going to be careful how they spend their time. Their highest fulfilment will be in doing work which they regard as developing them. If they can satisfy both drives, there is likely to be a release of energy and a high level of commitment.

If the work is not regarded as significant, then energy is likely to go into personal self-development, unrelated to organizational needs. Motivation involves making the work seem useful and spending time to ensure that this is so. However, as managers, we need to be sure we have no preconceptions about what is meant by interesting or useful. It is a truism that others will hold different views to us. Although we may appreciate this in an intellectual sense, it can still come as a considerable surprise to learn what others think is significant. Our job as motivators is to explore these views, then to accept them and to relate them to the organization. If we are unable to accept them, or if their views of significance are not synchronized with organizational goals, we are at some time going to see a parting of the ways. It can be helpful to appreciate this in advance. It is sometimes possible to ameliorate the difficulties by providing space for people to satisfy some of their need for self-development outside the organization, perhaps providing support. Relieving pressure in this way might be sufficient to keep people focused on organizational goals.

People with a high personal development need but a low need for interesting work will not suffer this constant anxiety as to whether or not what they are doing is worth while. We will still need to take time to make certain that their personal development goals are compatible with those of the organization. Again, where there is incomplete compatibility, we can consider giving some space for personal development.

Factor 12

Interest and usefulness

Highest score recorded = 97
Lowest score recorded = 15
Mode 41 Median 43

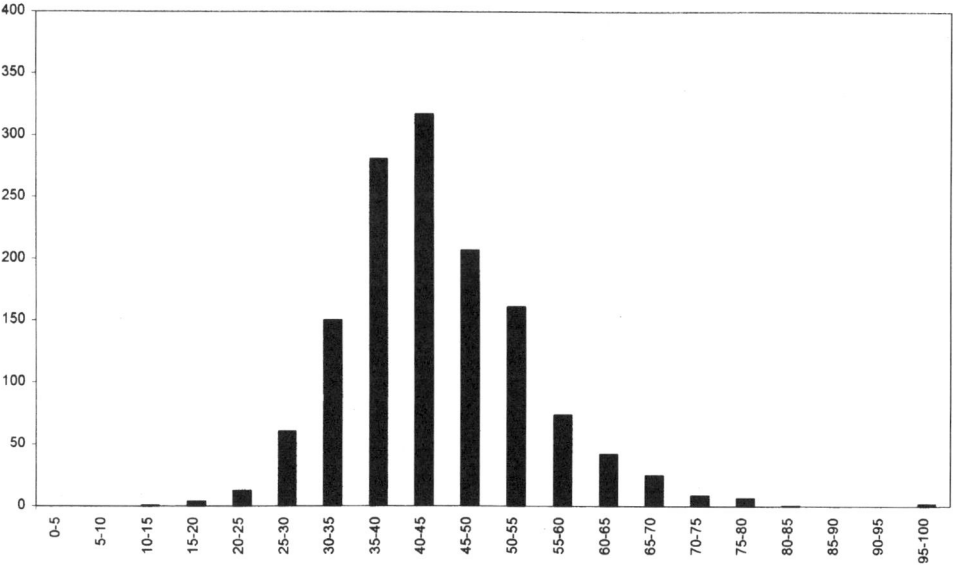

Figure 12   **Factor 12: histogram of scores**

Factor 12 (interest and usefulness)

The mode for this factor, 41, is the highest for any factor. That is to say that the need for job interest or usefulness is higher, on average, than the need for any other motivator. With this statement, we are saying something that has not been said so emphatically by any other researcher: that professional and managerial people are more motivated, for example, by a feeling of usefulness or interest than by opportunities for influence, achievement or recognition.

The implications for motivation are profound. If the strongest motivator is interest or usefulness, jobs need to be designed in such a way that they allow people to feel interested or useful. If that does not happen, a large component of motivation is missing. It is possible that if the job is not seen as interesting or useful, all other motivators will not work to their full potential. Thus, for example, high achievers will accept opportunities to achieve, but their hearts may not be in it. Their sense of having achieved something worthwhile will not be fully satisfied.

The further implications of this finding will be examined later in this chapter. But the question we need to consider first is what we mean by 'useful' and 'interesting'. Indeed, what do we mean by 'work'? Looking at 'useful', we have to ask 'who decides?'. The only person whose opinion can matter is the person who is to be motivated. The range of choices open to them is infinite, from contributing to what they regard as the public good, to indulging their skills and abilities in some artistic endeavour. That is, it can be outer directed or inner directed. It can be in some professional endeavour like law or medicine, or in foreign exchange trading, or in baroque music or carpentry. Some of the highest scores for factor 12 have been obtained from FX traders; their explanation of their high scores was that their activity enabled the world economy to function. Without them there would be no, or less efficient, world trade. Similar considerations apply to 'interesting'.

If the range of 'useful' and 'interesting' activities is wide, so is the range of activities which constitute 'work'. It can be the hyperactivity of the international business person, or the musings of the academic. Out of this range of activities emerges some sort of output, a business deal or a painting, or a computer program which tracks the migration of birds.

As far as motivation is concerned, the key point is that the decision as to what constitutes 'useful', 'interesting' and 'work' is made by each and every person. The problem for the motivator is that his or her assessment of these terms might be different from that of the person to be motivated. There may be no meeting of minds. This does not mean that people will not perform in areas which they do not regard as useful. It means they are not best motivated. It also means that to motivate them, we need to move in the direction of their understanding of usefulness. Either we change what we want them to do, unlikely in the world of business; or they change their job, which is of course possible; or we reach some sort of understanding. That is to say, we could attempt to improve interest and usefulness while still retaining the output required from the job.

How would we do that? The easiest aspect to deal with is job interest. That is, designing the job so that it is interesting, or so that someone can run the job in a way that is interesting to them. In the jargon, to empower them. Job usefulness on the face of it is more difficult. If the job is not useful, no amount of tinkering will make it otherwise. However, all is not lost. Most jobs have purpose, though their wider purpose for the organization may be unclear. This is simply because the jobs handle only part of the task, or because they are not, in the minds of those doing them, related to a wider purpose. Immediately we see a way forward. That is to increase job content, or to take pains to make explicit the wider context in which the job operates. Both these practices are now widely regarded as good employment practice. The motivation profile has made explicit why this is so.

Part of the process of motivation is thus to spend time with people establishing what they regard as rewarding and interesting. It means listening to their conversation and putting it in some sort of context. It means that when we listen formally, we do not betray our own feelings about what they regard as interesting, but consider what they say as putting their motivational needs in context. As always, we need to consider their other drives. In listening to them, we have to bear in mind that, if they do not find their work interesting, they are likely either to not do it, or to reduce their commitment. People with personal commitment who are not interested in the work are likely to grit their teeth and continue, but there are others who will simply give up and move on to something else, or retire on the job.

Factor 12, factor 1 (money and tangible rewards)

The most agreeable state must be the job which the holder regards as interesting and useful and which is well paid. There could be little which is more desirable, particularly if there is a high need for money as well. People in such jobs are probably self-starters. However, their tendency will be to pursue what is interesting, sometimes regardless of what is important to the organization. The organization could thus find itself paying well but not achieving its required output. It is important to maintain contact and to make organizational objectives clear. If the nature of the work makes it possible, that is to say there is a verifiable relationship between effort, output and reward, we should consider some sort of incentive scheme. All the time, though, we should bear in mind that the principal driving force is job interest. The advantage of a well-designed scheme is that the organization is not rewarding people for unproductive but interesting work.

If the need for money is low, but the job happens to be well paid, there will not be a problem. An incentive scheme would be of little benefit, and we may need to make a continuous motivational effort to relate personal to organizational needs. If (and this is perhaps more likely) the job is interesting but not well paid, we may find ourselves with no shortage of candidates. There are many such jobs, for example, in the public sector, at all levels, ranging from primary school teacher to permanent secretary in departments of state. Certainly, at more senior levels, there is a real possibility of obtaining much higher incomes at the head of a large business. But job interest is seen as of overwhelming importance and it is that which motivates even at the cost of reward. At lower levels, the difference in income between important jobs and jobs which are available but regarded as less significant can make the difference between reasonable comfort and near poverty.

In motivational terms, we have an absolute requirement to offer, as far as possible, the opportunity for people to work with substance and to celebrate and acknowledge the need for such work as a main driver. This is relatively easy to do (though we have to remember to do it!) when there is a congruence of views with those of the organization. Sometimes we may find that we are dealing with very strong views as to what is worthwhile and interesting and that those views are not consistent with those of the organization, or are even diametrically opposed. We can see such clashes, say, in the world of primary and secondary education, when the views of teachers and education authorities or even parents can differ. There are significant motivational problems here. Attempts to re-educate people, to change their views of significance, are likely to fail. Perhaps the most that we can hope to achieve is an accommodation, which is to say that they do the work but do not feel motivated. Ultimately, they may wish to leave, or we encourage them to leave, to find opportunities more to their taste.

In working with this factor, we should be aware that, in extreme cases, people are likely to give up regular employment so they can pursue their interest, regardless of the financial consequences. They will pursue their music, boat-building, or sport or charity, almost at any cost to themselves. Sometimes they can rely on a more financially solvent partner who will be prepared to support them. This gives us insight into the paramount importance of correct selection when we are recruiting people into jobs where the motivation comes from usefulness and interest and not from financial reward. Thus, although correct selection is always important, it is doubly so for these jobs. We need to take care that there is agreement of views before we bring them on board.

Factor 12, factor 2 (physical conditions)

It is unlikely that those who are motivated by factor 12 will be unduly worried by physical comfort. The median for factor 12, at 43, is more than two and a half times as great as that for factor 2. Provided the discomfort is not extreme, it will be tolerated and subordinated to the more significant need for interest. If factor 2 is raised as an issue, we are probably looking at another drive acting in compensation.

Factor 12, factor 3 (structure)

There is a potential tension between the need for structure and the need for interesting and useful work. Those with high factor 12/high factor 3 will want interesting work in which they have a clear expectation of what is required and how to go about it. Their sense of interest may well come in the way the job is structured. For example, it has to follow particular procedures and be undertaken in defined ways. The minutiae of the job may exert their own fascination. The usefulness of the job may be less clear, but may be illuminated by relating the pieces of the jigsaw to the larger picture. The tension will arise when they wish to explore the boundaries of usefulness, but there is no structure. They will feel uncomfortable until they have structure in place.

Motivation involves making sure that significance needs are met and that a supportive structure is created. It also involves mediating any tensions between the two needs; firstly, if the structure meets one need but undermines the other. For example, if the job is interesting but the rules or bureaucracy make it difficult to do, the high structure person feels unable to ignore them or does ignore them and feels stress. We will motivate by regular review, changing the rules if we need and are able to, explicitly recognizing the problems they create if we cannot.

Those with high factor 12/low factor 3 are in a different position. Interest and usefulness are at a premium. The internal structure of the job is virtually irrelevant. Attention will be focused on the output of the job and its perceived contribution. Any structure supplied will be that required to make the job work, rather than that imposed because of personal need. The low structure person will be happy to take the job as far as possible, rather than only to the boundaries of where structure will permit. In so doing they will be running the risk of all low structure people, of leaving no organizational traces that others can follow or build on. If structure is required to make the contribution accessible to others, they either have to supply structure, whatever their low personal need, or to work with others who will supply it for them.

We will probably not have any motivating to do, finding that we are dealing with self-starters. Our problem may be in ensuring that the energy expended actually provides the fullest possible benefit to the organization. This may be a matter of some delicacy as we work, firstly, to achieve congruence, relating organizational and personal needs; secondly, to be confident that necessary structure is created. We are in danger of seeming to impede rather than encourage. It will probably be beneficial to make this explicit and to try to create a situation where any tensions can be openly discussed. Ultimately, of course, in any organization the organization's needs will predominate and this understanding will inform all our discussions.

Factor 12, factor 4 (people contact)

The need for job interest has a median nearly twice as high as that for sociability. Factor 12 is much more significant. For those with high factor 12/low factor 4, the interest is in other than people, for example in computers, business strategy or design. People form the supporting cast at most.

Motivation will be to ensure that those aspects of job interest which impinge on other people receive attention; that there is perhaps a sharing of the interest with others so that motivation can be general. In other words, the intensity created by job interest at least does not lead to the de-motivation of others, and preferably does motivate them.

For those who are high factor 12/high 4, by far the minority, the interest will probably be focused on tasks, but for them people have more than a walk-on part. Their presence is vital for need satisfaction. But, overwhelmingly, the focus of high factor 12 is the task.

Factor 12, factor 5 (relationships)

Those with high factor 12/high factor 5 value job and long-term relationships. They may develop job interest through long-term relationships. An example would be the village GP, who over the years has come to know his or her patients and their medical history. The satisfaction increases as each generation succeeds the other and, in the end, the GP becomes a repository of the social and medical history of the village, sadly unable to publish an account of this experience for reasons of medical confidentiality.

With this combination, we are almost certainly dealing with self-starters. We will want to leave the longer-term relationship untouched, even to celebrate it. Our only problem is if it stands in the way of 'progress' or necessary change. Thus, if their interests, or those of the organization, change, to sustain motivation we may have to work to re-establish congruence. We may also have to find a balance between sustaining the relationship and changing it. We will need to emphasize both. If the job is interesting enough, they will join with us in trying to refocus the relationships, or we can let them get on with doing it themselves.

High factor 12/low factor 5 people are more task related. The interest is in the work. The people are merely background. We have no long-term relationships to consider.

Factor 12, factor 6 (recognition)

A person with high factor 12/high factor 6 wants interesting and useful work and to be recognized for doing it. It is the profile of the artist who craves the spotlight.

In a sense this profile is ultimately self-indulgent. The aim is to present an interest which provides personal satisfaction and gains approval. In one sense, people with this profile want it both ways. They want interesting work and they want to be praised for doing it. If they are not praised, they are still likely to want to continue with the work, but will try to find opportunities to do it elsewhere where they receive the recognition they want. If that is not possible, they will return non-recognition by failing to communicate the informal information which is so useful to organizations. It is obviously worth taking the trouble to give fulsome recognition.

Those with high factor 12/low factor 6 want interesting work for its own sake and do not care what other people think. At one extreme, people with such a profile will bury themselves, for example, in the desert of Oman working to save the oryx from extinction, taking a small salary and receiving almost no recognition from anybody. In more conventional terms, they will be fascinated with their area of technology or expertise, and feel no need to explain it to others. Their presentations, if they make them, will be replete with jargon and incomprehensible to the non-specialist. They may have difficulty in understanding why they have to communicate clearly and, if they do understand, they will find it difficult to write the speech. Their fascination with their topic means they will try to follow it regardless of the requirements of the organization. If the organization has no particular needs, that will be fine for them. There are not many organizations like that, and motivation will consist of spelling out clearly what the organization wants from them. They may spend time testing the boundaries, their low recognition meaning that the organization's opinion is of little account. If we can sit alongside them long enough, we are in a better position to establish a mutually acceptable division of effort.

Factor 12, factor 7 (achievement)

High factor 12/high factor 7 will want to achieve things that are interesting and useful. If they are not, they will not want to achieve them. In motivational terms, there is an absolute need to establish that what they are to do is, in their terms, worthwhile, otherwise they may be unable to energize themselves to move even to achieve the simplest things. Indeed, if there is nothing of interest requiring attention, the high achiever could actually sit around and achieve nothing. Their personal morale would be at rock bottom, but they would be unable to move. Usually, of course, they will find something interesting to do, but it may not necessarily coincide with what the organization would regard as worthwhile, and indeed might be something outside the organization. When they do find something interesting, they will be concerned to reduce it to measurable form. Part of motivation will be helping them, if necessary, to achieve just that. They will then have the satisfaction of knowing what they are working for and knowing when they have succeeded.

High factor 12/low factor 7 will absorb themselves in something interesting, but will be absorbed without achieving. In extreme cases, they will lose themselves in whatever engages them, ignoring the outside world. If we are not careful, there will be no discernible benefit to the organization. If the focus of their interest has no marketable value, they could soon find themselves in trouble. If it has a marketable value, they might, if they have tolerant clients, be able to make themselves a living advising others. There may be a tendency to give unfocused advice, which might create irritation and reduce the value of their contribution. They are best kept away from those areas of activity which require measurable results.

Motivating them will be difficult, not in the sense of needing to encourage them to use energy to pursue their interests, but in the sense of making it useful to the organization. If their expertise is valuable, we might tolerate their lack of focus and spend the necessary amount of time with them. If their contribution is not so valuable, we are likely to be coaxing them to focus in the hope that they may do so to the extent necessary. They are likely to be consumers of our motivational time.

Factor 12, factor 8 (power and influence)

High factor 12/high factor 8 are most likely to want to exercise influence in areas where they have high job interest or usefulness. They will, in practice, work with people whether or not they share their interest. Their interaction with these people will depend on what they see as significant and on their underlying purpose.

From a motivational point of view, such people have to be handled with care. A sense of significance and a desire to influence make a powerful combination. From our point of view we want to be sure that both are used to help to achieve the organization's purpose. We are likely to be working with self-starters. Because their impact on others can be so powerful, it is worth our while spending time with them to ensure congruence. Our starting point is with what they regard as interesting. We have to explore differences if we can, and to confirm their commitment to what the organization requires; or at least try to establish where we cannot rely on them. We might have to do this by observation. On their use of influence skills, we will want to encourage them to influence in an enabling sense, and in their turn, to establish others' points of significance. This is necessary to counter any tendency to use their influencing skills to attempt to impose their own view. In this way the organization also reaches an understanding of what drives those who work for it, and how they can, together, achieve the greatest impact.

There is one area which will require our particular attention. The roles people occupy frequently change as they progress through the organization. People start out in a functional role, say as specialists, or as accountants or marketers. If we assume that is the focus of their interest, as they progress, they are likely to move away from their initial skill base into a more general role. If the wider view sustains their interest and their need for influence, they can continue to be successful. If not, there will be a tendency to revert to function, to spend excessive time on their areas of interest, probably reducing their effectiveness in the more general role. Part of our motivational brief will be to keep track of what sustains their interest as they progress.

People high on factor 12 and low on factor 8 will be absorbed in their area of interest and will not want to exercise influence. Indeed, they will be tolerant of others who are interested in the same area and let them get on with it, even relishing the differences in view. We have to maintain dialogue to ensure that the organization benefits from their interests.

Factor 12, factor 9 (variety and change)

Those with high factor 12/high factor 9 will be sustained by variety. They are likely to give each organizational requirement fair scrutiny, and they will relate it to their overriding view of significance. If they cannot relate to what is now required, they are likely to have a low level of commitment. They will probably be able to sustain their effort for short-term unrelated activities, but are likely to have difficulty in the longer term. We can try to motivate them by helping them think through the implications of what we require and by helping them to relate it to their view of interest and usefulness. We may find we can assist them by modifying our requirements, perhaps by job redesign. The more information we give them about the larger picture, the more likely they are to make the connection. When they do so, we will see a regeneration of energy and purpose.

Factor 12, factor 10 (creativity)

Someone with high factor 12/high factor 10 demands creativity. The main drive is self-development. Creativity is instrumental in its achievement. This combination requires a great deal of personal space and freedom. Not only must the job provide interest and feel useful, but it must be possible to harness the creativity to the job needs without it feeling constrained. In other words, for motivational purposes, interest, creativity and job focus must work together. Obviously people in this position must be largely self-motivated and managed with kid gloves. Nevertheless, our role is to present the organizational point of view and to define outputs so that the maximum space can be given and the organization can benefit from all the energy expended. If we cannot guarantee interest, we are likely to find a diminution of commitment and a use of creativity outside the organization, particularly in furtherance of what is deemed interesting.

Those with high factor 12/low factor 10 demand a job that is intrinsically interesting and useful but not requiring a creative input. Such people will probably be tantalized by the intrinsic interest of the job but will not feel that they would like to do things differently. Probably less space is required.

Factor 12, factor 11 (self-development)

High factor 12/high factor 11 can be a powerful combination. Job interest powers self-development. Both drives working in the same direction will move mountains. The manager's job is to try to ensure that both are aligned, and then stand back. The commitment will be overwhelming, and the willingness to learn and to be trained impressive. Part of motivation will be in offering learning opportunities, both on and off the job. Where the inclinations diverge, there will be a faltering in commitment and management time needs to be spent refocusing. If training is not given, the employee will either try to obtain training from work, to undertake their own training perhaps part-time, or to move on. Generally speaking, this combination is likely to take a pragmatic view of learning, that is, the learning is for a purpose, usually to do better in this job or in later jobs.

Our research suggests there is a significant number who have high factor 12 but low factor 11. Presumably those with a lower need for self-development have reached a level at which the work sustains their interest. There will be less of an incentive to push the boundaries to see what else can be gleaned. The personal gain will be less apparent. Motivating them will not be so demanding, though there may be frustration at their failure to develop. Problems may arise when they feel that the job is not interesting or significant. In this case their development drive will quickly focus elsewhere and they are likely to become de-motivated very quickly. They will look to re-establish interest. We can help them do this, at the same time working to establish congruence with organizational needs. We may have to consider redesigning the scope of the job. We will always need to relate whatever we have asked them to do to the wider interest and the larger picture.

If they are unable to re-establish interest, then they should consider moving on. The problem is not so simple if the opportunities to do so are not available; for example, if funds are not available for early retirement. We have here the classic case of the individual on a plateau. At work they will make the minimum contribution and, although they may indulge their need for change elsewhere, even this is not guaranteed. They have lost interest and cannot be bothered to make the effort. If they have reached this state, re-motivating them is difficult and requires long periods of discussion with no likelihood of success. The most important thing to do is to try to prevent them from reaching this state. That requires continuous attention through their careers, making change and stimulation available and helping them move on early enough in their career if the interest and significance of the work has become irretrievably lost.

Part III
Motivation in action

Managing change

The one sure thing about the future is that nothing will be certain. It seems to follow that, if our organization is to be proactive, we must train people to appreciate the inevitability of change, to see how its impacts affect them; to withstand the stresses; and to develop a range of skills which will carry themselves and their staff forward into an uncertain future, while maintaining or even improving performance.

It is fashionable now to see change as a good, even a necessary, thing. From this perspective old habits, processes and structures can and should be unfrozen, complacent people shaken up and the organization rendered more flexible and responsive. People in the organization who are able to tolerate uncertainty and to operate well under it are valued. More of them are recruited and attempts are made to train those already in post to develop resilience. The converse is also believed, that people who are less able to tolerate change and uncertainty, or who attempt to do so but fail – in which case their work or health suffers – are a liability.

For managers the message is clear: recruit and select people able to work well under uncertainty, train existing staff to cope with it better and find humane ways of transferring or getting rid of those who are unable to learn the new behaviour or to change their attitudes to match the new requirements.

The successful change manager

Let us look at the kinds of behaviour and attitudes that characterize the effective manager of change.

Confidence in their own abilities and propensities

Lack of self-esteem and confidence is a barrier to the individual forming and maintaining good relationships with others; and this matters especially where others themselves face uncertainty and need to feel that they are trusted and esteemed by their managers. The word empowerment can be misused but only the genuinely confident (those who believe themselves to be powerful) can allow others the freedom to exercise personal power in their turn. But this is not a requirement particular to successful change management. All good managers need this. Is there any other quality or feature which we might expect a good manager of change to have which is not necessarily required in all managers?

Low structure needs

Here is the fit with motivation theory. If they are the kind of person who needs structure, likes to know where they stand and operates best under conditions of relative certainty, in a situation of change they will either do what the organization requires, suffering tremendous personal stress (with attendant health problems), or they will not do it. They may fail in the task but will preserve their own equilibrium. A person with *low* structure needs is tolerant of uncertainty, they prefer it to routine and rules. Those whose needs are extremely low even show contraindications: they rebel against structure, suffer frustration at petty rules and form filling or other administrative (bureaucratic) requirements as they see them. More importantly for those who work with them, they seek to avoid, even to disrupt structure where they find it, to make trouble to keep themselves stimulated and to avoid boredom. Such managers see themselves as active and unconstrained ('I do my best work from moment to moment').

And here is the rub. Most of the staff working for them are likely to have higher structure needs than their manager. Their jobs tend to be more structured and they were hired because of their propensity to do those jobs efficiently, consistently and accurately. Now they have a boss who sees the world in a different way, whose motivational profile is fit for the uncertainties ahead, but who is more likely to add to the uncertainties ('throw even more plates into the air') as the organization moves into the period of change. At each setback, or even if results are slow to appear, this manager will see the solution as more change. 'That hasn't worked too well, let's try this'. At what point for the staff does almost tolerable change become inexplicable chaos, change for change's sake?

Here is a mismatch of needs and a fertile bed for stress and low performance. To carry through change, especially an opening-up type of change programme where there is no quick unfreeze, rearrangement and then refreeze into the newer pattern, we need a low structure manager. Unfortunately, that person is not necessarily the best choice to give comfort and stability to the staff at a time when their structure needs are going to be raised even higher (by the additional uncertainties of change or the threat of it). Help is on hand though. Not all managers with low structure needs are so insensitive as to assume that their staff are motivated as they are. Some can build structure for others, while not needing it themselves. These skills are rare, but they can be learned. And here is where training for change comes into its own.

There are managers who are suited to uncertainty as though born to tread on quicksand. If they can be trained to harness the worst excesses of their own needs to build certainty for others, they make exceptional managers of change. If they cannot or will not adjust – and the catch is that it is stressful for them to restrain their motivational drives to meet the structure needs of others – they make good task drivers (the changes go through) but they leave large numbers of casualties.

This may not matter if you take the view that the 'weaker' staff can be weeded out this way. What is more likely is that those who are put under such stress will become less productive. They will be less able to learn new skills and processes as their energies will be used up managing their anxieties. They will not leave conveniently as they will have neither the self-esteem nor the energy to apply for another job, but will probably dig in like an animal going into hibernation. They will lower their arousal level and will try to let the storm pass over their heads. If they are forced to take part in little exercises, like applying for their own job, they will feel acute anxiety. They might become anxious enough to leave, like the examination candidate who withdraws from the exam rather than face the uncertainty of taking it and possibly failing, but they are more likely to stay, stressed and unproductive. And if the organization has gone through a period of massive restructuring where everyone has been through a similar mill, their low performance will not easily be noticed against a backdrop of all the other exhausted survivors.

A useful question at this point is, 'Can people be trained to withstand change at work better?' If we consider a continuum of increasingly proactive approaches to change, we can help people by first establishing where they lie on the continuum and then using a range of interventions to help them to move in the proactive direction.

At the far left of Figure 13 we are dealing with the causes of stress, how to recognize it in oneself and others, how to avoid it, lessen it, share it, compensate for having it, learn to mind it less and so on. This is almost at the therapy end of training for change where the facilitator struggles to help the corporate victims of restructuring, downsizing and other drastic job changes, such as partial or total status, skill or job loss. Further to the right training sessions cover some of the same ground with leadership and team-building skills to help managers handle

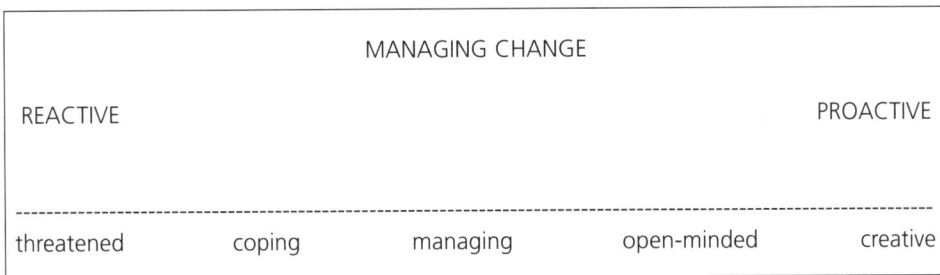

MANAGING CHANGE				
REACTIVE				PROACTIVE
threatened	coping	managing	open-minded	creative

Figure 13   **The spectrum of change**

de-motivated and/or confused staff, travelling with them into the uncertain future. The far right seems the ideal, that of people freed from the shackles of habit and routine, fermenting like a creative compost heap and permanently poised to take flexible advantage of opportunities.

Are there motivational factors which are good indicators for handling and managing change? The answer does seem to be yes but, conversely, some are contraindicators for it.

Factor 1 (need for money and tangible rewards)

Pay can motivate people to accept change, but it can be a powerful de-motivator as well. Think of the salesperson on high commission. Everything is progressing well, there is plenty of money coming in at the end of the month. Then the boss wants to change the way things are done. The salesperson sees his or her income being threatened. Change is something to be fought against, or negotiated to make sure earnings levels are maintained. The process of change makes the negotiations difficult, who knows where the change is going to end? Suppose the new pay structure is frozen before the change has been fully worked through? Those who have a high need for reward will be careful about accepting change, might even fight it, trying to make the organization carry the risk.

Such people can be motivated by change if they can see it enhances their earnings. But if the incentive schemes reward the wrong actions, these are where they will concentrate their effort, even if so doing undermines the benefits or the purpose of the change. An example is the conference centre which offered managers a personal bonus scheme if they obtained large volume training business at 80 per cent of list prices. Realizing that the best strategy was to sell only some items at 80 per cent and to include a number of other, small variables free (like flip charts, TV, video, photocopying), managers were able to achieve high levels of bonus. Only after the scheme had operated for a year did senior management realize that their objective should have been to encourage the maximum income per transaction, regardless of the headings the money was listed under. Similarly, if co-operating with colleagues, a useful approach at times of rapid change, threatens to reduce earnings, they will not co-operate, or will do so only to the minimum extent possible.

There is no easy answer. Guaranteeing earnings for the period of change is one, expensive option. And if the earnings are guaranteed, the performance may not follow. The other is to engineer the change so that the payment arrangements support what is required. In practice, that is possible but difficult. The process of change with high earners can be fraught with difficulty. In the end it can be easier to maintain the status quo than to negotiate for every penny. But if the pay can be made to support the change, the high earners will be the organization's best friend.

The training need is how to make money from the new situation.

Factor 2 (need for good physical conditions)

Not many of our respondents scored high on this factor. When questioned, some of those who did reported that good office accommodation and clean surroundings matter to them enough that change which adversely affects their surroundings would cause them serious unhappiness. Would someone like this be prepared to move jobs if this happened? Yes, appears to be the answer, unless a move is not possible, in which case stress would result and so would lowered motivation to do the job. Positive change was viewed as good, and not of much importance, certainly not a source of extra motivational drive to do better. It seems that Herzberg (1966) was right and that improved working conditions, even when of importance to someone, do not serve as reasons to work better or harder.

Factor 3 (need for structure)

Change driven by management

Managers who wish to drive change in their organization are likely to meet resistance unless they prepare the ground. The biggest problem will occur if those working in the organization either do not see the need for change or have previously experienced badly managed change. In the circumstances, even those who might be disposed to change are unlikely to be committed to what is being proposed. If managers are determined to go ahead, they will have to rely on their powers of coercion.

Management's chance of successfully implementing change is improved to the extent that it has a good track record. Staff will probably give them the benefit of the doubt. Chances can be improved even further if managers take the trouble to explain the reasons for the change and the consequences of not training for it. If the case made is convincing and the proposed change to meet the new challenges is defensible, staff will at least see that there is logic and good sense in place, and one element of their proposed resistance will have disappeared.

Staff will then be concerned about their own position. Each individual will want to know if they are a net beneficiary or a net loser from the change. Those who are going to benefit are likely to be the most enthusiastic, though there may, of course, be quibbles over whether they might have benefited more or differently. Those who are going to lose will be asking themselves whether or not they deserve to lose. If they feel they do deserve it, they will fight their corner, but their primary concern will be their dignity and any deserved compensation. For example, some of their 'failure' could reasonably be laid at management's door. Those who feel they do not deserve to lose will fight more strongly for compensation and, in a well-ordered organization, they are more likely to achieve it.

In summary, managers can successfully manage change provided they take a great deal of trouble to explain the reasons and justify their proposals, and take into account the personal considerations of those who will be affected. If they do not take these steps, they will find themselves using coercion to overcome lack of commitment.

Change driven by external events

Taking the extreme position, highly structured individuals will happily settle into a rut of repetition and predictability. Change will be seen as something threatening and will be resisted despite the clamour for things to be done differently and, where it cannot be resisted, there will be stress. Such individuals, in the face of overwhelming odds, or what we can call catastrophic change, may find the old ways of doing things so incongruent that they can no longer be maintained. In the jargon, they have been unfrozen. They may discover a new lease of life for themselves and maintain their new found flexibility, but return to old ways as soon as the threat recedes. Such, for example, is the experience of war. Some people who are comfortable and happy in their structures suddenly find they have new resources of energy and initiative and behave in ways which in normal times are uncharacteristic. Others are unable to cope and become casualties of stress.

The unpalatable lesson is that those with high structure needs may have to experience discontinuity before they will accept change. The problem for management is to manage the transition so that it is not destructive. This is best done in two ways: firstly, by having a clear view of what structure is required in the new situation, so that the 'victims' can see light at the end of the tunnel; secondly, as soon as those affected have internalized the fact that they are going to have to adapt to the new situation, providing assistance, training or whatever is required, to help them to get there. If there is no light, then we are looking at the possibility of illness or breakdown.

Factor 4 (need for short-term people contact)

Someone with a need for contact with others is likely to seek comfort from them during the process of change. Unless the change adversely affects their chances to socialize, they are unlikely to resist it, other factors being equal. Their response to the threat of change will be mitigated if they are able to discuss (perhaps at what seems exceptional length) the implications with colleagues. This desire to share with others comes from their propensity to ameliorate what they perceive as threatening by contact with others. There is a well-known series of 'misery loves company' studies which demonstrates that people under a perceived threat seek the company of others in preference to being on their own. These studies apply to the generality of people, not just those especially vulnerable to such needs as are these high-factor-four scorers.

In short, a manager wishing to make changes in the working environment or practices of staff with high needs on this factor must allow plenty of time for meetings and other briefing-type events, including a lot of informal discussions. The very act of assembling staff for such events reassures and comforts people high on factor 4, even if the quality of the information given and exchanged is not high.

Factor 5 (need for long-term relationships)

The need for long-term relationships can have two outcomes. As long as the relationships hold, they can provide a bedrock on which change is experienced and it can even deepen them. If change threatens relationships, it may be resisted. The question for the manager is, how beneficial are the relationships? Are they inhibiting the business; for example, do they help to enshrine bad working practices? If so, the process of change is through joint education, or if that is not deemed possible, by breaking the relationship and providing opportunities to re-build after unfreezing has taken place.

Training will be in team building, using the new job roles to provide the training structure, together with interpersonal skills to help people open out to each other.

Factor 6 (need for recognition)

Recognition, handled properly, can make the change process proceed smoothly; handled badly, it can derail it. Recognition becomes magnified in its impact. The key question for the manager is the extent to which the change is adding to or detracting from recognition. If the current job gives high positive recognition, there is going to be anxiety about change. Constant positive feedback can help such people through change, provided there is opportunity for recognition in the new situation. If the recognition is not given, if there is no understanding or explanation of the new opportunities, people with high recognition needs are likely to become, at the very least, silently obstructive. Likewise, if the present job offers poor opportunities for recognition, and the new job is seen as providing an improvement, change can be welcomed. The key is to supply information about what is coming. Finally, if the present job offers poor recognition and the new job is seen as bad or worse, there is little real hope.

The manager may have different priorities. Change might be seen as stimulating and provide excellent opportunities for recognition. The need here is for sensitivity to the feelings of those who are undergoing change but who do not have control. Training should look specifically at the new job or situation and overtly at the indicators of recognition.

Factor 7 (need for achievement)

If the change process can be turned into a project with measurable indicators of progress, those with high achievement drives will co-operate all the way. The problem comes when the change is messy, there is no clear sense of direction, or it appears out of control. High achievers have a natural difficulty in coping with the ambiguity thus created. They want to get a grip on it, halt it, measure it, set a firm course and get on with it. They may be continually frustrated. Whenever they think they have clarified the situation, they find in a very short time that they are going in the wrong direction.

High achievers may try to stop the process too early, or focus their effort in those areas where measurement is possible, when the really important happenings are immeasurable and, perhaps, need more subtle handling. In the midst of frenetic change, high achievers will probably be bewildered, unable to manage, needing to have trends explained. As soon as events slow and start to take some recognizable form, the achievers will come into their own, measuring indicators, setting targets, displaying enormous energy and making progress.

The lesson for managers is that a lax approach to change will probably de-motivate both high achievers and people with high structure needs; two failures for the price of one sloppy piece of work.

What training will work for them? When they are not in control, they will be miserable. They need to have explained what is happening to them. Giving them an insight into what motivates people will help. It will not completely satisfy them, their feelings are too intense, so some relaxation training will not come amiss. Perhaps also, if enough is known about the end conditions, some technical training will help them towards achievement when the time is ripe.

Factor 8 (need for power and influence)

Those with a high influence drive love change. It is a time of maximum opportunity, especially if the drive is accompanied by a clear vision of what is to be achieved. The real frustration will come if the change is out of their control and their efforts are just whistling in the wind. The ideal state is one in which there is sufficient confusion to provide the opportunity to exercise influence, but not so much that nobody is in control! The training effort should be focused on strategic matters, to ensure that the exercise of influence actually helps the organization to achieve and does not hinder or even mislead.

Factor 9 (need for variety and change)

By definition, those with a high need for variety will welcome change. They will seek it and, if their jobs seem boring or if nothing much has happened for some time, they will probably find means of livening up the situation by changing things. For the manager wishing to make changes, this is relatively good news: a high drive on the need for variety and stimulation means that change is rarely seen as threatening and to be resisted. Such people will often be good change drivers to the extent that they will push it through, not always sensitively, but certainly with enthusiasm. With some, however, change is both enjoyable and an opportunity to avoid commitment. The manager's job is to make sure that change is not seen as an excuse for staff to amuse themselves. The absence of clear standards of performance in all the confusion can hide poor performance. The manager needs to maintain a clear view of what needs to be done. The training effort should again be focused on the organization's strategic objectives to ensure that the change effort is directed where it is required.

Factor 10 (need for creativity)

Creativity and change clearly go together. Creativity can be undisciplined, adding confusion to potential chaos. There is a danger that people low on structure needs and high on the creativity drive can generate unbridled change. With a careful mixture of encouragement and restraint, the manager can harness the benefits of new idea generation while preventing the drawbacks of too much open-ended suggestion. One obvious drawback to unbridled creativity is the paralysis that it can cause in some people when they are faced with too many options.

People high on both the creative drive and on the need for structure (factor 3) are likely to be frozen into impotence if change is handled badly by management. Needing structure, their needs will probably rise even higher if their anxieties are raised by open-ended change. An example is the announcement by management that 'The organization is moving into a period of change where we cannot offer more than an outline of a future vision'. This will be perceived as threatening unless staff/management relationships are strong and there is high trust in the organization. Needless to say, the high creativity drive of such an individual will be unavailable to the organization until and unless their structure needs are met.

Creativity harnessed to planned change can widen the options – how things should be done and what should be done – and can be beneficial. The management role is to focus creativity, without a peremptory dismissal of the wilder offerings. Training, again, involves focusing on the organization's needs.

Factor 11 (need for self-development)

Change provides an opportunity for self-development. The advantage is most obvious when the resulting self-development meets already established personal objectives. Where it does not do so, the role of the manager is to help re-focus personal objectives. If this can be done successfully, motivation will be enhanced. If not, the change will be seen as annoying and de-motivating.

People high on the need for self-development will seek change for themselves if it is not offered. A team leader in the construction industry, scoring 49 on this factor, expressed ambitions for 'becoming a commercial manager within two years' and asked if an MBA would help him to achieve this. His job required him to work on-site a great deal of the time and his weekly hours were punishingly high. He was willing to pay high fees to a university and to study during his evenings and weekends if he could gain new knowledge and skills. On a micro level his motivation to learn and to expose himself to new ideas was so high that he attended three courses back-to-back, one on Wednesday, Thursday and Friday, another on Saturday and Sunday, another on Monday and Tuesday, and was restrained with difficulty from attending yet a fourth on the following Wednesday, Thursday and Friday (this one being less relevant to his work).

Factor 12 (need for job interest and usefulness)

People scoring high on the need for intrinsic job interest and usefulnes will welcome change if it benefits their work: it is not enough for change to result in an expansion of duties or responsibilities or in a multiplication of similar tasks. Such people require in-depth enhancement of the interest level of the work. This could mean increased perceived-difficulty level, higher technical requirement or other intellectually challenging content.

For example, a geologist working for a multinational oil company scored 53 on this factor. He was well paid, happy with colleagues and working conditions and had moved to the city with his family to take up the job 18 months before. He sought career development advice as he was concerned that, on casting around for the next interesting project to work on (the current one had about three months to run), he could see nothing that equated to the present one in interest level. He wanted to know whether he should move house, after having bought one he liked very much only four months before, as he could see that some projects based in other parts of Europe could meet his job-interest criteria. In discussions it became clear that he would suffer large amounts of disruption to his personal and working life to avoid the possibility of doing a project that did not fully engage his talents.

It is clear that people with high needs on factor 12 do need personal counselling on their work and future. In the case outlined above, the manager responsible for the geologist's work should have been keeping a continuous eye on his needs. It may be too late if there are now no interesting projects for him to join without moving country and, possibly, employer.

The manager who tries to reconcile the needs of the individual and those of the organization and who keeps a watching brief will at least be forewarned of such problems and may be able to prevent them. Training effort should be directed to personal counselling, and an attempt made to align organizational and personal development needs.

Coping with stress

We will define stress in some detail, but the message of this chapter is that although stress can be caused by many external factors, for example job loss, for our purposes, a powerful internal cause of stress is the blocking of our motivational drives.

Stress manifests itself very differently from person to person. Take the case where an executive is required to make decisions and to direct operations without guidelines or clear instruction, and where very little feedback is given either during the work or after projects are completed: a situation that occurs quite often. If the jobholder is both low on the need for structure (factor 3) and average or low on their need for recognition (factor 6), they are probably not too concerned about either the lack of direction or the paucity of response. Someone scoring higher on both of these factors would find this job stressful. Without guidelines and with the impression that effort just disappears into a black hole without acknowledgement, they will resolve their stresses as best they can. Assuming that they cannot easily move jobs or employer, they will probably reduce effort, while maintaining a façade of 'busyness'.

In order to avoid stress for the high structure, high recognition scorer, a manager needs to offer good guidelines at the beginning of a task and during the course of the work, and to offer frequent feedback along the way, including a final summary of outcomes and results after the work has been done.

Stress, like motivation, is not an absolute; all of us will find certain events stressful, an accident, for example. But people differ markedly in both the things that cause them stress and in the effects that such stressors have.

What is stress?

For many years stress was described and defined in terms of external, usually physical, forces acting on an individual. Later, theorists such as Lazarus (1976) suggested that the individual's perception of, and response to, stimuli or events was a very important factor in determining how that individual might react, and even whether or not an event would be considered stressful in the first place. Since the 1970s most researchers acknowledge that both external and internal factors affect stress. One definition is that stress is: 'A response to external or internal processes' which reach levels that strain physical and psychological capacities 'to, or beyond, their limit' (Cooper *et al.*, 1988, quoting from Basowitz *et al.*, 1955).

A range of phenomena act as stressors: from external events, such as accidents and illness, to internal states, such as low self-esteem and conflicting drives. Some of the more common are listed below, but for the purposes of this book the most important stressor listed is that of motivational mismatches.

External threats	*Internal threats*
accidents	motivational mismatches
bereavement	anxiety from internal psychological processes
illness	low self-esteem
work overload	ambivalence
work underload	conflict
family/relationship problems	

What are the implications of blocking or denying our motivational needs? Many people are in situations they do not feel comfortable about; for some people even the circumstances of their lives are uncomfortable. What is the stage at which discomfort becomes stress? At what point does not getting what we want or need become a serious block or frustration? There are two ways of approaching the problem. One is that people will adapt to the situation, the other that they will not and will experience stress. We will also consider the case of those who deliberately, for reasons that seem valid to them, frustrate their motivational drives.

The first view that someone, if deprived of something, will learn to live without it, is that they will become so accustomed to being denied that they will no longer seek to satisfy the need. For basic, physiological needs there is no doubt that deprivation has few benefits: a baby that is not fed does not learn to do without, but becomes ill and dies. For social needs the picture is less clear, but evidence seems to point to similar results. A child that receives no love, but is neglected and abused, is likely to warp its needs to adapt to a hostile environment. Having received no love, it will find it hard to recognize, appreciate or be capable of feeling love towards others. Its need for love may be converted into a stronger drive for immediate satisfaction in other areas, a form of compensation. The adult that results could be very instrumental in relationships. Conversely, human beings are adaptable and many intelligent adults have been able to overcome both physically and socially deprived childhoods, learning how to give and to receive affection and love and to develop consideration for others where little was shown to them. There is thus no definitive answer, though it seems likely that while some people do not recover from motivational deprivation, others can do so with effort.

The second view is that motivational frustration causes stress. Consider someone with a high need for interesting, useful and rewarding work. If they work in a boring, repetitive job which, although highly paid, seems to have no particular purpose or value, they are likely to feel stressed, particularly in the longer term. They will be bored and frustrated because they are blocking or ignoring their need for interesting work in order to earn a large amount of money. If they have a low need for tangible rewards, including money, they will be even more stressed, as they find themselves in the position of favouring something they do not value above something they do.

They will feel better about the situation if they are in need of money for other reasons, for example, they have just acquired a large mortgage which they wish to reduce quickly, especially if they are aware of what they are doing and if the problem is short term (Festinger, 1957). They will reduce their stress by such a stratagem as it puts them in control. If they do this, they have made a decision to offset some current discomfort for a later gain. This displacement of satisfaction (deferred gratification) is something that we have learned to do from childhood; those children who do not learn how to do it experience many problems later in life (Goleman, 1996).

This leads directly to the questions: 'To what extent should we consciously ignore our motivational needs?' and 'What price do we pay for doing so?' The short answer might be: *By all means ignore one or two needs in the short term for the sake of a later gain, but do not do so in the long term.* We also need to be aware of exactly what we are doing and the price we are likely to have to pay.

It is one thing to suppress a need for interesting work while earning enough money for the holiday of a lifetime; it is another to work in a succession of boring but well-paid jobs to accumulate a great deal of money for which there is no immediate use. In case you think that someone is unlikely to do this, bear in mind that it is not only motivational drives that dictate life choices. Many people have a strong urge to do (even in adulthood) what their parents told them was the right thing and, if their parents were brought up in a society where poverty and debt caused misery, a well-paid job will outrank factors such as social satisfactions from the working team, or the opportunity to do challenging work. Such people may seek well-paid work at the expense of interest or value, allowing their adherence to the family code to outweigh their personal needs. They prefer mental peace from the superego (or parental voice) to satisfaction of their own needs. The benefit is suspension of guilt, the price is frustration.

According to Freud, the psyche is divided into three main areas – the id, the ego and the superego. The id represents our instinctive, animal nature and drives us to satisfy our appetites. Many motivational drives come from the id. The ego is a construct which lets us perceive ourselves as individuals, separate from others, and enables us to map out our unique place in the world. The superego is a set of instructions, positive and negative, built up over time and derived from authority figures in our lives which operates as a rough rule book in guiding our decisions and actions. These three operate independently and often conflict.

Motivation is linked to the id. Parental instructions can, therefore, seem to operate as brakes on motivation. It would be tidy to consider instructions from the superego as part of motivation, after all, if you have an urge to follow the code

Always keep out of debt, surely this is a component of your motivational set? Something you want to do? But it is not. It is something you feel you *ought* to do. This distinction is important if we are to understand motivation, which in this book means what you *want* to do. Denying your innate needs to satisfy the urgings of your superego is likely to lead to considerable stress, particularly in the longer term.

The mechanics of stress

We now need to understand the mechanics of stress, particularly why blocking motivation can cause stress. The fundamental reason is that blocked emotion leads to a permanent state of arousal and inhibits repose which body and mind require for regeneration.

One of the most useful models for defining and assessing the impact of stress is based on the scale of arousal, described by Rycroft (1968). The horizontal line in Figure 14, based on Rycroft's work, represents that scale, from low on the left to high on the right.

When we are asleep, arousal is low. The body is efficient and will use only the minimum necessary to maintain basic functioning; rest and repair take precedence. Moving on we wake and gradually move to awareness, probably doing some task on 'automatic pilot' like preparing breakfast or washing ourselves when we get up in the morning. Further yet is alertness where we are conscious of background stimuli, able to scan the horizon for possible threats, but still operating comfortably with some task, like driving a car, in the foreground of our minds. This state is known as vigilance.

Anything unexpected, and especially something perceived as threatening, say another car looking as if it might drive into our path from a side road, moves us further along to the right of the scale, to minor, or even major threat level. At this point we start to feel uncomfortable; our physiological reactions to the perceived threat operate before rational thinking, and the results can be felt even to our fingertips. Our heart beat increases, our breathing becomes shallow and we experience a range of unpleasant sensations. We are a considerable way along the scale of arousal and our body has prepared us for the classic readiness to respond known as the fight, flight and submission state. Realizing that the other car driver

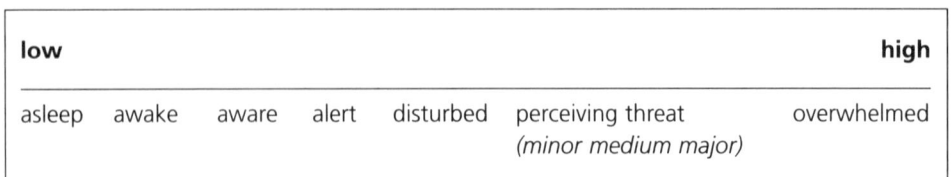

low						high
asleep	awake	aware	alert	disturbed	perceiving threat *(minor medium major)*	overwhelmed

Figure 14   **The scale of arousal**

has seen us, is slowing down and that there is now far less likelihood of an accident, we start to relax and begin the slow process of retreating back down the scale. Unfortunately, it takes longer to back down the scale towards relaxation than it does to gear up towards the threat level.

A really serious threat, as when we find ourselves inside a burning car, will force us along to the extreme right of the scale and will probably lead to instinctive and panic reactions, unless we can force ourselves to think and act logically in spite of our fear. Energy is expended increasingly towards the right-hand end of the scale. This helps to explain why anyone emerging from a very stressful event usually displays exhaustion.

Stress and performance

Stress impairs effectiveness as we can see from Figure 15. Bearing in mind the body's tendency to conserve energy, some functions only operate along a certain range of the scale. Short-term memory, for example, is not available when we sleep. It also begins to be affected adversely to the right of the scale, from minor threat onwards, indicated by a solid line that changes to a dotted one, cutting out altogether as the threat becomes overwhelming. Similarly, rational and logical thought operates over a range: it seems to be available 'on standby' but is summoned up only when, say, the milk for breakfast coffee and cereal cannot be found and a decision must be made as to what to use instead. Our immune system is also efficient. It begins to be impaired as threat levels increase. Both viral and bacteriological defences are affected from minor threat onwards, especially if we maintain ourselves at that level of arousal for a long time.

Against this background, let us now look at each of the factors in relation to stress level.

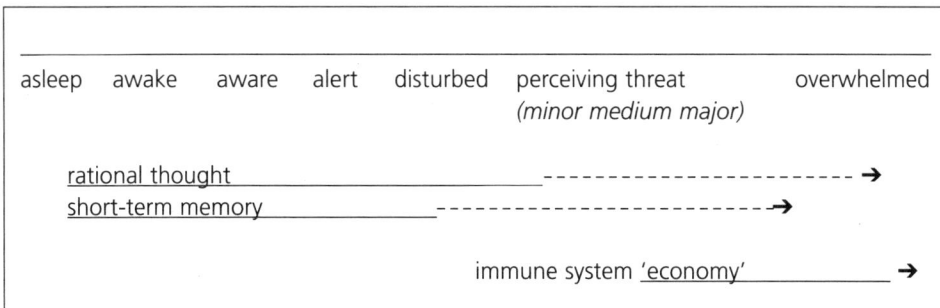

asleep	awake	aware	alert	disturbed	perceiving threat *(minor medium major)*	overwhelmed

rational thought _____ - →
short-term memory _____ - →

                                        immune system 'economy' _____ →

Figure 15   **Efficiency of physiological function**

Factor 1 (money and tangible rewards)

Someone who scores high on the need for tangible rewards, including money, and who works in a job that is badly paid, will probably feel aggrieved. If they cannot move jobs to a better paid one, they will probably resent their employer and will take various measures to make themselves more comfortable. One possibility is to cheat: from overt stealing ('It is only part of my proper wages') to shaving time off the working day and extending breaks, from acts of minor sabotage to just not doing tasks as well as they are able. The problem here is both for the employer and for themselves. They are minimizing effort as a punishment to the employer.

If someone scores low on the need for tangibles, they will not suffer stress as a result of being paid highly, but may suffer if the company uses money as a substitute for other beneficial job features. A very good salary for a boring and trivial job does not compensate for long, as Herzberg and other researchers have proven with regard to professional and managerial work (Herzberg, 1966). It is an interesting question whether people suffer stress if they feel overpaid. Probably, yes. Guilt may cause them discomfort, but their behaviour may adjust to avoid this. The first likely result is busyness and over-justification of their work. Anyone who spends time complaining about how they are overloaded is probably underoccupied.

Factor 2 (physical conditions)

Someone with a high score on the need for good working conditions will probably suffer stress if they work in a draughty, dingy office with a lot of noisy machinery and telephones. That much is obvious. But what conclusion can be drawn if they work in a relatively pleasant office and still score highly? Perhaps they need a carpet with pile up to knee level before feeling comfortable. It is possible that they are compensating for something else that is causing them discomfort in the working environment? One respondent scoring 63 on this factor revealed that there was no problem with her surroundings, but that she disliked the way her boss behaved towards her and others. There is nowhere to record *dislike of superior* on the profile; perhaps she expressed her feelings here; for 'working conditions', read 'working relationships'.

For low scorers on this factor, no one seems to suffer stress as a result of excellent working conditions! They may be wise to capitalize on their tolerance of poor conditions, but then few organizations reward people for suffering such things. Usually the rewards go to those enjoying more luxurious surroundings.

Factor 3 (structure)

Those who score high on the need for structure, and do not get it, tend to suffer stress in the form of anxiety. This can be mild, from a vague desire to know more about a task they have been asked to do, to severe, such as a generalized confusion over too wide a choice of options. Unfortunately, someone with a high need on this factor is rarely able to rescue themselves. It may seem obvious that someone presented with, say, a new and unfamiliar computer software program, should read some of the manual, play a bit with the program and generally jump in and 'have a go'. Any anxiety about lack of knowledge will, therefore, be gradually dissipated as they go along, gaining more knowledge and confidence. Not a bit of it. People with high structure needs tend to sit, mesmerized, before unfamiliar things; in Hofstede's (1994) terminology on uncertainty avoidance 'what is new and unfamiliar is dangerous'. Instead of reducing their anxiety by action, such people freeze and become increasingly dependent. They look to others for help.

People low on the need for structure suffer stress when structure is imposed upon them. A job with not only well-defined procedures, but also constraining and limiting rules, where the slightest deviation is prohibited, will cause them serious problems. Their lack of need for structure has an obverse of great importance: a need for freedom. If they are not allowed any leeway, they must repress their need for freedom, suffering frustration. Any form of conflict uses energy and internal conflicts use it up doubly as the individual devotes energy first to planning escape and then to recognizing the possible adverse consequences of obtaining freedom and to dampening down the desire.

This STOP / GO dilemma can be seen in the following example. After working for only ten months in a job, David was made redundant. Using industry contacts, he found a new job within three months of finishing work. This job was at management level with a large national company. The salary and perks were very good, better than in his previous job. After four months he began to come home tired. He rationalized this as travel fatigue as he was commuting to London taking one and a half hours each way. In the sixth month he came home and announced 'I've handed in my notice. I'll be leaving as soon as the notice period allows.' He had no other job in view and had heavy financial commitments. Within four days his energy levels rose. He worked out his notice with enthusiasm. His Motivational Profile is given in Figure 16.

David disregarded his need for freedom (low factor 3) and his love of variety and stimulation (high factor 9) for the sake of a quick solution to unemployment and a good set of tangible benefits. He suffered stress from the frustrations of a bureaucratic organization and a lack of leeway in his job without being able to enjoy the benefits of a good salary and the security of a large, stable company. With a score of nil on factor 3 there is no point in his acquiring security if he does not value it. His tiredness resulted from the energy he was expending to repress frustration. As soon as he handed in his notice to leave, his energy levels began to rise. He was opening up his options and being true to his needs.

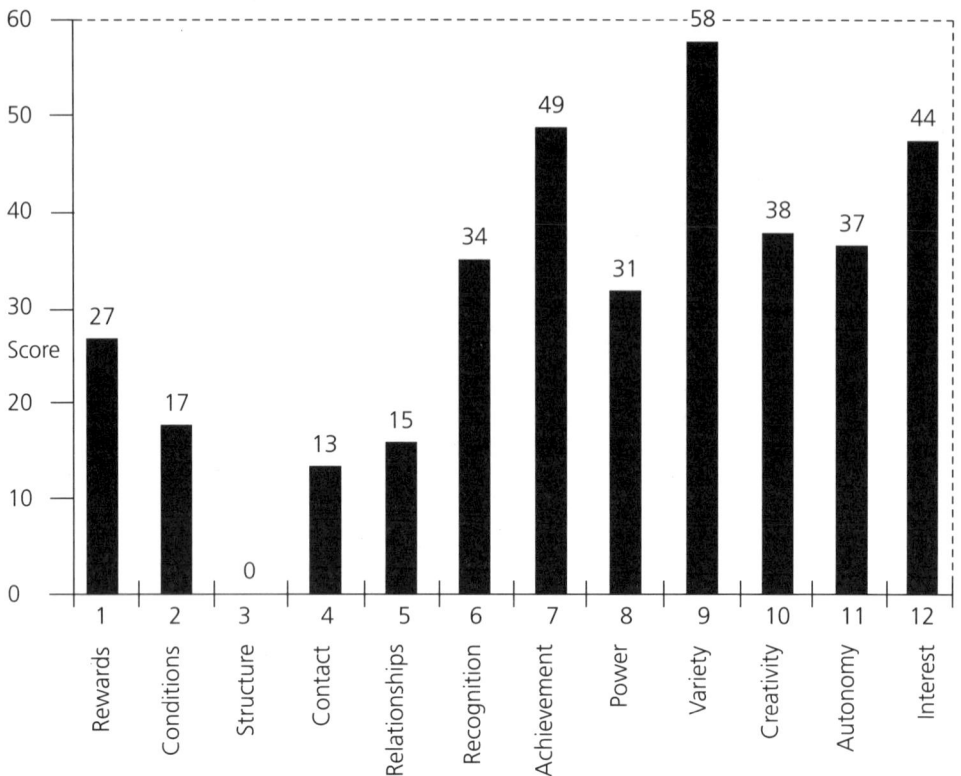

Figure 16   **David's Motivational Profile**

Factor 4 (people contact)

A stressful situation for someone high on need for contact with others is where they are forced to work alone for long periods. Where satisfaction is gained from the presence and approval of others, isolation becomes a form of sensory deprivation.

Conversely, people very low on the need for contact with others can suffer stress if placed in working circumstances which require extensive social interaction. We must be careful here to identify exactly the kind of social interaction that is stressful. The mere presence of others is no problem and a low score on this factor does not indicate that the person is a recluse or suitable only for isolated working. They may be socially adept. It is the behaviour of those others that is the crucial issue. If they are not just present, but overactive in engaging the time and energy of the low scoring person, then they will probably be perceived as intrusive and irritating. Low scorers do not like what they call 'idle gossip'. For them talk at work should be about work. To others such exchanges are vital, the content of the messages irrelevant as their purpose is to oil the wheels of social intercourse and to maintain relationships.

Factor 5 (relationships)

People high on the need for relationships work best in stable work teams where they can get to know others well. It might be stretching the measure too far to suggest that someone high on this factor would suffer stress if they were working with a large number of others in circumstances which did not allow relationships to form, but it is probable that they will not work as well as they might. People, after all, form relationships outside of work, and these are usually their most important ones. The possible exception to this rule is the person who is high scoring on factor 5 but who has no close relationships outside work. Someone could usefully research the question of whether our increasingly single-living population is likely to derive more of their relationships needs from work than those in partnerships or families.

That someone low on relationships need might suffer stress if placed in close proximity with a number of others is a possibility. It is more likely that they would avoid the problem of enforced intimacy by engaging in as few interactions as possible with others and by distancing themselves mentally, if not physically, by various means. There are many people who do not like the idea that relationships at work should be anything other than formal and strictly work-related, even to the point of outside life not being discussed. Interestingly, this view is held by some people who score low on factor 5, whether because they are either already in satisfying personal relationships or because they are generally happier being alone. The difference seems to be that the former group can appreciate that others may hold alternative views, the latter often push for workplace schemes that reduce interpersonal interaction.

Factor 6 (recognition)

People who need recognition strive to get it, and the higher their need, the less discriminating they are about how they do so. For them stress levels rise if their behaviour seems to elicit no response from the boss, others perceived to act *in loco parentis* in organizations, even from society at large. No response at all is perceived as worse than a negative response. At least that is notice, attention of a kind. The worst fear is that of the vacuum, the black hole, into which efforts and energy pass and from which nothing emerges. As a strategy to extinguish behaviour patterns, this is quite good. It is surprising that so many managers ignore people's need for this attention, sometimes feeling that if they cannot convey good news, they should convey nothing. It is lack of attention and feedback that causes discomfort.

Where does this leave the style of management: 'I'll tell you when you get it wrong'? Usually criticized for being negative, a more serious complaint may be levelled. If you as a manager only tell someone when they are doing things wrong, you are not telling them when they do them properly and you are missing the opportunity to reinforce good behaviour. More worrying still, you are giving them attention only when they perform badly. As all of us need attention, for those who require recognition (and bear in mind the median and modes for recognition are 36 and 35 so the need is common), you run the risk of reinforcing the behaviour you do not want: the negative. If in any doubt about this, listen to the next naughty child in the supermarket being threatened by an irascible parent along the lines of 'If you don't stop pulling those cans off the shelf, I'll ...' and then a few seconds later making equally idle threats about another misdemeanour. You can thus observe the child being trained to misbehave by the successive rewards of little bits of attention for bad behaviour.

Low scorers on this factor do not experience stress when they are noticed or praised; it is a matter of relative indifference to them. They would suffer stress if subjected to public or gushing praise, or if put into the spotlight and required to perform in some way with the attention of others upon them. Many such people have an internal value system and inbuilt self-confidence that allows them to validate their own actions. They do not need the judgement of others and may resent it.

Factor 7 (achievement)

High scorers on the need for achievement are uncomfortable in situations where there are no clear objectives and they are prevented from forming their own. Such situations occur where organizations have vague aims and where much politicking replaces the achievement drive. High achievers also feel stress when the targets they were encouraged to go all out for are suddenly changed, especially if the reasons seem capricious.

Those scoring low on the need for achievement may not suffer stress working in a job where there is pressure to achieve targets, but will be less than enthusiastic about them. This lack of enthusiasm once known, may cause secondary stress as their boss tries to find other motivators, possibly negative ('Meet the quota this month, or be paid less money').

Factor 8 (power and influence)

A need to influence others, when frustrated, will probably arise from situations where someone feels that their opinions are of no account or that they are powerless to affect either the circumstances of their work or the decisions made by others.

These can range from the minor irritations of dealings with petty bureaucracy to more serious cases where their wishes and needs appear to be irrelevant.

For those low on power drive, stress can come from being in situations where they have responsibility for others. An example is having staff reporting to you where the successful performance of your job depends on theirs. A surprisingly large number of managers have people whose work they are responsible for, but whom they do not really wish to influence. This is not to say that such a manager wishes the staff to do badly, only that he would prefer them to do well without any input from him, and certainly not if that input is likely to be continuous.

Factor 9 (variety and change)

People high on the need for stimulation, variety and change can suffer the frustration of boredom easily; there is an abundance of boring jobs. Even interesting jobs entail some chores and routine tasks. People high on this factor avoid stress by not doing the boring bits; sometimes to their cost later as the chores pile up and eventually require a long stretch of hard work to clear the backlog. If the word backlog causes someone to yawn, they have a low boredom threshold. Managers who try to push such people into doing their fair share of the routine work have set themselves one of the most energy-consuming tasks an organization offers. It will probably fail, unless continuous amounts of heavy pressure are applied. Those who deliver training in time management know the near-impossibility of trying to cajole people with high needs on factor 9 to force themselves into dealing with chores on a regular basis, knowing that negative methods do not work for long and that positive methods ('Treat yourself when you have done each item on your list') rarely offer enough reward to surmount the inertia. One suggestion is to harness their need for variety by providing a range of short, different chores successively. This may help but cannot succeed in the long term if the person is intelligent.

Low scorers on the need for change and variety are stressed from having large or successive changes providing more stimulation than they can cope with. The problem for them is how to stay in a comfortable rut when the world seems to conspire to get them out of it. All forms of change can cause problems, from domestic upheaval (moving house, people moving in and out, people changing their ways of working or routines), to changes at work (reorganization, new processes and procedures, people leaving jobs or arriving as new team members, disruptions to the job, new or changed relationships). Stress results from successive changes as the person tries to adjust to each new situation, consolidating time after time only to be disturbed again. It seems to be less stressful to make one large change. Acceptance, settlement and reorientation are then achieved more quickly.

Factor 10 (creativity)

Those scoring high on the need to be creative will obviously feel under stress in jobs where there is no freedom to think with an open mind or even to consider new ideas. This could include a very large number of people.

Low scorers may feel pressurized if put into situations where creativity is required, but are not likely to suffer long as their lack of performance will act as the cure. They will soon be moved out. We suspect that all people are latently creative given the right circumstances and many people who are thought not to be creative have had experiences which have discouraged it. Perhaps it is something that our socialization undervalues and, as other attributes tend to be rewarded more highly, like giving the *right* answer to many problems, the unexpected, unusual or different answer is usually marked as plain wrong.

Factor 11 (self-development)

Someone high scoring on Factor 11, the need for autonomy and a chance to grow in the job, is stressed by tasks which allow little leeway. Rigid and prescribed jobs, and certain organizational cultures, such as those which do not encourage initiative or which reward dependence, will cause discomfort. A manager whose style is autocratic, allowing an employee few opportunities to influence their own work, or even to express views about how it should be done, will probably wonder why they obtain poor performance from someone with a high need for this factor.

Low scorers on this factor do not suffer stress or manifest problems if offered a chance to control and influence their work and to develop within the job: they are not likely to take advantage of the offer, unless it causes them no effort.

Factor 12 (interest and usefulness)

High scorers must be very high to exceed a mode of 41 and a median of 43 for the need for intrinsically interesting, useful and rewarding work and, if in jobs where instrumentality reigns, are likely to be alienated and stressed. Jobs without interest to them and with no obvious good or useful elements or outcomes will impinge heavily on such people. If unable to leave, they will be disruptive, if intelligent and bored; apathetic, if conscientious; and depressed and/or absent on sick leave, if unable to openly rebel; either because of fear of job loss or as a salve to their consciences.

Those scoring low have little problem. If they have an interesting and rewarding job thrust upon them, it is unlikely to cause them stress. An exception is the person very highly motivated by tangible rewards – factor 1 – who, if also low on factor 12, would not welcome added interest or social utility at the expense of the salary and benefits package. There are, of course, many jobs where the salary and benefits package is nil. Voluntary work, for example, offers no monetary rewards at all.

Conclusion

In summary, people have developed to be able to manage short-term stresses but will have difficulty with those which are longer term, especially if unable to settle down, recover and relax from time to time to let those stresses dissipate. Most awkward are continuous stresses, either from outside, perhaps a long-drawn-out and disruptive corporate reorganization which affects the job adversely, or from within, perhaps a domestic disturbance which cannot be resolved and which drags on indefinitely. The individual motivational profile gives strong clues to the kinds of stress someone will suffer.

Teamworking

As individuals differ markedly in their motivational profiles, the manager interested in team formation and working can benefit from understanding both the process of group dynamics linked to motivation and the benefits and problems that differing motivation produces.

Team formation and building

Starting from scratch is a wonderful, and rare, opportunity. A real fresh start is where you are able to define the task for the team clearly and to choose freely people who are individually capable, experienced and suitably motivated for it. Not only that, but to choose people whose motivational profiles indicate that they will work together well, not just with one or two preferred people, but with all of those in the team. The people chosen to join the team need to understand their own motivation so that they appreciate why others not only may, but will, work very differently. They need to feel that their needs are understood and that their unique contribution will be valued. The following example demonstrates the point.

A true story

Two senior managers in a local government department have been asked to plan and to execute a major reorganization. The aims of the changes are to save money and to respond to customer needs better with improved and better targeted services. There are 600 staff.

The more senior manager, labelled A, is the Chief Executive Officer of the Department. The other manager, B, is in charge of Customer Services and acts as Deputy in the absence of the CEO. Their Motivational Profiles are given in Figures 17 and 18. Taking person A first. Highlights are recognition, 12 above the mode; achievement 15 above the mode; and variety and stimulation, 8 above the

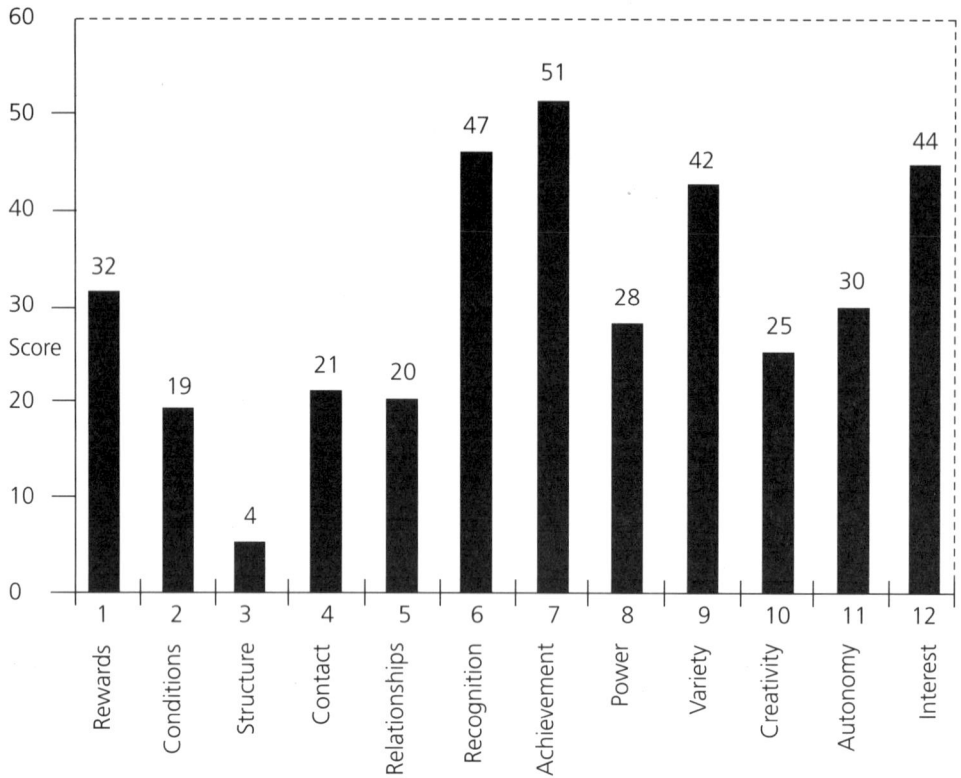

Figure 17   Motivational Profile for person A

mode. Low points are structure with a notable 22 below the mode and, to a certain extent, creativity, 7 points below the mode. A is a low structure need, high achiever who would like to be seen to be performing and noticed for it. With a very low need for structure this person wants plenty of leeway to operate and can tolerate a lot of uncertainty. The high need for variety and stimulation means that they will probably seek to make changes in whatever job they do, whether asked to or not.

Person B has a similar profile in some respects. Highlights here are achievement, 8 above the mode, and variety and stimulation, 19 above the mode. Like person A, they are low on need for structure, 12 below the mode. They are also 12 points below the mode on creativity. Here is another low structure need, high achiever with a desperate need for variety and stimulation.

Put these two people together and they are likely to augment each other in certain ways. Firstly they will approach change and the job of reorganization with relish and few anxieties. So far, so good. They will relish it so much that they are likely to want to make sweeping changes and to change everything they can. Untrammelled by structure needs, their ideas will probably be whole picture,

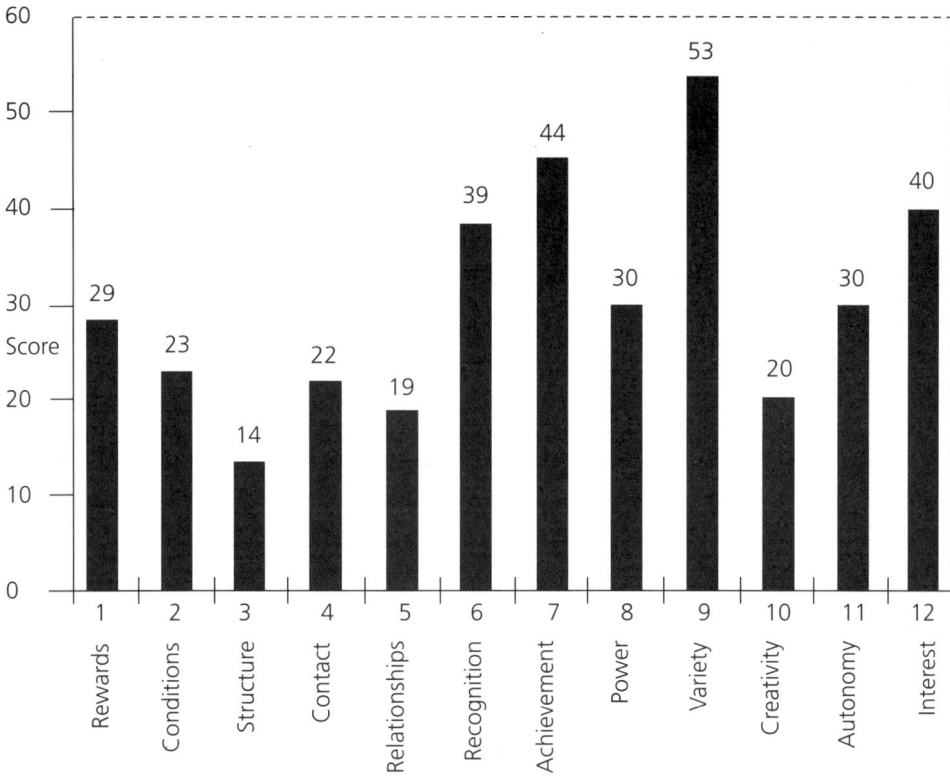

Figure 18 **Motivational Profile for person B**

broad brush and low on detail. They will take the view that the main objective is to stir things around and that the last thing they want to do is to leave things alone. They will see change as good and as offering lots of possibilities and opportunities. If they pause to consider difficulties, they will think in terms of how to avoid, steamroller or get rid of them. Resistance from people will be swept aside as 'stick in the mud' or reactionary.

For our intrepid change makers progress will be rapid and plans will have short time-scales. There will be no prototypes built or small sections of the department tested out first. The whole vision will be put into operation like a living and real-time experiment. Any problems will be bludgeoned out of the way or swept underneath an organizational carpet. If difficulties arise and the patent stupidity or impracticality of any aspect of the plan becomes impossible to ignore, our energetic duo will pause, think again and try something else. As before, this new change will not be tested.

As this is happening, 600 people are at the receiving end of the plans. To put their staff in the picture, the management pair announced early on in the process that there would be wide-ranging changes both in the service and in its delivery and that this would have effects on many staff. The way this news was conveyed was by a meeting in which the senior management told the staff that the time-scale for Phase 1 of the reorganization would be seven months and would work as follows:

> D-day (Deadline day) will be the 16th of December this year (today being mid-May). We cannot tell you at this stage what the new service will look like, which service points it will operate from or in what respects it will differ from the service we operate now, nor can we tell you what job you will be doing, where or with whom. But we can tell you one thing: *Whatever job you are doing now, in seven months' time your job will be a different one and in a different location.*

As some of the staff had been in their jobs for over 25 years, in the same location and with long-standing colleagues, anxiety and confusion arose. For the next two months these anxieties rose further and, although A and B did hold monthly meetings and outline a few more details of their plan, they did not address the central question of importance to the staff. This could be summarized as:

> Never mind grand visions and improved services for less money, *who will I be working with and where and doing what on 17 December this year?*

Two months later there was a strike.

At this point a third person, C, Profile in Figure 19, was added to the management team. Highlights for C are need for structure, 6 above the mode and creativity, 22 above the mode. The most obvious low score is for people contact, at 13 below the mode. C is a manager with strengths to complement those of our duo, if they will let him. He has higher structure needs than theirs, although he is only six points above the mode. He will show more tolerance for seeking detail and the careful working out of plans. He will also sympathize with other staff, many of whom will have even higher structure needs and who see the senior partnership as being gung-ho and too open ended. He possesses very high needs to be creative, something A and B distinctly lack.

As he arrives, we have a group. The original pair will now need to adjust their habitual two-way dialogue to accommodate a very different third. Chastened by the strike and other difficulties, A and B are ready to listen to C, especially in regard to suggestions for progressing the changes or preventing resistance and problems. This is the good news and a period of constructive team work can begin. Unfortunately A and B are human, fallible and driven by motivational needs which are very different to C's. They are likely, after initial good intentions, to revert to their usual mode of 'bull in china shop' style of management. C will remind them of the need to spell out the implications of change in terms understandable by their staff: he may be perceived as pernickety, even obstructive and will be the object of remarks like: 'We got you in to help, not hinder us'; 'If we need someone to put the brakes on, we'll ask you'; and so on.

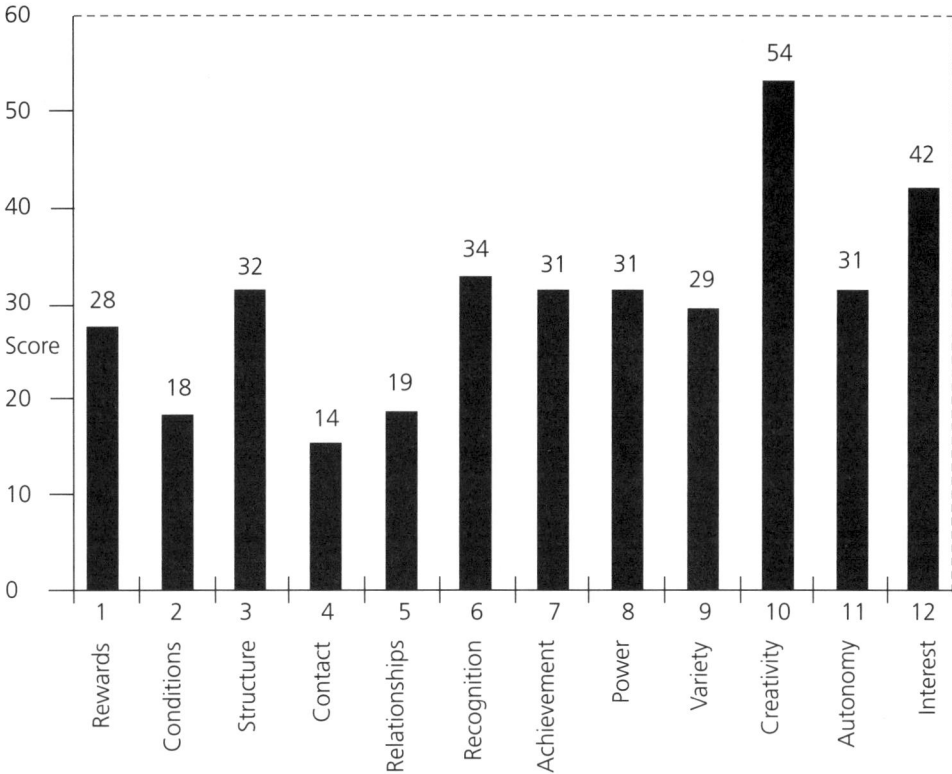

Figure 19   Motivational Profile for person C

C is not the only source of creative ideas, but could be a very rich fund of them. For other reasons, such as his low need for people contact, he may not be very adept at communicating such ideas in a group. If he offers one, and it is rejected, he will probably not push it further. In this team ideas may not even be heard. A and B both have profiles that are geared to action more than reflection. The only way that these managers will find a workable basis for sorting out their problems is if they are honest from the beginning about the process issues of their motivational differences and how these can affect their discussions and work if not recognized and acknowledged.

When this team later added a fourth person, D, interaction between the members changed yet again. The Motivational Profile for D (Figure 20) shows someone with a high need to influence others and a below average need for recognition. If of suitable maturity and experience, D could be the chairperson for the team. With roughly average structure needs, the new team member could tolerate the low structure behaviour of A and B, but would be tempted to regulate and to organize things to meet his high influence drive.

And so we build up the team. Predicting behaviour and interaction is hard and

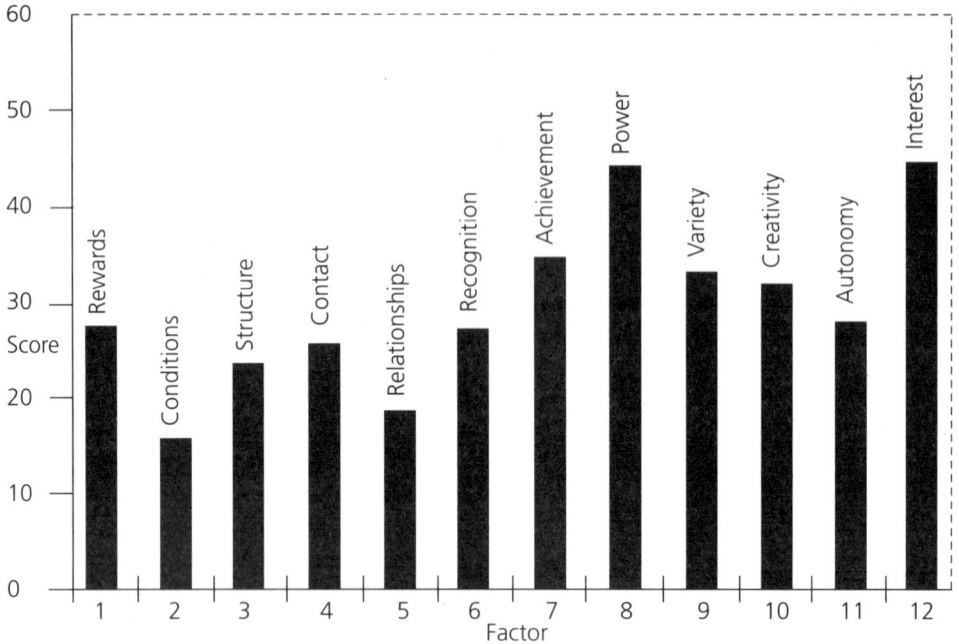

Figure 20   Motivational Profile for person D

there are no guarantees of success, but you have the consolation of knowing that if you do put a team together purposefully, they stand a chance of working together well. However, the Profile will help you even if your team is the result of random agglomeration. If each person in it knows their own motivational tendencies and those of the others, then at least understanding can form the basis of agreed ways of working together.

Starting up

Teams are usually assembled in an *ad hoc* manner: there is an existing group to which are added other people with the right knowledge and experience, representing the right organizational section. Rarely are people chosen with an eye to their knowledge and technical capability *and* their personality and motivational needs.

When building up a team, primacy favours the first member and, as subsequent team members are added, each new person is chosen more as a creature of the team's needs for balance and complementarity according to an increasingly tight individual specification, than for their intrinsic qualities and skills. Nonsenses often occur, like the near-impossible specification which results from assembling seven team members and then looking for the perfect jigsaw-piece person to just fit the gap for number eight. This task-oriented approach to team building will usually result in an exercise of increasing concentration and difficulty as the team expands.

The alternative? There is another way of team building: to select and train competent and experienced people while checking that they are either already interpersonally skilled or are potentially able to benefit from such training. Their Profiles can be used to help them to understand their own approach to work and their likely interactions with others. When a new team is forming, almost any selection of staff can be chosen, according to experience and knowledge, with confidence that, with some facilitation support, this group can be helped to work together well.

This recognizes the reality of organizational life, which is that there simply is not the luxury or even the possibility of building teams out of an ideal matrix of skills, personality profiles and Belbin-type roles (Belbin, 1981). Organizations usually (certainly in the short term) have to work with whoever has the right knowledge and skills and is available. Training people to understand their motivational profiles and their likely impact on others, and others' likely impact on them, makes effective teamworking possible, even if an ideal mix of personality profiles is not present. If there is some choice, we would recommend managers to both try to match personal profiles to the required objectives of the team; and to consider the team's internal process needs. Thus, if the team has to achieve, there should be achievers present; if it needs to exercise influence, people with a need to exercise influence should be present, and so on. The managers can meet team process needs by ensuring that its membership, and preferably its leader, demonstrate a deep understanding of the interpersonal processes which contribute to the dynamics of the team. Even then we can expect problems, but we will have at least established a common language which the team can use to discuss what is happening, and it is in a good position to work towards solutions.

Someone leaves the team and has to be replaced

When someone leaves a team, the usual response is to fill the vacancy almost as soon as it occurs. This is done for speed and for ease. Management hope for as little disruption as possible. If there is to be no replacement, readjustment is usually left to chance: management rely on existing members of the team to fill the gap by adopting some of the departing person's work. With luck, all the pieces will be taken up and the team will have absorbed the job. What management should do, of course, is to recognize that a fresh look can be taken at the whole of the team's working. This can best be done by considering the following issues and asking some questions.

Firstly, can a team be flexible in its behaviour? For a team to be flexible, some or all of its members must be able, and willing, to change their behaviour. Not only that, but each person who changes their behaviour requires a change in that of the others, if only that of acknowledgement. If the other members go further, by responding positively to the new behaviour, change is possible. Several other requirements must be met:

- The new behaviour exhibited must be appropriate to the new circumstances or needs of the team.
- Old or inappropriate behaviour must cease or decline.
- When the new behaviour is no longer useful, it must, in its turn, be discarded.
- Group behaviour is established very quickly and is resistant to change once formed (Tuckman, 1977).

There is one overriding question which will concern both the manager and the team members: Who decides when it is time for change?

Other considerations are:

- What does the team do about someone who will not change either their own behaviour and/or will not allow others to do so? There is no definitive answer to this question, but ...
- We cannot just substitute someone for another person and assume that they will fit exactly into the space created.
- No matter how good the match between the old and the new team member, some adjustment will be needed.
- We do not want too close a match between the old and the new team members (unless the old team has been conspicuously successful); usually the whole point of changing the membership is so that the new person behaves differently.

Solutions include:

- Existing team members will need to change their behaviour, and not just to the new person but to each other as well.
- The results of the changes are unpredictable; the complex dynamics of interaction will ensure that unforeseen forces operate.
- Time needs to be allowed for relationships to form.
- It may be better to take the opportunity of changing the whole team to meet the new needs, rather than just one person in it.

In selecting someone new to join a team, it is wise to establish a picture of the new person's motivational needs before they join the group. To borrow the example given above, imagine adding yet another person low on structure needs and high on achievement, variety and stimulation to the A and B partnership. This triumvirate would certainly get things done, but they would probably 'take no prisoners' and could cause large-scale damage. Any attempt to moderate 'headless chicken' behaviour by adding someone with a different Profile, especially someone high on the need for structure, would probably not work; the latest addition would have to apply very strong influence to achieve a result and could suffer stress, with likelihood of failure, in the attempt.

Research on decision making demonstrates that groups tend to be more extreme in their decisions than individuals, taking a 'shift to risk' when faced with certain decisions (Wallach *et al.*, 1962). Motivational tendencies such as these multiply leading not only to unbalanced outcomes but also to teams who think that they have become invincible.

In summary, the first principle in selecting a replacement or a new member for a team is to remind the team of their motivational needs and of any apparent imbalance in the team's motivational drive. The next step is to translate that awareness into knowledge of what action should be taken to prevent, avoid and neutralize problems from motivational mismatches. The message may be hard to hear; for example, low structure need people will best serve a group if they limit their need for freedom by building in some organization and structure. Often they can perceive a need for it, but the further stage of exhibiting enough self-discipline to put restraints on their powerful drives for freedom and to allow themselves to be bound by rules and procedures, can prove too much for them to sustain. And here is where facilitation and training proves its utility for team building: even small and intermittent movements towards the desired behaviour can be recognized and rewarded: 'John did not rush off to design another interesting feature on his own, but stayed to help Sarah to finish doing the foundations.' It may seem to operate at a very detailed level, but significant behavioural changes are based on such modest beginnings, followed by frequent and appropriate reinforcement.

Team development

We consider now the five stages of team development and their interaction with the high motivational drives. The five stages proposed by Tuckman (1977) are:

1.   Forming (awareness)
2.   Storming (conflict)
3.   Norming (co-operation)
4.   Performing (productivity)
5.   Dorming (separation)

The characteristics of these stages are outlined below.

1. Forming

Team members need to understand and to become committed to group goals and also to become acquainted with each other. But getting to know each other does not create a team, there needs to be activity directed to setting goals, which give the team meaning. People need to know how the team fits within the organization and how they personally relate to the team goals. In achieving this they look to the leader for the way forward and then form subgroups. Any personal issues or objectives which might distract from commitment to team goals, need to be brought out into the open and explored. The outcome of stage one is acceptance by the team members of each other, followed by commitment to the goals of the team.

The key motivational drivers are as follows. Factor 8, influence, tries to establish agreed vision, purpose and goals. People high on factor 3, structure, look for guidance on rules and expected norms of behaviour and feel uncertain or anxious. Those low on factor 3 are not worried one way or the other. People with a high score on factor 7, achievement, in the presence of those they consider outrank them, can be inactive because goals have not yet been established, and their primary contribution is finger-tapping nervousness and a surfeit of undirected energy. If there is no higher-ranking person present, they are likely to burn off energy in any way that suits them, perhaps by starting to work on an area of interest, or by recruiting someone with high structure needs to help them to do something under direction. This behaviour may or may not be beneficial to the team; it is a matter of chance.

Those with high factors 4, social contact, and 5, relationships, are looking at the human dimensions. For them, 'Am I comfortable in this group?' is the key question. Factor 9, variety, likes the possibilities for change. Factor 11, self-development, wonders what can be learned and brought within control, and if learning is possible, commitment will follow. If not, the group will be tolerated. Factor 12, interest and significance, tries to establish if there is congruence between the goals of the team and personal goals. If not, there will again be minimal commitment. Those with high factor 1 will be looking at the implications for earnings. High factor 6, recognition, is wondering what is the best way to gain personal significance.

2. Storming

The storming stage of group development is one in which competition and conflict emerge naturally. Individuals have to adjust to group needs. They form defensive subgroups with people they identify as of like kind. There is conflict over leadership issues. 'How should we go about things?', 'Where do we stand in relation to each other?' are key questions. Team building at this stage includes acknowledging and confronting conflict openly at the task level, and listening with understanding at the relationship level. It is important that the group encourages a diversity of opinion and allows expression of disagreement. This will further clarify purpose and begin to define the most effective means of working together.

Factor 8, influence, again plays a key role, for good or ill. It is malevolent when competitive and someone tries to impose their own ideas on how the team should develop. It is beneficial when acting as an enabler, helping people think their way through the variety of available choices. A person with high factor 3, structure, is immobilized by the ambiguity of it all, but with luck, may be able to direct their energies towards rule making or adhering to any form of agenda available. The problem is that rule making may start too early, before the team has decided on its direction and mode of operation and certainly before it has aired a range of creative options. Low factor 3 might decide to be constructive and help to create rules, or might let the discussion pass him by. Factor 7, achievement, is still uneasy with the formlessness of it all and is waiting for a clearer view of the target or is getting on with some other task in the corner. Factor 9, variety, is enjoying the confusion and may not be totally constructive. Factor 11 is still looking for self-development opportunities. Factor 12, interest, is trying to subvert the team purpose towards their own goals. High factor 6, recognition, is, politically, keeping options open, and beginning to be dissatisfied with the lack of opportunities for attention. Factor 10, creativity, contributes insights and attempts to synthesize the process. Factors 4 and 5, the social drives, have a major part to play in keeping people on side.

3. Norming

At this stage, norms develop, those unstated but tacit rules of behaviour which the group colludes to impose upon itself. The theme is co-operation and people willingly explore each other's contribution. There is a flow of ideas and creativity; subgroups disappear; people learn the parts they are to play and the contribution they are expected to make. This is the stage where the work of Belbin can be used most beneficially (Belbin, 1981). Appropriate behaviours are including others in the decision-making process and recognizing and respecting individual differences. At its very best, members at this stage are more able to give and to receive feedback.

High factor 3, structure, starts to come into its own and to attempt to codify rules and expected behaviours. Care has to be taken that such behaviour does not snuff out the vitality in the team, nor that creative possibilities are ignored. Factor 7, achievement, is becoming visibly more relaxed as it becomes clearer what is required and is beginning to take useful action towards team goals. If all goes well, we can shortly expect a huge surge of energy. Factor 8 is keeping a watching brief, at best intervening with good humour to keep the ship afloat, at worst, trying to impose rules or to suppress ideas. Factor 1, money, is trying to manipulate the rules in favour of his or her pocket. Factor 6, recognition, starts to know the rules and what to do to receive attention. Factors 11, self-development, and 12, interest, have either decided the team is going to work in their favour and we can expect heavy commitment, or it is not and they will simply mark time. Factor 9, variety, might start to become bored.

At the norming stage, certain motivational drives can exert influence which causes adverse consequences for the team. High structure needs (factor 3) and high achievement needs (factor 7) will both be pushing for a quick resolution of the main aspects of the team plan and, once in place, there will be strong resistance to any change. In extreme cases, the group will also establish rigid behavioural rules, all the stronger for often being unstated. These norms can become so powerful that anyone infringing one will be disciplined by the group. The team needs to steer between the disorganization of no norms and rules, which makes work and decisions time-consuming and tiring, and the rigidity of ossification which creates unnecessary barriers and can be the enemy of action.

4. Performing

This stage is not reached by all teams. In successful teams, members are challenged to work to their greatest potential and to collaborate with each other to achieve goals and objectives. True interdependence and trust is achieved. People make themselves vulnerable to each other, but do not take unfair advantage of each other. There is a problem-solving approach and issues of personality are avoided. There is experimentation to try to achieve optimum results and failure does not produce recriminations. There is a preoccupation with sustaining momentum and enthusiasm. There is intense group loyalty. Milestones are established so that success at each point can be recognized and celebrated.

When the team has reached this stage we can expect factor 8 to be empowering and building people up, not keeping them down. Factor 7 is totally committed and working flat out, with a clear sense of what is expected. Provided he can rely on the others, we can expect him to be a good team member. If not, he will revert to type as a loner, deliver what is required, but will not accommodate himself to the team processes. Factor 6, if receiving the recognition required from fellow members, will contribute generously to the team, but may sulk or be disruptive if ignored. Factor 3, structure, will be content with keeping the records and watching the deadlines. If also high on creativity (factor 10) this person will be contributing ideas of some worth; unfortunately, it may be a little late for the team, which has moved beyond the brainstorming stage and may have converged on the 'one right answer'. There is wasted potential here, probably only avoided if the team can provide the platform of security needed by this person earlier on in its life. Factors 11 and 12, self-development and interest, will be contributing positively if the team has reached this stage of development. There is congruence between their development and interest needs and what the team is required to achieve. Factor 1, money, if on an individual incentive scheme has the potential to disrupt the team, but on a group scheme could be a good contributor. Factor 9, variety, has long had her thoughts elsewhere; a wise group would have capitalized on her energies long before now.

5. Dorming

The Dorming stage occurs at the completion of a key task, or when new members are added to the team or new tasks established. Some teams do not conclude at stage five but cycle from stage five to stage one without pausing. The objective at stage five is to recognize and appreciate team performance. People benefit from closure, the feeling of a good job well done. Evaluation of team accomplishments provides important feedback regarding job performance and working relationships. People may regret the termination of the group, but it needs to be buried so that they can move on to other things.

Factor 7, achievement, relaxes in a glow of self-satisfaction and will want to move on soon to attack the next target. Factor 6, recognition, revels in the review, enjoying the praise and happy to learn from gentle and constructive criticism. Factor 1, money, is planning to get back to accumulation. Factor 3 is comfortable during the review, but there is incipient anxiety about what will happen when the team finally disbands. Factors 11 and 12 are considering what they have learned and the degree of interest, and what they should be doing next. Factor 9 has already left the room, in spirit if not in body. Factor 10 is pondering how it could all have been done better, given the chance again. Factor 8 feels some of the regret of a parent when the children grow up and leave home.

The message is that in changing the membership of the team we should pay attention not only to the motivational profile of those remaining, but to the profile and commitment of those joining, and the stage of development reached by the team.

Training and development

It is important to re-emphasize that development is in the hands of the person being developed and the role of the professional helper is to facilitate. The purpose of this chapter is to provide the insights which make for effective facilitation.

In exploring the topic, we will need

- to define what we mean by development and training;
- to review the interrelationship between people's needs and organizational needs;
- to see if organizational competencies can help us;
- to remind ourselves of the relevance of learning styles; and
- to consider the significance of the motivation profile scores.

We can help the person being developed by explaining that the development process is complex and that it will take as much time as we spend on such matters as pricing, strategy and so on.

What do we mean by development and training?

We differentiate between development and training.

Training is perceived as a process necessary to the acquisition of the skills associated with a particular management level or role (for example, budgetary development and control), management development tends to be viewed as a broadening, educational process by means of which the individual is initiated, shaped or fitted to the attitudes, values, rites and rituals of successively higher levels within the organization. As such, management development may or may not encompass formal training, and it may be self-managed (Robinson, 1986).

In using the Profile, do we need to distinguish between training and development?

Up to a point. Using the Profile will take time, which will be used most effectively in providing insight into the development process. Thus, if the Profile shows someone has a zero need for rules and structure, we would not want to give them extensive training in the technicalities of document custody. There is a built-in safeguard, of course, in that they would not let us! The gap between their ability to undertake the technical training and their low need for the structure required, would almost certainly be too great. In summary, using the Profile to establish development needs will usually tell us what we need to know about training needs.

This brings us back to the purpose of development. We do not believe it is to change the shape of the Profile. We think this may be possible in the short term. In the longer term it will cause intolerable stress: people will be stressed if they work in a job with a motivational Profile different from their personal Profile. We aim then to:

- harness the Profile to personal development;
- make people aware of the impact of their Profile on their personal development and on their job performance; and
- help people discover the extent to which they need to redesign their job, and even their leisure, to ensure peak performance in their job.

Reviewing the interrelationship between people's needs and organizational needs

This area requires considerable attention. Our concern as managers is to establish congruence between individual needs and organizational needs, which means that as people satisfy their own needs the organization benefits. If people's needs are satisfied, but the organization derives no benefit, that is bad business. Our job as motivators is to establish first of all what the organization requires, then to establish individual needs and skills and see how best we can match them. The question of skills is important. Somebody might have a strong influence drive, the organization might need people with such a drive, but if they are technically incompetent, their exercise of influence might be damaging. The first requirement in motivation is to ensure that either the technical skills are there or that they can be acquired. The second requirement is to see if the organization can use the motivational needs on offer. How we might do so is suggested in the chapter on Selection. Competencies, if they are available, can help us to define motivational needs. If the answer is 'yes' to an organizational need, we are then in a position to think about individual motivation.

Can organizational competencies help us?

According to the Industrial Society (1996), the best description of a competency is that of authors Boam and Sparrow (1992) who define it as 'the set of behaviour patterns that the incumbent needs to bring to a position in order to perform its tasks and functions with competence'. The article adds that the benefits of competencies include:

> Improved individual performance: working with a competency approach allows employees to be very clear about the standard of work expected of them.
> Business alignment of the human resource system: by providing HR systems which focus on standards of performance identified to improve individuals and the business.

Those organizations which have a well-developed set of competencies will be in a good position to, at least, start the discussion. There will be available a clear statement of the behaviours required at their own level and by those at a level more senior to that of the person being considered. Thus, for example, to quote from a very good range of competencies produced by Vickers plc (unpublished), competencies for team orientation range from 'Prefer own company. Tend to work by themselves' at one extreme to 'Ensures team members clearly understand their role and responsibilities' at the other. Taking another example, 'Prefer to tackle problems themselves' at one end of the spectrum through to 'Actively encourages and participates in team working within own team(s) to seek collective solutions to problems' at the other end.

Knowing the behaviour required will provide an insight into those motivational needs that will most encourage that behaviour. Thus, in the examples above, those who 'ensure team members clearly understand their role and responsibilities' are likely to have a strong influence drive and we can use the section on motivational components in the chapter on Selection for further analysis.

The relevance of learning styles

Before embarking on management development, we need to remind ourselves about learning styles. This wide subject is best encapsulated by Honey and Mumford (1992).

They posit four learning styles:

- *Activists* who involve themselves fully and without bias in new experiences. They enjoy the here and now and are happy to be dominated by immediate experiences.
- *Reflectors* who like to stand back to ponder experiences and to observe them

from many different perspectives. They collect data, both first hand and from others, and prefer to think about it thoroughly before coming to any conclusions.

- *Theorists* adapt and integrate observations into complex but logically sound theories. They think problems through in a vertical, step by step, logical way.
- *Pragmatists* are keen on trying out ideas, theories and techniques to see if they work in practice. They positively search out new ideas and take the first opportunity to experiment with applications.

The development implications for the individual are obvious as are some of the development risks. For example, the activist may enjoy immediate involvement, but the organization has to consider the potential for organizational damage. What is not so obvious is the organization's preferred learning style, an important part of culture. For example, some organizations are activist and pragmatic by nature. Reflectors will be given short shrift and theorists would be frozen out. In such an environment, theorists would need to move out, possibly to business school, to acquire their theory. However, that might not be a particular problem, in that theorists are unlikely to have been selected.

The message is that the facilitator needs to bear in mind constantly the interplay been individual and organizational learning styles and that, ideally, development should take place using the preferred learning style.

The significance of the motivational profile for development

The Motivation-to-work Profile is a powerful development tool. The main limitation on its use is the quality of our imagination. We can brainstorm ways of using it, but some suggestions are given below.

First of all, people have to complete it, then have it explained to them. People are absorbed in the explanations and compare themselves enthusiastically with the norms. The best of these for training use are the figures for mode, median and the range which shows the spread of the distribution for each factor. Then there comes an extra layer of interest when they compare themselves against the histograms. What this means is that they look to see where their score falls on the curve, comparing themselves with the number of others scoring similarly. For those at the extreme ends of the curve, they see clearly just how few others accompany them.

Very roughly speaking, two-thirds of people are found within a range of plus or minus ten points around the mode. If they are outside that range, they are always keen to know the development implications. They will then want to know what the Profile tells them about the work situations they should seek and those they should avoid. They like to know how they are likely to behave in the job and what sort of interaction there might be between themselves and others. What people find hard to do, of course, is to decide, for example, that they have a deficit of achievement need and that they need to sharpen it up. If there is a deficit, it can probably be stimulated in the short term, but most certainly not in the long term. The attempt will probably be repaid in deteriorating health and increased stress. What they can do is accept their Profile and compensate for deficiencies by working with other people who have what they lack.

Before using the Profile for development we need to ask ourselves three questions. How reliable are our scores, and once we are satisfied about reliability, which of the factors should we try to develop? Then, how do these factors influence the way in which we go about development? We will consider the question of reliability in the section below headed 'The Motivation-to-work Profile and development'. Before we consider these questions, we should note that when we are making serious demands for development, demands that, although they may be exhilarating, still take time and effort and involve sacrifice of personal time, we need to be sure that the need for development is real. For major development efforts, we would expect the score for factor 11 to be significantly above the norm, preferably around 40 plus. If not, we would need to satisfy ourselves that the effort will be expended, even though the score is low. Acceptable explanations would be along the lines that other needs, for example, the need to influence or achieve, were significantly above average and would provide the motivation necessary to undertake development.

We also need to ascertain the extent to which the needs for autonomy and self-development do or do not relate to the organization's needs. Thus, development and growth, integral components of factor 11, look as though they can potentially be captured by the organization, so people will undertake development even though the main beneficiary will be the organization. Autonomy needs to be considered with care. It can encompass the need for autonomy within the job or autonomy regardless of the needs of the job. Usually, consideration of someone's track record will give the necessary insight, so that in their job history to date they have shown an awareness of, and directed their efforts to, the needs of the organization. However, there are some industries, for example, publishing, where many of the employees regard autonomy in terms of their own needs and not those of the organization. The point is made succinctly in a *Financial Times* case study by Virginia Matthews (1997).

Assuming we are satisfied with their organizational focus, we need to establish what the employee concerned means by self-development. Do they believe its purpose is to maintain the shape of the Profile, strengthening and deepening existing needs, or is it to try to change the needs relative to each other, to change the shape of the Profile? Most will not know precisely. They will have a feeling that things are not as they want them to be and that they want to make progress.

It is not possible to give them a definitive answer. However, we think that no amount of development will change innate drives. That, for example, if somebody has no need for achievement, it is possible for them to develop consciously a high innate need. We do think we can teach them about the dynamics of achievement, about topics like the need for measurement and so on. We also believe that we can train them to achieve. We do not believe we can develop an innate drive for achievement, so that there is a significant change in the shape of their Profile.

Thus, it would not be a sensible use of development time to try to shoehorn a low achiever into a job requiring high achievement. Similar considerations apply to all the other factors.

We suggest that development builds on existing needs, but teaches people to be aware of and to compensate for weaknesses.

The Motivation-to-work Profile and development

The purpose of the Profile is to form the framework for a structured intelligent review, leading to an informed analysis of needs. It is not able, and neither are any other psychometric tests, to give a definitive statement of somebody's motivational needs. The Profile is at its best when we use it as the basis for asking further questions. We consider the answer to these questions in the light of our own experience at work, bearing in mind the constructive comments of those who have seen us in operation. We then make a judgement as to the significance of, and weight to be attached to, each of these factors for our personal development. In this section, we will suggest the sort of questions that should be asked.

The obvious starting point is an individual's scores. We should carry out an initial review by comparing the individual's scores with those from the full database. This can be followed by comparing individual norms with those of the company, if available, to see how the individual relates to the culture and if anything needs to be handled differently. These considerations suggest the following questions, which we can usefully consider before undertaking a detailed analysis of a particular Profile and its meaning for training and development needs. The questions are addressed to the person who completed the Profile:

Do I believe the Profile reflects my relative needs adequately? If not, what relative adjustments would I make? But, before I do so:

- Do I believe that my score for any factor is lower than it might have been because that particular need is fully satisfied in my current job? Would my score change if the existing motivational demands of the job – think of examples – were significantly increased or reduced? How significant would the change be?
- Do I believe that my score for any factor is higher than it might have been because that need is not satisfied in my current job? Would my score change if the existing motivational demands of the job – think of examples – were significantly increased or reduced? How significant would the change be?

In exploring the Profile, we always need to consider the intensity of the person's needs. For example, does a high relative need mean that, at one extreme, he or she requires constant high level stimulation or, at the other, intermittent low level stimulation, or something in between? The first means that we need to be absolutely sure that the job for which the person is destined offers opportunities for the required high level of stimulation. If it does not, there will be tensions and difficulties and the work or development should probably not be undertaken. At the other extreme, it will probably be easier to work with a mismatch between personal needs and the opportunities of the job. The chapter on Selection which describes the components of motivation will help us with our thinking.

We can sharpen our thinking on the importance of our motivational drives to us by asking questions like:

- Do the requirements of my job differ from my needs? For example, do I *genuinely* believe that my need for, say, achievement cannot be satisfied in the job I am doing? Can it be satisfied in the next job? If not, what are the implications for my personal development?

- What would I be like if my principal drives were missing; or my minor drives strengthened? In what way would my life have been different?

- In practice, I use certain drives in the current job, but my score shows that I do not have a strong need to do so. Is this creating a strain for me, or can I handle it easily? Are there any implications for my moving to other jobs?

- What happens, if anything, if my needs are not satisfied at work? Do I make sure they are satisfied outside work, or perhaps by unsatisfactory performance or behaviour at work? For example, non-recognition of high recognition people at work can lead to disruptive behaviour as attention is sought at almost any price.

- Is there any further evidence I can develop about my motivational drives? For example, completing a life and career chart. This might also give me some insight into how I am changing over time.

- What level of stimulation is required to satisfy my needs? Where does it stand on the spectrum constant/deep to intermittent/shallow? (*draw a grid*)

If I want to move into a job, what do I need to do technically and in personal development terms to make this possible?

- Looking at the job I am doing, what are, in my view, the relative strengths of key motivational factors required in the job? How different are they from my Profile? Do I enjoy or dislike the consequences? What are the implications for a future job?

- How would my boss and colleagues draw my Profile? Is there an opportunity to ask them to assess their view of my Profile and to discuss any differences with them?

- What are the last six occasions on which the boss has given me work? In motivational terms, how was the work presented? In what ways could my motivation have been harnessed better?

- What are the last six occasions on which I gave work to other people? In motivational terms, how do I present the work?

- Is there a lack of congruence between my motivational drives and my competence in the job? For example, if I have a strong achievement drive but no technical skills, what does that imply about my security in the job?

- What technical training/experience do I require to develop?

- In motivational terms are there any different approaches I can experiment with? For example, if I have high needs for variety and change, but a low need for achievement, and wish to develop the achievement drive, what should I do? The section that follows suggests a way forward.

We can use these questions to help develop a clearer view of our motivational Profile. Then we can work through the twelve factors which are discussed below, starting with factor 1.

Whenever we use the Profile, we need to relate it to what is happening at work. How do the profiles of individuals and departments relate to their performance at work? What are the profiles of the more successful departments and bosses? And the less successful? Can we explain what is going on?

We will now consider each factor in turn, looking at building on strengths, compensating for weaknesses and how each factor affects the way people develop.

Factor 1 (money and tangible rewards)

A high need for money can facilitate the development process, especially if successful development is seen to lead to more money. However, money can, in certain circumstances, inhibit development. Thus, time spent on development can reduce current earnings, particularly if there is an incentive scheme and time and energy is diverted from paying work. And if development leading to promotion is seen to lead to less money, as can sometimes be the case in selling and financial trading, the urge to develop might falter. The effect needs to be addressed at the outset.

Those with a high relative need for money benefit by working in a good, clearly defined and measurable individual incentive scheme. If the need for money is relatively low, they should try to obtain a salary, or perhaps a salary with a relatively undemanding group incentive scheme. If high factor 1 is accompanied by a low need for variety, creativity and self-development, it is probably possible to tolerate endless boredom provided the money is good. The development taking place could be minimal, certainly the drive will not be there. There may also be a willingness to cut corners if that will help achieve the earnings required. Part of development consists of ensuring that compliance with appropriate regulations becomes second nature. Beyond that, development continuously sharpens the technical skills that will help to earn more money, and makes sure that incentives are effective.

If the need for money is relatively low, then development should concentrate on more significant factors.

Factor 2 (physical conditions)

The need for good physical working conditions does not usually provide any clues for career development. The need appears to be relatively low both for those who work on construction sites and for those who work in offices.

Factor 3 (structure)

The need for structure is paramount. People with high factor 3 need to work in as stable an environment as possible. Since, however, stability is in short supply, they need at least to have some body of rules to refer to in their work. They need to know that they are doing the right thing even in the most difficult circumstances. Preferably they should find a core activity for themselves, a sort of bedrock from which they can venture to deal with that instability from which there is no escape. They can often help themselves by nurturing a stable family background. High factor 3 people, in the most extreme cases, develop by becoming more technically competent in their chosen field. They can be exceptionally effective, provided they stick to their area of competence and allow others to handle uncertainty. Generally speaking, they should aim to be number one in their chosen field, but number two in more general areas of management.

Low factor 3 people should avoid situations requiring structure. If they can, they should even avoid having to fill in forms. Typically, they will fill in the form and read the instructions later. Then, armed with scissors and Tipp-Ex®, they will try to make good and end up by sending away for another blank form! Low factor 3 people can tolerate uncertainty. They can, in theory, aim for the top. Whether they succeed or not depends on how much uncertainty and lack of structure they will tolerate. If they are too tolerant, they will end up like the director who, being examined for bankruptcy, pleaded that he had not been dishonest, he had merely failed to keep proper records!

Low 3s can be successful provided they recognize, with humility, their deficiencies in this regard and are able and willing to work with people who will supply the structure they need. They can be providers of structure for others, but often are not, for the sensible reason that they do not need it themselves. They need to look with care at their other motivators. For example, if they also have a high need for variety and a low need for achievement, they are in danger of fecklessness. They might be rescued by a creative streak which will enable them to earn some sort of living writing, provided the publisher doesn't mind waiting for the manuscript!

Low 3s are best developed by putting them into positions of uncertainty and stretching them. Then putting them into even more difficult positions and stretching them further. They will resent control, but to perform at their best, they need to be clear about what is required. Low structure without any underlying vision could fritter energy away.

Development has two main purposes. The first is to make the vision process instinctive. The technical training they are given should not only enable them to do the job but also to develop a sense of direction. The second is to help them understand the role of structure and to learn to reach out to, and work successfully with, those who can supply the structure which they cannot, but which is necessary for effective organization.

How does factor 3 affect the way people learn?

The strength of the structure need will have a significant impact on the learning process and needs the fullest consideration. Those with high structure needs will prefer to learn in a structured way; they will benefit from learning presented in packages. There will need to be clarity of learning objectives and possibly prescribed marking schemes. Structured learning has benefits. It means that significant amounts of knowledge can be acquired efficiently and relatively quickly. Its limitation is that it is confined to measurable knowledge. This limitation is important. For example, softer skills cannot be acquired in structured fashion. They require an approach in which the learning objectives necessarily lack the clarity of 'hard' knowledge objectives and where progress is made through the experience of ambiguity. Yet softer skills are an important part of management and have to be learned.

The problem for the Development Manager is to explain the purpose of the learning. Highly structured people cannot comprehend soft learning objectives and the experience of apparently purposeless ambiguity is disturbing. There is a twofold approach. The first is to create such an environment of trust that the person concerned will take the plunge. Generally speaking, people will come out of such an experience having learned something and this provides a sound platform for further development. The second, which can be used with the first, is to provide structure initially which will be reduced as development takes place.

People with high structure needs who fail to progress with learning in an unstructured environment, face a considerable development problem. They confine themselves to situations where the parameters are known. They are likely to have difficulty in ambiguous, unfocused business situations. If they cannot learn without structure, they may have ruled themselves out for promotion to the highest levels. In terms of Honey and Mumford's four styles, highly structured people will have a preference for reflector, theoretician and pragmatist styles. They will tend to avoid the activist approach.

Factor 4 (people contact)

Factor 4 concerns the need to make contact with a variety of people, but a low score is not a contraindication meaning that the person is unsociable and does not get on with others. It means that they are able to work with people but are not driven to do so more than is necessary. Unfortunately, some organizations see people only as factors of production. Some say there is little point in training managers to be more sensitive and open to others if the culture does not encourage or is even hostile to such behaviour. More positively, training can demonstrate that good people skills are always worthwhile, starting with the most basic, that of good observation: the art of knowing what it is one sees and being able to appreciate the implications of it.

People high on the need for contact with others will readily volunteer for training, especially if it involves group discussions and exercises, and the possibility of going to a pleasant training centre away from the office where sociability is one of the benefits. Low scorers may need to be encouraged to participate, and will be keener if the programme is clearly task oriented, with not too much emphasis on soft, and possibly formless, discussions.

The trainer faces a problem when trying to handle the process issues of people management skills in groups where the need for people contact is low. Usually such groups are hell-bent on the task, ignoring the process and people aspects. Even when this is brought to their attention, it can take some time and persuasion before they realize that many working problems can be solved by attention to people's needs and relationships before too much emphasis is put on the task. For training purposes, if someone does not need or value something, they may need help to appreciate that others do and, just as important, that they may need to take account of others' views when planning and organizing work.

Factor 5 (relationships)

Factor 5 involves getting to know other people well and the mode, at 18, is very low. Not needing to get to know others well does not imply an inability to work with other people. It means working with people when necessary but not being driven to do so more than is needed. Taken to extremes it means taking an instrumental view of people. They are one of the factors of production to be utilized as required.

The problem is that people have a habit of wanting more than to be utilized. For example, apart from common observation, unpublished work with repertory grid interviews suggests that people like their managers to be approachable, to give feedback. Some managers they enjoy working for, others they work for because they have to. Some managers have staff support, for others their staff just put up with them. Some managers have much appreciated good listening skills, others are unable to listen. Some know how to stretch and challenge their staff, others de-motivate people.

The development implication is to place the people dimension high on the manager's agenda. First of all, take theory. A manager should accept that part of being a manager is understanding motivational and interpersonal skills theory to a fair level of sophistication. It is, of course, true to say that understanding the theory does not guarantee the practice. Theory can, however, inform instincts and provide confidence and there should be an expectation that the professional manager has a firm grounding in the best thinking of the day and is able to relate it to the practical business of management. A good understanding of motivational theory can also provide useful insights at times of stress. This approach is in contrast to the situation which sometimes occurs where motivational studies are often seen as a kind of add-on, an interlude before getting on with the 'proper' topics like strategy and marketing.

Second, practice. Managers' attention can be drawn to their obligations in respect of people by ensuring that their motivational and interpersonal skills are given prominence in the appraisal process. Managers must also be aware that they are required to assess their staff in terms of motivational needs and that they, in turn, can be judged on the quality of their assessments as well as their practice.

Factor 6 (recognition)

The recognition need is important and requires careful consideration. The development imperative is awareness of the need and its impact on behaviour. Do some people have such a high recognition need that their ability to act effectively is impaired? For example, are decisions made to prompt applause, regardless of whether or not the decision is appropriate to the task in hand? Or more sinister, if no applause is possible, was the action designed to provoke confrontation? In each case, motivation should ensure that the manager is seen centre-stage. In contrast, the need for recognition can be very positive. It can lead people to great achievements. Outside work, it can, for example, lead people to dedicate themselves to service to the community.

Where recognition is a significant need, regular review will be seen as beneficial as will a request to provide regular reports on the experience. At the same time, it is important to ensure that senior management are seen to be informed about the development work being undertaken. If the recognition need is low, review should take place only as a way of monitoring the effectiveness of the process and need not have PR overtones.

In development terms, we can ask people to question themselves as to the strength of their recognition need and where it might lead them. They need to be sure from whence they draw their recognition. We can help them learn about themselves by considering significant moments in their career and how their need for recognition impacted on their decisions and their behaviour. For example, did their need for recognition lead them into making a decision which they suspected was wrong but which they made anyway because they could not face the loss of recognition? In particular, we can encourage them to question if there are other ways of acting which would achieve better results, and how might they handle the loss of recognition, if any, that this could entail?

We would use the opportunity of the discussion to make them sensitive to possible future occurrences and to the necessity to take the impact of their recognition need into account. In spite of their increased awareness, they may still make recognition-related wrong decisions in the future. They need to be advised to review and learn the lessons they can and to consider how to react differently, experimenting if necessary. In discussing the recognition need the facilitator will require great sensitivity. It is not easy for people to admit that they are too easily influenced by others. In development terms, however, they need to know where they stand and how they might improve.

An additional aspect of recognition is that people with high recognition needs try to avoid giving recognition to others, not only being dishonest with them but also de-motivating them. Again, the facilitator should help them to explore their behaviour and admit the extent to which they do this. The best approach is to consider the consequences of passing on recognition. In practice, those who recognize the achievements of others usually benefit themselves, not only in terms of the increased motivation they engender, but in that recognition of others also reflects back on them. They need to be helped to experience this for themselves and the problem will, in time, disappear.

We should encourage them to undertake regular, systematic review of their own behaviour and the practical steps they can take to change it where necessary. Review with a boss, colleagues whom they trust, or with a mentor, will greatly increase their understanding. In due course, their understanding will become second nature and improve their effectiveness with others. Similarly, those with low recognition need should consider their situation. Are they allowing themselves to be too insensitive to the needs of others, perhaps as a result damaging their own prospects and relationships? As before, the recommended approach is for them to think about critical events at work and how they handled them. The facilitator can help them think through how they might have handled situations differently and, particularly useful to those who lack a natural sensitivity to the needs of others, provide some theoretical underpinning to their thinking about how they might behave differently.

Factor 7 (achievement)

For achievement, the development need is, in principle, simple, though there is a subtlety. The drive with high achievers is to achieve measurable objectives. Development is a matter of offering appropriate technical training, setting more demanding objectives and reviewing progress, particularly where objectives have been set to overcome areas of weakness. If we are thinking of external development, we might be thinking of a full- or part-time qualification such as an

MBA. People with high needs on this factor often have histories of success in academic achievement. They will probably enjoy the challenge of new learning and will be more motivated to seek it if it is accompanied by certificated and, especially, graded courses.

There are two problems with high achievers. The first is that while they can 'gobble up' huge chunks of work, they have difficulty in seeing what cannot be measured. The softness and ambiguities of work and life can escape them. Unfortunately, one of those softer areas is that of people management and interpersonal skills. Unless this area can be presented as a challenging learning opportunity, those high on achievement may not realize its importance. The second problem is that they tend to want to work on their own more than as part of a team and, in organizations, that can be a weakness. In training and development terms this deficiency needs to be addressed.

As far as ambiguities are concerned, the development approach is to keep them on a high diet of achievement; relying on the motivation and security this provides to introduce them to softer areas which need to be seen in shades of grey, rather than in black and white. They will need to be coached. At first, it is safer to let them work on projects and tasks where there is time to consider and to debate the subtleties. Then, as they improve, let them establish objectives in the more subtle areas where measurement is difficult. In other words, we are trying to use their need for achievement to help them to seek out the softer areas which they are likely to overlook. We can help them think of the subtleties by discussion and by using techniques such as brainstorming.

There is no guarantee of success, of course. This approach will make the high achievers aware that there is another dimension, beyond simple measurement, but nonetheless important. It is the most likely way of awakening in them an understanding that the world has more complexity than appears at first sight. It is the very concentration of effort in high achievers that is the weakness; in pursuing one objective with vigour and intensity, they are inclined to ignore, or maybe not even to notice, other ways of proceeding. High achievement drives seem to lead to convergent thinking and action.

For teamworking, we can help by choosing a team-based learning environment. Internally, we will be looking at working parties. High achievers need clarity of objectives and roles before they can begin to perform in a team environment, so we will form properly constituted working parties. As they improve, we can put the onus on them to ensure that role definition occurs. If we are looking for external training, we will choose courses in which there is a significant team culture. Whenever possible, we give more and more demanding targets, always remembering that they have to be achievable or they will not be attempted. What is achievable is a matter of judgement and discussion but always requires consideration.

Finally, although the achievement drive would provide the motor for self-development, we need the person to understand the limitations of personal achievement for those who wish to move into management. Achievers want to do everything themselves, but managers want things to be done by others as well. We help the process of development by reviewing their work with them and encouraging them to recognize the work that can be done by others. We coach them in delegation best practice and ensure that the work is delegated. If necessary, we overload them so that the real choice they face is of delegating or going under.

Developing the low achievers is something different. They shy away from measurement. They can be chatterers. If they have high structure needs they can be fed on a diet of routine and will be perfectly satisfied. Training for people with low achievement drives means giving them objectives well within their capability, and these objectives should be gradually increased in difficulty and complexity; they should be varied in method; they should be short in duration, rather than a long haul; and they should address as many other motivation factors as possible; the first choice being recognition, supplied as frequently and as effusively as is decent. It will take time and in the worst cases might not achieve much success. But if the time is available, and the routine work is being done anyway, the effort can be worthwhile. At best, it might awaken latent achievement drives and take people far further than they expected.

Factor 8 (power and influence)

The influence drive is most beneficial when it is allied with competence. Without competence it can be disastrous and the first development need is technical and personal management training. Even with basic competence there is a need to ensure that technical awareness, if not the actual ability to practise the technical skills, is up to date.

The personal drive will be to exercise more influence, over more people, at a higher level. The development need is to establish credibility, both technical and personal. In the developed business world, where the irresponsible exercise of power is likely to bring retribution at the hands of either the market or the authorities, we are talking about the exercise of purposeful, responsible power.

The first part of development, then, is to ensure that the technical skills required are in place and that technical advice is available. The second is to recognize that the growth of the capability to influence requires practice. The problem is to permit its exercise in an environment where the inevitable mistakes do not cause severe damage. Although mistakes are permitted and are probably necessary, the damage to the organization could be compounded by damage to the person being developed, either in terms of their self-confidence or in terms of management not being prepared to give them further opportunities. The choice of an appropriate area in which to exercise influence is crucial.

Assuming competence, the most fruitful development approach is to provide formal channels for the exercise of influence. Something like this is best practice in the UK's Administrative Civil Service. The junior officer will write a paper, which will be submitted to the next higher officer who will make a contribution and so on up to the Permanent Secretary. The industrial/commercial equivalent is to identify the potential influence brokers and allow them to contribute to working parties, formally assessing both the quality of the thinking and their ability to carry others with them; or simply to observe, dispassionately, their impact in meetings on both their colleagues and their seniors.

Particular attention needs to be paid to their impact on their seniors, not only on the quality of their contribution, but the acceptability of the way they exert their influence, and its appropriateness to the organizational culture. There is a problem, or certainly a need to be addressed, if it appears they can influence downwards and perhaps sideways but not upwards. They should be given every encouragement to influence upwards. It should at first be made as easy as possible so that they can enjoy the taste of success, thus reinforcing the behaviour. Otherwise, development should be in terms of exercising the influence they are capable of, but they will inevitably be deprived of access to the inner counsels of the organization. As in all development, the tasks they work on should increase in magnitude and difficulty. As they develop, they should move from influencing others who make decisions to being made fully accountable for the influence they exercise.

The development of influence is quite unlike the development of knowledge. It is not possible to re-read the textbook. The potential lessons can quickly vanish if not reinforced. Therefore, although those who exercise influence may not like the process, it is worth encouraging them to keep a regular log of events, if necessary, password protected on the computer, so that events can be reviewed and lessons learned. Review should take place not only with the development manager, but also with senior line managers.

Factor 9 (variety and change)

The need for variety and change seems an ideal attribute in today's organizations where constant fast change is the norm. There are two development approaches to factor 9. The first is to manage the need, the second is to utilize it.

The danger with factor 9, when taken to extremes, is the temptation to create variety and change for its own sake. The development need here is again awareness. Establishing how much of the chaos is a result of the manager's disorganization is a good starting point. If the problem lies with the manager, then a good antidote is the introduction of good time-management procedures, whereby the future receives constant attention and management is not always 'by the seat of the pants'. Time and personal management training is a must. If, however, the change occurring is in the circumstances of the job and the personal management is as good as can be expected in the circumstances, then the management need is to ensure that amid all the chaos there is purpose. Given purpose there is the possibility of creating order or, at least, reducing disorder. That becomes the management task.

The development need is to improve the ability to relate disorder to purpose. The first part of development consists of instilling a full understanding of organizational purpose and, as far as possible, its measurement. Next comes an understanding of which aspects of the disorder contribute to, and which detract from, achievement. There is a mixture here of classroom study and observation; observing which actions help and which actions hinder. Development here consists of regular debriefing and review. As the ability to reduce disorder and achieve purpose improves, so the challenge is increased. The outcome of the development is the ability to 'control chaos', but to use it for the ends of the organization.

The development process is one which is stimulated by variety and change. It means learning on the job and off the job, using as many learning media as possible. It means an eclectic approach to learning, introducing different topics and aspects of the organization so that there is no opportunity for boredom or lack of attention. We bring back the key topics as often as we can, but move on when concentration wanes. We use this approach to try to increase the attention span. We probably do not, however, wish to reduce significantly the need for variety and change. It is possibly one of the principal drivers in helping people cope with the increasing pressures of organizations; but we want people to learn to control it. That needs to be an underlying theme of our development effort.

What development is required when the need for variety and change is low? Obviously, for people with this drive to be effective, there needs to be a core area where there is stability. If we, and they, are satisfied with this situation and it is sustainable, there may not be a development need. However, such situations are rarely sustainable and development, leading to the ability to handle variety and change, will be required. The recommended development approach is to work around the areas of stability; to train people to observe and analyse change and to establish with clarity the new outputs following on from change, preferably before it is put into action. Once people have learned to do this, they are in a position to use change to create a new stability. When the approach has become internalized, they will feel more able to manage change and less need to avoid it.

Factor 10 (creativity)

People with the need for creativity and the ability to explore ideas welcome the opportunity to create. However, creativity takes time and costs money. Productive creativity can recover its costs many times and probably carry the cost of the unproductive.

The management task is twofold: to provide an environment in which people can make creative contributions and to identify those priority areas where the creative instinct can make the most impact. The development task likewise is twofold. In general, there needs to be a recognition that organizations cannot afford the costs of making creative those who are uncreative. After that, the task is to nurture the basic creativity resident within the organization. This can be done by ensuring that managers understand how organizational culture can impact on creativity. For example, a blame culture discourages creativity. In the same way the culture needs to be tolerant and open with a recognition that an 'office hours' approach is unlikely to be successful. Creative people need space. Their approach to work can be a mixture of apparently uncontrollable peaks and troughs, bursts of energy followed by passivity. Development does not try to alter that approach, it tries to ensure that amidst what sometimes appears to be chaos, creativity is taking place.

The best approach is to recognize that people learn by their mistakes, while being aware that mistakes cannot be allowed to damage the organization. Good delegation allows mistakes to provide learning without seriously damaging the organization. This sounds glib, but is workable where delegation is practised well. In part, then, the process of developing for creativity is ensuring that managers understand how to delegate and are expected to do it properly. The right culture also requires that managers, as a matter of good practice, encourage people to establish systematically and openly the possible benefits of all suggested ideas, before allowing the ideas to be shot down. The potential benefits hardly need prolonged discussion. They avoid the 'yes, a good idea but...' syndrome, allow ideas to be expressed and encourage tentative ideas which otherwise might not be offered. There is also benefit, on appropriate occasions, in using creativity techniques like brainstorming and quality circles. This means finding time for creativity when it appears that it might make a contribution.

The second opportunity for development is to use the identifiably creative to work in those priority areas where high level creativity can make a significant contribution. Indeed this may be the only way ahead. In these areas we give people the time and facilities to use their creativity and try to ensure it is channelled. Architects are an obvious example. Given basic technical competence, we can rely on them not to create buildings likely to fall down. An additional development tool is to have people contribute to matters outside their immediate areas of responsibility, alongside those who are more directly involved. We should look at formal creativity techniques like, for example, reverse assumptions (list the assumptions associated with an approach, reverse them and see the consequences); forced combinations (mixing the properties of two or more 'trigger ideas' to spark remote associations); and so on. In addition, there is value in using formal problem-solving techniques which encourage creativity.

In summary, we need to identify the areas where creative input will be of most benefit, bring in those known to be creative, and stimulate them from time to time, using formal creativity techniques.

Factor 11 (self-development)

We have discussed this factor at the beginning of the chapter. The development need is obvious and is, on the one hand, to offer opportunities for people to develop their technical skills, through on-the-job training, distance learning, courses, and so on; and on the other, to offer the opportunities appropriate to the other motivation needs as outlined above.

The strength of a person's development drive will be confirmed by the tenacity with which he or she works to achieve their development goals. The drive will be reinforced when it is identified with success. The development task is to identify those areas where success is possible and to focus people's development efforts in that direction.

People high on this need can be a pleasure to train. Eager for new learning and open to new ideas, they often make training events more enjoyable for colleagues. Where factor 11 is low, we have to work to motivate people to learn as much as is sufficient for them to do the job in hand. We try to encourage development on the back of their other needs, to encourage people to do what is necessary for them to be able to fully engage those needs.

Factor 12 (interest and usefulness)

The drive for intrinsic job satisfaction and usefulness is a strong one with a mode of 41 and a median of 43. The development need can be described simply as 'good management practice'. In other words, let people see the relevance of their jobs to other jobs and to the organization. Keep them informed. Try to give them whole jobs and not just parts of larger jobs.

We need to be aware that those who have a high factor 12 simply will not engage with anything which is not, in their terms, interesting. They might be able to do so in the short term, but most certainly not in the long term. We also need to consider what they regard as 'interesting'. That might be quite remarkably different from what we think is interesting. We have to accept their definition of 'interest'. A major part of our development effort will be establishing their view of 'interest' and ensuring that it is relevant to the needs of the organization. We may find ourselves spending more time than we want painting the global picture. But if we can establish congruence, there will be a considerable effort at self-development and the organization will be the beneficiary. If we cannot, then we can expect a development effort to take place but it will not be related to our needs.

One recent high scorer on this need observed that he wished to work on projects that stretched his capabilities; he did not mean that he sought to achieve targets, but that he wanted to feel that the work was complex and difficult. He was not keen to undertake training unless it led directly to more interesting work.

Interacting with others

There is a further part of the development task, beyond that described above. It is to consider how people with different motivational Profiles interact with each other. In general, there is a tendency to project our own needs on to other people, sometimes regardless of their needs. Thus, for example, the person with a low need for structure will project that low need on to somebody who has a high need, resulting in the potential for friction. They will assume that the other person likes freedom of action, as they do, and that offering guidelines is unnecessary. Or the high achiever will feel let down by the low achiever ('How could he not be keen to do such an obviously valuable task?') and so on. The tendency will be most pronounced at times of stress.

The question, in development terms, is how can that tendency be controlled? With difficulty, is the instant response. The preferred approach is through developed self-awareness, perhaps reinforced with mentoring. The first step is to learn to depersonalize the issue by asking what the job requires and by trying to establish an objective answer. Then to recognize that there will be differences and that, for example, people with high structure needs are likely to both need and put more structure into the job than someone with low structure needs. The second step is to ask if what they have assumed differently about the job is positively damaging, or is it, on the contrary, within some margin of tolerance? In that case, the development need is to learn to tolerate the differences in approach and, even better, to work with them.

Development succeeds when jobs are being done, competently but differently, and where there is an absence of interpersonal conflict between those with different Profiles. It fails when there is a lack of reasonable tolerance and those who work differently are regarded, in extreme situations, with contempt.

The limits of our imagination

The most obvious way to use the Profile for development is to work with the individual on his or her own Profile. Comparing the individual's scores with those of the full database is the starting point. This can be followed by comparing individual scores with those of the organization, if available, and seeing how the individual relates to the culture and if something needs to be handled differently. On a one-to-one basis, there is development benefit in boss and subordinate each sitting down and discussing how their own Profiles might influence the way they act and react towards each other. Perhaps the same can happen with colleagues.

From an organizational or departmental point of view, it is worth seeing if there are any excesses or deficiencies. Is there an influence deficit, meaning a possible tendency to follow the leader without the constructive challenge that could improve the quality of decisions? Is the structure need too high considering the flexibility of attitude and response demanded by the market-place. Does this mean there is a need to improve the systems and planning, or should there be an injection of more low structure need people?

The Profile presents an almost unlimited format for thinking about motivation and how we can use it to benefit both the organization and the people who work for it.

Selection

The Profile can give an additional layer of sophistication to the selection process. It helps us to look not only at whether people are able to perform in the job, but also the extent to which they are likely to have above average performance and the ability to develop the job. Using the Profile for selection requires us, in the usual way, to ascertain the technical and professional skills and behaviours required in the job. We then establish the motivational Profile of the job and identify those motivational aspects which will encourage above average performance. In doing this we will break down each factor into its motivational components.

Obviously, we need to start with the skills and experience required. What technical skills are necessary to do the job? If the applicants lack those skills or experience, no amount of commitment or motivation will make it possible for them to do the job. It may be possible to train them, but that is a different matter and means that they might be able to do the job after training. As for experience, the position may not be so clear cut. If they have the experience but not the specific skills, it may be that they will be sufficiently flexible and alert to manage the demands of the job. The motivational Profile will give us clues as to whether that is likely or not.

We then look at effective behaviours, which we establish by consulting stakeholders. These are the people who actually do the job, those who manage the job and those who are affected by its performance. We can either do this by discussion and interview, or by using sophisticated techniques like repertory grid. Whichever approach we use, we will want to prioritize behaviours in terms of effectiveness. We will want to know which behaviours have most impact on job performance and which have least. As we are interested in the impact of motivation on performance, we then list behaviours under whichever of the twelve motivational factors seems appropriate.

We need to disentangle 'ability to behave in the required way' from the drive which impels people towards that sort of behaviour. For example, we might find that a job requires the holder to be able to achieve; and that a particular person without an achievement drive is unable to perform adequately in that job. On the other hand, we might find somebody else with a relatively low need for achievement who is actually able to achieve to the extent necessary to perform well in that job. What we want to know from the point of view of selecting effective performers is whether the possession of the right motivational drive enhances behavioural effectiveness and whether its absence inhibits effectiveness.

The Profile gives us insight into how to proceed. It can do this despite the fact that it measures needs relative to each other and not absolute needs. It is possible for two people to have the same relative needs, for example for achievement, but for one to have a significantly stronger achievement drive than the other. We are now talking about absolute needs. It is obviously extremely difficult to measure absolutes, whether of need or ability. The task has been attempted in some areas. For example, mountain climbs are graded according to difficulty, as are ski runs. Thus a novice skier, setting out for his or her first run, would be ill-advised to attempt an icy black run. Something similar is possible in the world of work, where points are allocated for tasks and these form the basis for job grading. This can be effective where the tasks are measurable, though doing this becomes more difficult with complex tasks or in jobs where there are elements of judgement not so susceptible to measurement.

Can we apply the same approach to measuring the strength of a motivational need? That is, with the same accuracy that the Profile estimates the strengths of one need relative to another, and does so statistically with a high degree of confidence. There are a number of possible approaches, mainly impracticable, but one approach which is workable and which is used to predict likely performance in the job. Impractical approaches mainly consist of training people to the same level of competence to perform tasks which relate to each motivational need. We deprive them of the opportunity of spending their time elsewhere and then urge them to undertake the tasks. The extent to which people continue in the task we take as a measure of the strength of their need. The flaws in the approach do not need further emphasis.

A more practicable approach is to break each factor into its components. We do this by analysing the questionnaire and the chapters which describe each factor. The components are listed in Table 1 on pages 227–44. Briefly, achievement will be broken down into such components as:

- achieves over a range of activities,

- achieves a single activity,

- has a need for constant achievement,

- has a need for occasional achievement,

- develops by increasing range of activities,

- develops by increasing frequency of achievement,

- develops by slight increase in difficulty of achievement,

- develops by significant increase in difficulty of achievement.

For factor 8, power and influence, we use headings like 'uses influence to create dependency'; 'uses influence to empower', and so on. Under factor 9, 'variety and change', we use headings like 'enjoys variety but moves on, leaving work uncompleted'.

We want to use the components to give us insight into how people's motivational need will impact on their job performance. For each of the critical behaviours required in the job, we ask the simple question: 'Given the same resources in the job, which motivational component, if enhanced or reduced, would be most likely to double or halve job effectiveness?' We can take the questions further by asking: 'Which is the next motivational component which, if enhanced or reduced, would be next-most likely to double or halve job effectiveness?' Finally, we can ask the question: 'Which motivational component, if enhanced or reduced, would make no difference to job effectiveness?' If we restrict the number of people who are invited to contribute answers to these questions, it becomes clearer as to who is responsible for selection. We are most likely to restrict the number successfully by choosing people who either are regarded as good performers in the job or are most affected by its standard of performance.

The questions pose very stark choices. This is deliberate. No psychological or motivational questionnaire is sensitive enough to predict small changes in job performance. Asking which component has the potential to double or halve performance forces a harder and more realistic choice than asking which will enhance or reduce effectiveness by 10 per cent. At the end of this exercise, we will have a detailed analysis of which aspects of motivation are most likely to enhance or impair performance.

We are now able to say, looking at, for example, the component for achievement, that the job will be performed more effectively 'if there is a significant increase in the range of tasks handled'. With a detailed job analysis we might even be able to say which tasks would make the greatest contribution; or if there was 'an increase in the difficulty of achievement'; or for factor 8 that there would be a job improvement if 'influence were exercised in an empowering and not a controlling way', and so on. We can also make the very reasonable – and critical – assumption that if improved job performance requires a significant increase in a particular behaviour, especially if it requires that behaviour to be sustained, then there is a considerable advantage in having the motivational drive that supports that behaviour. People without the drive will probably not be able to sustain the required behaviour and will succumb to stress. We now have to match the personal Profile to the job.

We need to satisfy ourselves that the applicants are not so informed about motivation and about the required job Profile that they can cheat. There are never any guarantees. (Appendix 2 on The making of the Profile addresses this question of respondent honesty in detail.) However, it is unlikely that applicants will have such detailed knowledge of the job or of motivation and, of course, they face the dilemma that if they focus the Profile on one job they may disqualify themselves for another. It is a workable assumption, particularly when taken into account with other information on which to base selection, that the Profile is neither easy nor worth cheating on.

We now come to a distinct advantage of the Profile, which can help us to resolve some of the principal dilemmas in selection. As we have said, it is possible for two people to have identical Profiles, or relative needs, but for one to be significantly more effective than the other. Thus although, in personally relative terms, each of them is satisfied with a score for achievement of say, 40, one of them moves mountains and the other molehills. Even more confusing, one can have a lower achievement score than the other, but achieve in the job twice as much.

How can we distinguish between applicants? We approach this initially in the standard way. That is we ask them and perhaps test them; and ask others. As always in selection, we have a particular interest in the accuracy of the information given to us and we want to predict performance.

The first thing we can do is to ask applicants to list the three or four key behavioural and motivational demands of their current job. They will have already completed the Profile so they will have been alerted to the topics that might be considered. We do not ask them to comment on behaviour and motivation without any priming, because it is our experience that most applicants are unable to give an unprompted reply. We give them some additional information so that we are all talking about the same issues (pages 245–6, Table 2). We then ask them, given the same resources in the job, to describe 'the behaviours and motivational drives which if enhanced or reduced would be most likely to double or halve effectiveness in your job'. We ask them to write 200 to 500 words. Note that in this question we deliberately do not ask them about their own contribution to the job. We invite them to make an objective comment on performance in the job and it is possible that their reply will contain some element of projection. We do not, however, depend on projection. We read the statements and classify the comments made under what we judge are the appropriate motivational factors. Thus statements about the need to 'exercise greater influence with other departments' will be classified under factor 8; and statements about the need for 'increased self-development' will be classified under factor 11 and so on. We further compare these replies against the motivational components listed in Table 1 on pages 227–44.

We are now in a situation where the job stakeholders have a great deal of information about the motivation and behaviours that they believe will enhance effectiveness in the job. The applicants have a view as to the behaviours and motivation that will enhance effectiveness in the job they have just done. We now have the basis for very focused interviewing, that is, to make the best use of the time available. We can ask about behaviour and motivation in the existing job; what the applicant sees as the difference between the existing job and the new job under consideration; and the motivational or behavioural differences. We will certainly establish the extent to which the candidate understands the basis of their performance in their existing job and the extent to which they have thought about the job for which they are being considered. In establishing the similarities and differences, we can ask the candidates to rate themselves and we can add their rating to our own assessment.

In general, we can take the view that if the job requires more or particular behaviours, and these are not supported by the motivational drives of the applicant, the applicant will not be successful in that job. Likewise, if the required behaviours are supported, their chance of successful performance and personal growth in the job are enhanced. At the end of this process, both we and the candidates will have a sophisticated understanding of what makes for effectiveness and the contribution made to it by their motivational Profile. The time spent in analysis will help to focus the interview and to enhance the likelihood that we will achieve a match between what the candidate offers and what the job requires.

Components of motivation

The components of motivation are used with the question:

> Given the same resources in the job, which motivational component, if enhanced or reduced, would be most likely to double or halve effectiveness?

The answer is subjective and is based on experience of the job. If there is agreement on the conditions for effectiveness, they should be explored closely in the selection process.

Table 1   *Components of motivation*

Component **Components of factor 1 (money and tangible rewards)**	Comment
accepts management direction/does not accept management direction	
non-conformance/conformance	
own effort/team effort	
low tolerance of boredom/high tolerance of boredom	
job needs short-term relationships/job needs long-term relationships	
self interest/business interest	

Component	Comment
accepts detailed targets/own initiative	
accepts change/resists change	
strict link between effort and reward/loose link between effort and reward	
tolerates boredom/seeks variety	
narrow focus/wide focus	
risk averse/risk seeking	
influence seeking/influencing averse	
accepts a brief/self-directed	
seeks self-development/avoids self-development	
other	

There are no motivational components for factor 2.

Component	Comment
Components of factor 3 (structure)	
rules and guidelines required and adhered to/rules and guidelines not required	
up-to-date job description essential and used/job description not required	
work fully specified and structured/work not specified and unstructured	
clear statement of expectations/no statement of expectations	
actively seeks rules/resents rules	
wants rules to be provided/creates own rules	
plans forward/reactive	
copes with administrative aspects of work/unable to cope with administrative aspects	
works with uncertainty/quite unable to work with uncertainty	
able to work with others/not able to work with others	
self-sufficient/not self-sufficient	
systems before people/people before systems	
need to comply undermines achievement/need to comply does not inhibit achievement	

Component	Comment
strong preference for stability/strong preference for change	
learns in a structured way/learns in an unstructured way	
more interested in the job/more interested in the job structure	
other	

Components of factor 4 (people contact)	
works with a wide range of people/works on own	
transitory contacts generate business/transitory contacts do not generate business	
short-term relationships/long-term relationships	
sociability/lack of sociability	
sociability reinforces achievement drive/sociability undermines achievement drive	
recognition needs reinforce business/recognition needs undermine business	
other	

Component	Comment
Components of factor 5 (relationships)	
forms and sustains good relationships with colleagues/does not form good relationships with colleagues	
long-term commitment to team/short-term commitment to team	
independent/interdependent	
trusting/not trusting	
relationships high priority/money high priority	
long-term relationships/short-term relationships	
long-term relationships impair achievement/long-term relationships enhance achievement	
forms business effective long-term relationships/does not form business effective long-term relationships	
competitive drive impairs relationships/ competitive drive enhances relationships	
is dependent in relationships/creates equal relationships	
makes others dependent/creates equal relationships	
independent creativity/team-based creativity	
independent learning/group learning	
other	

Component	Comment
Components of factor 6 (recognition)	
organizational recognition enhances performance/organizational recognition does not affect performance	
receives recognition and is dependent/receives recognition and is not dependent	
need for recognition undermines effectiveness/need for recognition enhances effectiveness	
need for recognition undermines ability to recognize others/need for recognition does not undermine ability to recognize others	
need for recognition distorts focus/need for recognition does not distort focus	
need for recognition satisfied outside the organization/need for recognition satisfied inside organization	
low need for recognition makes organizational control difficult/low need for recognition does not affect organizational control	
lack of need for recognition creates insensitivity/lack of need for recognition does not affect sensitivity	
lack of recognition need means poor presentation of work/lack of recognition need does not affect presentation of work	

Component	Comment
recognition needs require excessive management attention/recognition only requires reasonable management attention	
requires recognition for exceptional work/requires recognition for unremarkable work	
recognition needs create inability to do what is unpopular/recognition needs do not affect ability to do what is unpopular	
recognition needs inhibit creative contribution to business/recognition needs do not inhibit creative contribution to business	
recognition enhances self-development/recognition does not impact on self-development	
other	

Components of factor 7 (achievement)	
sets own targets/requires others to set targets	
able to co-operate with others in achieving their targets/unable to co-operate with others in achieving their targets	

Component	Comment
will only accept achievable targets/will accept targets where there is a possibility of failure	
will only perform where measurement of performance is possible/will perform where measurement is difficult	
ignores non-measurable areas/takes account of non-measurable areas	
focuses on single targets/focuses on a range of targets	
defines targets/does not define targets	
spends time at beginning defining possible obstacles/does not take time at beginning defining possible obstacles	
target driven, ignores routine work/target driven, attends to routine work	
achievement driven but can delegate/achievement driven but cannot delegate	
prepared and able to adjust objectives/not prepared to adjust objectives	
disregards other than financially rewarding targets/will consider other than financially rewarding targets	
can achieve targets and fulfil compliance demands/can achieve targets but cannot fulfil compliance demands	

Component	Comment
recognition need enhances ability to achieve/recognition need inhibits ability to achieve	
achieves and influences/achieves and does not influence	
cannot resolve tension between need to achieve and need to create/manages tension between need to achieve and need to create	
uses projects as learning opportunities/does not use projects as learning opportunities	
other	

Components of factor 8 (power and influence)	
greater sense of purpose would enhance influence/greater sense of purpose would not affect exercise of influence	
greater technical and commercial skills would enhance influence/technical and commercial skills adequate for exercise of influence	
uses influence to coerce/uses influence to empower	
greater interpersonal skills would enhance influence/greater interpersonal skills would not enhance influence	

Component	Comment
greater willingness to take risks would enhance influence/willingness to take risks adequate for exercise of influence	
exercise of influence high profile/exercise of influence low profile	
exercise of influence in own interest/exercise of influence in organization's interest	
exercise of influence depends on personal qualities/exercise of influence depends on official position	
empowers and achieves required outputs/empowers but does not achieve required outputs	
exercise of influence rule based/exercise of influence not rule based	
influence based on expediency/influence based on integrity	
exercises influence in environment of uncertainty/exercises influence in predictable environment	
influence exercised sensitively/influence exercised insensitively	
need for recognition inhibits exercise of influence/need for recognition does not inhibit exercise of influence	
exercises influence and delegates fully/exercises influence and does not delegate	

Component	Comment
exercises influence in a controlling way/exercises influence in a non-controlling way	
exercises influence to task completion/exercises influence but tasks not completed	
exercises influence at times of rapid change/exercises influence in stable environment	
exercises influence creatively/exercises influence predictably	
other	

Components of factor 9 (variety and change)	
high boredom threshold/low boredom threshold	
thrives on constant change and stimulation/reacts adversely to constant change and stimulation	
never completes before moving on/always completes before moving on	
defines and uses formal objectives/does not define formal objectives	

Component	Comment
thrives on change and has clear understanding of organization's goals/thrives on change but has no clear understanding of organization's goals	
frenetic but poor administrator/frenetic but on top of administration	
wants space, accepts direction/wants space but does not accept direction	
wants variety, works well with others/wants variety, does not work well with others	
sensitive to others' concerns about change/not sensitive to others' concerns about change	
explains need for change to others/does not explain need for change to others	
introduces change for its own sake/introduces change for sound business reasons	
seeks variety and change but dissipates effort/ seeks variety and change and focuses effort	
creative and focused/creative but unfocused	
self-development wide but unfocused/self-development wide but focused	
other	

Component	Comment
Components of factor 10 (creativity)	
creative and focused/creative and unfocused	
creative and team worker/creative and lone worker	
creative in solving problems (range of valid solutions)/creative in solving puzzles (only one solution)	
creative and requires personal space/creative but will accept direction	
creative and willing to make and admit mistakes/creative but not willing to make mistakes	
creative and entrepreneurial/creative but not entrepreneurial	
creative and self-starter/creative but not self-starter	
creative and needs personal creative space/creative and does not need personal creative space	
creative and requires structure/creative and dislikes structure	
creative and communicates ideas/creative and cannot communicate ideas	
creative and fights for ideas/creative but does not push ideas	
creative and ideas in mainstream/creative and ideas out of mainstream	

Component	Comment
creative and wants to help develop and exploit ideas/creative but no interest in developing ideas	
creative and diffused/creative and concentrated	
manages changes of focus suggested by creative ideas/cannot manage change of focus suggested by creative ideas	
creative and influence drives together focus on organization's objectives/creative and influence drives together ignore organization's objectives	
creative activity very narrowly focused/creative activity wide ranging	
creativity stimulated by need for personal growth/creativity separate form need for personal growth	
creativity stimulated by job interest/job interest irrelevant to creativity	
other	

Components of factor 11 (self-development)	
effective when job and personal development needs concur/effective when job and personal needs do not concur	

Component	Comment
self-development and work financial goals converge/self-development and work financial goals diverge	
demands autonomy within a defined (professional) area/demands autonomy in all areas	
need for self-development occurs in defined area/need for self-development occurs in wide area	
need for self-development towards deep and narrow/need for self-development towards wide but shallow	
high self-development and self-contained/high self-development but develops as part of team	
uses self-development to gain recognition/does not use self-development to gain recognition	
actively learns self-development lessons from work/fails to learn self-development lessons from work	
likes self-development to take place in measurable areas/likes self-development to take place in non-measurable areas	
likes to learn on the job/likes to learn off the job	
uses self-development to increase influence over others/uses self-development for own purpose	

Component	Comment
attention to self-development inhibits ability to delegate/attention to self-development does not affect ability to delegate	
need for self-development inhibits ability to undertake repetitive work/need for self-development does not affect ability to undertake repetitive work	
high self-development high creativity/high self-development low creativity	
strong personal development weak organizational goals/strong personal development strong organizational goals	
needs personal self-development space/does not need personal development space	
self-development requires interesting work/self-development does not require interesting work	
other	

Components of factor 12 (interest and usefulness)	
requires job interest to be committed/does not require job interest to be committed	
interested regardless of the personal financial implication/interested but committed to personal financial targets	

Component	Comment
has deep understanding of their personal job interest/has poor understanding of their personal job interest	
concentrates on personal job interests regardless of organization's needs/concentrates on organization's needs rather than personal job interests	
effective when personal interests and job needs coincide/effective when job interests conflict with organization's needs	
tension between job interests and organization procedures/no tension between job interests and organization procedures	
job interests exclude others/job interests embrace others	
job interests focus on people/job interests focus on tasks	
job interests influenced by need for organizational recognition/job interests not influenced by need for organizational recognition	
requires job interest to achieve/does not require job interest to achieve	
pursuit of their job interests beneficial to organization/pursuit of their job interests does not benefit organization	
focus of job interests narrow/job interests wide	

Component	Comment
narrow focus of job interest prevents wider view/able to take wide view	
development of job interests increases ability to exercise influence/development of job interest has no impact on ability to exercise influence	
focus of job interest changes/focus of job interest constant	
pursuit of job interest leads to creative insights/pursuit of job interest does not lead to creative insights	
learns regardless of job interest/only learns when interested	
other	

The selection interview

As part of the interview process, after they have completed the Profile, we ask candidates to think about the motivational aspects of their *existing* job. Since it is difficult for candidates to think unprompted, we give them this outline of the motivation process and ask them to write up to 500 words, using the list given in Table 2 on pages 245–6 as a prompt. We explain that the list is not comprehensive and they may introduce any other motivational factors they think are relevant, or ignore factors which they regard as irrelevant. We ask candidates to give their name, job title and brief (three line maximum) description of their existing job. The questions we then ask candidates to consider are:

- Given the same resources in the job, which motivational need, if enhanced or reduced, would be most likely to double or halve job effectiveness?
- Which is the next motivational need which, if enhanced or reduced, would be next most likely to double or halve job effectiveness?
- Which motivational need, if enhanced or reduced, would make no difference to job effectiveness?

Table 2   *Using the components of motivation in a selection interview*

Factor/Need	High need	Low Need
1. Money and tangible rewards	Obsessive need for high salary and tangible rewards; desire to have a job with good benefits and perks; concentrates energies and conversation on monetary rewards of job	Spends little energy thinking about monetary reward; largely indifferent to money as a motivator
2. Physical conditions	Needs good working conditions and surroundings; constant complaints if not physically comfortable	Largely indifferent to physical surroundings
3. Structure	Need for rules and structure; need to reduce uncertainty and establish guidelines; wants to know procedures and rules for compliance	Finds rules and structure restrictive; wants freedom; happy with ambiguity; feels no need for compliance
4. People contact	Need for light social contact with a wide range of people	Feels no compelling need for company (not to be confused with inability to work with other people if necessary)
5. Relationships	Need to form and sustain long-term relationships with a small number of people	Feels no need to establish or maintain deep relationships (again not to be confused with inability to work with people over the long term if necessary)
6. Recognition	Overwhelming need for constant recognition and appreciation by others; can inhibit effectiveness, unwilling to give recognition to others	Indifferent to other people's views about them; possibly insensitive to others
7. Achievement	Deep personal need to set self challenging goals and to achieve them; unhappy if nothing to achieve; requires constant achievement stimulation; may be loner	No motivation for achievement; world passes them by
8. Power and influence	Strong impulse to influence others, sometimes to empower, sometimes to control; power drive dominates personality	No wish to attempt or to exercise influence

Factor/Need	High Need	Low Need
9. Variety and change	Need for constant variety, change and stimulation; avoids routine; keeps a high level of arousal and vigilance; can tend to leave projects and tasks incomplete	Happy to tolerate the mundane and boring
10. Creativity	Explorative, creative and open-minded; curious and thinks divergently	Little need for creative thinking and not much practice; lacks curiosity; can be closed minded
11. Self-development	Passionate need to grow and develop as an individual; assesses work in terms of its contribution to his or her personal growth	Does what is required, does not assess in terms of contribution to personal development; little personal growth takes place
12. Interest and usefulness	Needs to feel work is intrinsically interesting and useful and wants an element of social utility before committing to do the work	Will do work regardless of its intrinsic interest or usefulness

Working with others

Our motivational needs influence how we interact with other people. More precisely, we tend to project our own needs on to others, whether or not our needs resonate with, or are even remotely relevant to, what they need. Thus the person with high structure needs is likely to project those needs on to others. The message is simply, 'I have high structure needs. I will treat you as if you have high structure needs too'.

As you can imagine, if both parties have similar needs, matters can progress smoothly. The problem starts when one party projects dissonant needs on to the other. The low structure recipient of high structure demands may resent the demands that are being imposed, and immediately we have the possibility of conflict, or at the very least, a lack of empathy. In order to get on with others, certainly motivate others, one should bury one's own needs and concentrate on satisfying theirs. The situation varies with each factor, so let us look at each in turn.

Factor 1 (money and tangible rewards)

As far as projection is concerned factor 1 has all the properties of corrosive acid. It affects everything. At one extreme high factor 1 sustains the view that everybody else is motivated by money. Those who share similar views are either seen as complicit, with the attitude that we will judge others accordingly, or the relationship is seen as potentially exploitative. Alternatively, it is instrumental; that is we will relate to the extent that there is financial benefit. In contrast, if people do something that does not have a monetary outcome, then the people concerned are foolish and probably being exploited. Alternatively, there is always a hidden motive and the payoff will come later. 'All the world has its price' is the watchword. Midas was right. Everything turned to gold, never mind the consequences. Cynicism will rule the day.

At the other extreme, we have those for whom money is not a primary motivator. Their outlook is probably mixed. They may attempt to project their non-monetary needs, but could find themselves exploited and learn some hard lessons. Most will either glumly regret the fact that some seem to make money but they cannot, and they are disadvantaged, or they will surround themselves with those of like mind and put the subject as far out of sight as they can.

Some, of course, will have low motivation but plenty of money. They probably feel removed from the pressures that affect so many others and are likely to have a relaxed attitude, though perhaps learning to be on their guard against those who need money and are prepared to fight for it. In the middle, there are those with a moderate need for money. They would like to have enough to maintain what they regard as a fair standard of living, but they are not prepared to sacrifice other needs which they regard as important. University teachers could find themselves in this bracket. They might find themselves projecting a sense of unfairness on to others.

It is reasonable to say that in modern society money influences the choice and attitude of everybody, whether or not they have a high need. Even the supremely indifferent have to adapt to a lifestyle that reflects their situation.

Factor 2 (physical conditions)

There are probably no particular lessons, within the world of work, to be drawn. It is possible that the boss with low factor 2 will house her staff in the business equivalent of the pigsty. On the other hand, if business requires a pleasant physical ambience, she is likely to supply it. Conversely, the boss with high factor 2 may well house himself in a plush office, but regard the expense of housing his staff in equivalent accommodation as financially unrealistic. He will suppress his need to project his own feelings on to others!

Factor 3 (structure)

We will look at the outer limits first and then at the more common position. Taken to extremes, projection can be an uncomfortable experience. Consider somebody, and there are fortunately very few in this position, with very high factor 3. Such is their need for imposed structure that they almost require institutional living, with their lives guided by detailed rules of behaviour. What are they likely to project on to others? On to those to whom they have given, or those who have taken, the authority to control their lives, they project a need to be told what to do. They can be seen standing there waiting for instructions. To those outside the nexus of control, they may project passivity. They already know what is required.

Those with the same intensity of need who are unsatisfied probably project their desperate need for structure on to almost anybody with whom they come into contact. They may prefer to join rule-bound organizations. Their conversation is likely to be sprinkled with 'oughts' and 'musts'. Those who deal with them may have the feeling that they are victims of a take-over bid, that they are being ushered into somebody else's area of control. You may have experienced the feeling when somebody from a religious sect knocks at your door and tries to convert you.

At the other extreme, there are people who have no need for structure. They will project no expectations on to others and are probably extremely tolerant. Given the chance, they will, for example, set up private schools (they do exist but will not be named for legal reasons) where, as a matter of philosophy, there are no rules and people can do exactly what they want. They can learn if they wish to, play sport all day if they can persuade others to join them. They will be given the opportunity to explore their way through life and, it is hoped, establish sensible minimal rules for living. Such tolerance, to be completely consistent, should extend even to those who may cause them harm. Since this is an unlikely state of affairs, except to those with masochistic tendencies, how is it managed? Most likely, people will withdraw themselves from those whose behaviour may damage them. Their preference will be to associate with those who have low structure but whose behaviour, whatever it may be, will not harm them.

Low structure people will not feel the need for order, but some of them will still be perfectly capable of imposing the organization necessary for a job to function. It is just that imposing order is not their preference. Others, of course, will be incapable of imposing even the minimum order. Those in the middle will project a medium need for structure on to those with a very high need and recoil at attempts to drag themselves further in; and likewise when they project on to those with very low structure.

To motivate others, we need to think about those other people's structure needs, irrespective of our own preferences. To be fully successful we will have to balance their personal needs with the structure needs of the job, sometimes that can be quite a delicate business.

Factor 4 (people contact)

The highly sociable will naturally project sociability on to others. From those who are like minded, sociability will be projected back. Even those who are less sociable are probably given the benefit of the doubt. Some of those in turn, and in spite of themselves, may be minded to respond positively; others will move away quickly in order to restore their relative peace and tranquillity! Those who are highly sociable but empathic will respond sympathetically. The less empathic will carry on regardless until they infuriate. Those with low sociability probably take an instrumental view of others. Their expectation is that affairs will be conducted correctly, but there will be no expectation of chitchat beyond what is necessary to get the job done. Any attempts to go beyond that will be greeted with a wan smile and withdrawal.

Factor 5 (relationships)

This is an interesting factor. By definition, all attempts to form social relationships require reciprocity. With factor 4, sociability, this may not be too much of a problem. People just move on. To form long-term relationships requires time. Those with high factor 5 are likely to be projecting the need constantly. Relationships are likely to begin on the basis that potentially they might continue and there will probably be an element of sociability. People will be encouraged to come back. No doubt there is constant disappointment, but probably in the nature of things not too much hard feeling.

Those with low factor 5 may or may not be sociable. In their dealings with people there will be no expectation of longer-term horizons. There may be a small core of people with whom there are long-term relationships, family members and one or two others, but generally there will be no drive to establish a more permanent position in the scheme of things. Possibly, to the extent that commitment implies the long term, there will be reduced commitment and actions will be ordered accordingly. The job will be done, and perhaps done very well, but there may be a tendency not to give the last drop of blood.

Factor 6 (recognition)

The need for recognition which, in terms of projection, we might think of as the fight for self-esteem, is an important player in life. Those with the extreme need attach a reply-paid card to all their communications, which ends with the question 'Haven't I done well?' The response to their request depends on whom they are communicating with. If it is to somebody with an equally high need, the question will probably be ignored and perhaps even returned. We could then either have an endless dialogue of the deaf, which is not very interesting so people move on or switch off; or the formation of a mutual admiration society. In the most successful of these societies, the rules are very simple. Each takes it in turn to express approval, taking care not to detract from the approval of others. This last condition is hard to achieve, approval given to somebody else frequently being seen as approval withdrawn from 'me', and the society AGMs are likely to be stormy.

High recognition needs probably introduce a competitive element into relationships. People are not enjoyed for their own sake, but are regarded as instrumental in the fight for attention. Failure to fulfil the need can lead to disruptive behaviour, if it is possible to indulge in it, or sullen acquiescence bolstered by a feeling of deprivation. Unrequited high recognition needs are the precursor of poor personal relationships.

For those with a low need for recognition, there will be, in extreme cases, an indifference to how communication is presented. 'These are the facts and that's that!' will be the approach. However, the low recognition drive means there is no competition with others for attention and a more profitable approach, well in keeping with the low drive, is to communicate in a way which recognizes the needs, including the recognition needs, of the person being addressed. For those whose recognition needs are in the middle, failure to oblige them will lead to a mild feeling of disappointment. Life will not be as good as it could be, but we can cope. If recognition is provided, life is suddenly so much better.

Factor 7 (achievement)

Projection in one sense is not a major problem with the achievement drive, which concerns 'doing it myself'. If others do not want to achieve, that is up to them. But, from the comfort point of view, the high achiever probably wants to associate with those of like mind. After all, they will all be talking the language of achievement. Whatever the response from others, the high achiever will not let go of this wish to do it him or herself. Thus with other high achievers, we will see, where possible, competition. 'Let's see who can do it best'. Both sides will be happy with the arrangement.

In interacting with medium achievers, where the competitive challenge is not picked up quickly or well enough, the task will be removed and completed by the high achiever. The medium achiever will not be happy but will have to put up with it. The low achiever will let them get on with it. 'You want to achieve, fine by me, I have some serious dreaming to do.' Both sides again will be happy with the arrangement. High achievement finds low achievement dull. There is none of the excitement of effort expended and targets attained. Low achievers wonder what all the fuss is about.

The position with low achievers is more complex. Taking low achievement on its own, the tendency may be to project low expectations on to others. However, if combined with a high influence drive, the tendency may be to attempt to empower others. The situation will be explored more fully in the next section.

Factor 8 (power and influence)

Factor 8, the need to influence others, by definition, involves projection. In the chapter on Power and influence, we discussed how this need can be used, for good or ill, to empower or to dominate, with or without purpose. Where influence is used to achieve a purpose, and the drive is strong, it can arouse the achievement drive in others. Achievement is a significant aid to purpose. Likewise, the influence drive can be used to energize all the other factors necessary. For example, it can reinforce people's need for money, or variety, or structure or whatever is necessary for the purpose to be realized. Where somebody has a very high purposeful influence drive, its projection is likely to override all the other drives that are simultaneously being projected.

Where the influence drive is strong and is used without purpose, it has more connection with dominance than empowerment. It can mean frustrating other people's drives. The projection will be negative. Others' legitimate attempts to achieve will be undermined by, for example, a deliberate failure to give clear objectives, thus making non-achievement an opportunity for recrimination. Others' need for influence, which in a benign situation can be used to help realize goals, will be suppressed as an unwelcome challenge. Unnecessary structural demands will be imposed as an aid to creating frustration. The objective will be to dominate and create dependence.

Where the influence drive is weaker, what is projected can compete with all the other factors that are being projected at the same time. Thus, for example, it will compete with structural and achievement needs. It is possible to argue that the influence drive is weak to the extent that it is undermined by projection of all other competing drives, some of which may happen to work against what is required.

Factor 9 (variety and change)

Projection here is very straightforward. Those with a high need for variety will project that need on to others and expect reciprocation. If it is not forthcoming, they will move on or stay with scarcely disguised intolerance; they have failed to achieve the stimulation they require. People whose need is low will project a desire for stability and, if it is not reciprocated, will suffer stress, probably avoiding the person who caused it if they can. The position is simple, fast movers get stimulation from fast movers, and those who like to stand and stare prefer the same. This does not mean that fast movers cannot form good relations with those unlike themselves. They can. The classic example is Mrs Thatcher and Denis. However Mrs T surrounded herself with other fast movers. Denis clearly satisfied some other need.

Factor 10 (creativity)

As with those who need variety, the creative like to surround themselves with the like minded. That is where they get their stimulation. Those with low creativity may not be in the same position. They may not feel the need for creativity, but can still enjoy, as a spectacle, the creativity of others. Otherwise they will be happy to be associated with the less creative.

Factor 11 (self-development)

The need to develop and have sufficient autonomy are powerful drives. The message we will project on to others is 'help me to develop'. At one extreme, people will be used as if they were learning opportunities. At the highest levels we will be talking of a community of scholars. Self-development will be perceived as reinforcing autonomy and self-sufficiency. It will not quite be *cogito, ergo sum* (I think, therefore I am), more that, 'if I can be confident within myself, I can relate to you in a relaxed manner'.

The trouble is that the drive rarely reaches satiety. There is always more to learn, there are always people more developed than ourselves. There are momentary plateaux, then the sunny uplands beckon us and the struggle recommences. At worst, the high self-developer could project anxiety, 'I haven't quite arrived'. Or, 'You are infringing my autonomy, back off'. At best, the drive could work as a partnership. 'Let us work together and both of us can develop.' If the projection is on to others who themselves do not have such a drive, then the echo is likely to fade away. The message is 'You have nothing to contribute', and the relationship withers.

Factor 12 (interest and usefulness)

This factor has the highest average scores. The tendency will be to project and hope that the response is positive, 'Yes, we share a concern for usefulness and interest'. Of course, views as to what is useful and interesting vary. Probably, the greatest resonance will be found with those on the same wavelength. But even for those who are not, there will probably be sympathy if not empathy. Where the others have little concern for use or interest, there will be puzzlement as to how people can live in what is seen as a mental and moral vacuum; followed by withdrawal.

Summary

Interpersonal relationships can be seen as a Darwinian struggle between competing projections. Of these the influence drive is the one which overtly seeks to master, for good or ill, all others. All the other drives attempt, implicitly, to realize themselves by imposing their imperative on others. 'I need structure, you need it too' is the message and the reply ranges from 'Yes please, let's tango', to 'Go away, I would rather do business on my terms and they are different'. The constant interplay, benignly, leads to motivation, or perversely, to frustration. The path to motivational success is to play to others' needs, not to our own. But the path is rocky and our needs are great. So we ignore others' needs and the result at work is that many lead lives of quiet desperation.

If managers wish to change this situation, to reach the pleasant pastures of mutual recognition of diversity of interest and motivation, how do they do it?

Firstly, by recognizing that the diversity exists. This alone helps you to stop trying to motivate others with incentives couched in your own terms. The manager must offer what is valuable to recipients in their terms and in a manner which meets their perception of what makes the offer acceptable. For example, to offer an employee more money for doing work because you feel that you would like someone to do the same to you, is not wise if that person rates money low on their motivational scale of values. It could, at best, leave them feeling unimpressed, at worst to put them off the task you are offering. For success you put aside your own set of values and offer them an incentive to do the work that reflects theirs.

In motivation you do *not* do unto others what you would have them do unto you. Motivation is neither charity nor fair dealing; motivation involves putting yourself in the place of the other person and seeing the world as they see it. It is the first, essential stage of good negotiation.

Appendices

Appendix 1

The theoretical framework

In this appendix we show how our own thoughts and some 60 years of work by others helped us arrive at our own definition of motivation which is that *motivation is the drive behind the satisfaction of basic human needs and that such drives are specific to the individual*. We will discuss the difficulties inherent in working in the field of motivation and how we and our predecessors have attempted to tackle them. As we are interested in motivation study applied to work, we describe the major theories, relating them to our study and to each other, and give a brief description of some of the minor contributions. We start with a general discussion of motivation.

The background

In one sense all behaviour by human beings is motivated, but the term excludes unconscious or subconscious movements, such as reflexes and automatic reactions. Motivation implies an element of purpose and so is volitional. It is a drive or impulse to act and sometimes not to act at all. This urge to satisfy a need or want or to avoid pain or danger can be assumed to lie beneath all human actions.

Motivation is a complex subject, and a difficult area of study. Unfortunately, something so basic and all-pervading is not easy to define, classify and measure. For example, when we say that a person lacks motivation (and we usually do so in relation to something *we* wish them to do, like work), we really mean that they are motivated to do other things, like not to work, or at least not to work very efficiently or effectively. If a person is motivated by things which do not seem sensible or acceptable to us, we consider them to be unmotivated (or if their satisfactions appear to arise out of behaviour that is illogical, incongruous or disgusting, we may consider them to be mad). Generalizations about what motivates people are unwise. It is far more fruitful to assume that individuals are all motivated differently as a result of particular ancestry, background and experience. For this reason, theories of motivation which attempt to make general laws of wide applicability are not very useful to managers seeking to understand the behaviour of the individuals they work with.

Difficulties in measuring/studying motivation are as follows:

- The words used to define motivation are imprecise and open to different interpretations. In this appendix we show the approaches used by workers in the field as diverse as Freud, Maslow, Hull, Herzberg and Vroom.

- It is virtually impossible to separate the person as a worker from their other social roles. One difference between work and non-work is compulsion or necessity, another is the payment given by an organization or one person to another to perform tasks for them; yet another is that many people leave home and go to a place where their time and energies are, at least theoretically, at the disposal of someone else. We have looked at motivation at work, though we recognize that non-work drivers, like achievement, are probably present both at work and outside work. Freud and Hull do not distinguish between work and non-work. Maslow, Herzberg and Vroom look specifically at motivation at work. We recognize that to be effective at work requires not only motivation but capability, skill and competence.

- Measuring motivation at one time gives insight only into current feelings; a reading at a later date is likely to be different; recently experienced feelings (of anger, annoyance or pleasure in achievement) affect the way an individual responds, giving a Profile biased towards current events. We have tried to distinguish between the effects of current and long-term influences on people's motivation Profiles. For example, we thought structure needs might have increased between 1989–93 and 1994–98, times when the demands of restructuring and change seemed to have exacerbated the stress on the workforce. We found no such increase (see Appendix 2 on The making of the Profile).

- Differences in scores recorded at different times may be accounted for by a change in the attitudes and feelings of the individual, but the reason for the changes may be hard to establish. For example, structure needs (factor 3) seem to vary slightly over time for some people, especially with life changes. There is no way of checking whether differences in scores have occurred because the person has changed or because their circumstances are different.

- People find it hard to distinguish their true motivation for actions; we have very effective methods of defence and rationalization, including denial, to maintain mental equilibrium. Festinger (cognitive dissonance) and Vroom (expectancy theory) write about this and we describe their theories later in this appendix.

- The job and the work itself will affect motivation. We are all influenced by our experiences. The culture and structure of an organization will also enhance or inhibit our motivational drives. This is again described very well by Vroom.

- There are no realities or absolute measures possible. Motivation involves feelings on the part of those who are motivated and those who are assessing their motivation, although in the work environment, competence, capability and potentiality are influential. We consider the extent to which it is impossible to assess 'absolute' measurement in the chapter on Selection.

We will now look at how recent research and writing on the operation of the brain support the idea that needs and emotions have temporal primacy over rationality.

Motivation and the brain

As a general rule the brain evolved in a successive manner with the oldest part at the base (top of the spinal cord) and later parts superimposed. Part of the ancient limbic system, the *amygdala*, is the emotional centre. Primitive and instinctive, it is the part involved in feelings. The two-layered *cortex* is the part of the brain that plans, understands information coming from the senses and is able to co-ordinate movement. The *neocortex* is the most recently developed part which gives us the ability of being able to think. Here information is gathered and processed, allowing us to comprehend our thoughts and to make sense of them (Goleman, 1996).

When a signal is perceived by the eye, the message goes straight to the *thalamus* where it is relayed to the visual cortex for processing. At the same time a shorter and cruder message is sent to the amygdala, but this is received before the neocortex receives its message. The amygdala gets a few precious split seconds' prior notice of anything which may have an emotional aspect. In this way something perceived as threatening, say an approaching car, can be dealt with very quickly. The amygdala sends a signal for us to respond to the threat by freezing where we stand, to run or to lie down in the road and submit and is able to do it before the neocortex has even decoded the information, never mind produced a rational response. In other words, our emotional brain gets the chance to react to signals first (Le Doux, 1992). Similar considerations apply to those messages received via the other senses.

This is of the utmost importance for motivation. Broadly, the message is, look after the emotions and feelings first, let rationality follow. In so far as motivation concerns feelings, the brain gives a temporal primacy to motivation. Now let us look at how Freud saw the conflict between the forces of rationality and feeling.

Freudian psychology and motivation

According to Freud, the psyche is divided into three main areas: the id, the ego and the superego (Freud, 1934 as interpreted by Stafford-Clark, 1967). The *id* represents our instinctive, animal nature and drives us to satisfy our appetites.

Many motivational drives come from the id. The *ego* is a construct which lets us perceive ourselves as an individual separate from others and map out our unique place in the world. The *superego* is a set of instructions, positive and negative, built up over time and derived from authority figures in our lives which operates as a rough rule book in guiding our decisions and actions. These three operate independently and often conflict, leading to the popular joke that the Freudian view of the mind is a dark attic where a sex-crazed monkey and a frigid maiden aunt are locked in eternal conflict.

This is the realm of motivation, where the id and its instinctive drives underlie superimposed layers of individuality and inhibition. Suppose you want to buy a new car. Your id is likely to be the part of your brain urging you to have the sporty, red, gas-guzzling roadster capable of 0–60 miles per hour in 4.5 seconds. Your ego may be leaning towards a metallic silver-blue piece of super-engineering which announces to the world that you are someone to be reckoned with, especially if you can add some individualistic styling that marks your car out as unusual. Your superego will be cautioning you to pay less, make certain it has good safety features, get a long warranty and choose the large boot space and adult-sized rear seating. The car you eventually buy will depend on your management of these three warring factions as well as the added urgings of those family and friends who feel they have a right to comment on your purchase decision.

Let us assume that our product is a standard, family, cheap, mass-produced saloon and that our prospective purchaser is a man aged 28 with a partner and one child. Although he may wish to buy a red, sporty model (id), he is likely to be under strong influence to buy something 'sensible' (superego). Adding in his needs for individual distinction from the crowd (ego), how can the makers of a car reconcile such motivational differences? Firstly, the car must be cheap, with reasonable petrol consumption. Secondly, space must be well-planned with fancy styling and aerodynamics subordinate to internal comfort. So far the superego is winning. What about ego needs? How about offering a range of 'personalization' possibilities? These can be minor and cheap, but their importance can far outweigh their cost. Then, and only then, the id? We can use this thinking to analyse a typical car advertisement.

We could show an advertisement with a man driving his car to a remote beach where a glamorous woman meets him. As they kiss he bends her backwards against the bodywork of the car, she submits … *fade to heavy atmospheric music* (id). Cut to the man back in the car arriving home at a very large and pleasant mansion (old stone, ivied walls, long driveway). He goes into the house, greets two little children (hug and kiss) on the way. '*Hello, where's your mother?*' (superego). Cut to the interior and the same woman from the beach shot appears, smiling mysteriously against soft, gold backlighting (Mona Lisa?). Well done, Renault! Building on motivational research into car purchase in America in the mid-twentieth century – 'every man buys a wife, but really wants a mistress' – two conflicting drives can be reconciled.

Motivation and work performance

One of the first useful pieces of work on motivation applied to work performance was published by Yerkes and Dodson (1908). They formulated their law of the optimal level of arousal for motivated behaviour. According to this law, high motivation leads to good performance on easy tasks, but moderate motivation leads to the best performance on complex tasks.

Learning theory and motivation

Learning theory has close links to the study of motivation: many of the things that impel us to action rest on previous learning. For example, success in a task, even if inadvertent or accidental, will predispose us to want to do the task again. Conversely, failure in a task or an unpleasant experience while doing it, will predispose us to not want to do it again. If the failure was caused by the fact that we could not affect the outcome, no matter what effort or stratagem we adopted, we would be likely to learn helplessness and, in certain cases, to become depressed (Seligman, 1975). Although it is not realistically possible to separate the motivation of the individual at work from their motivation in social and domestic settings, some landmark work has been done over the years. One of the best known is that of Maslow.

The hierarchy of needs

Generally regarded as the father of modern motivation theory applied to work, Maslow formulated his 5-factor theory of motivation around 1940. Alternatively sketched as a pyramid (Figure 21) or as a series of superimposed waves, this simple but clever classification has had wide application and great impact on management thinking over the past 60 years (Maslow, 1943).

The first three needs are most closely related to Freud's id; esteem and self-actualization relate broadly to the ego. The theory is that you will satisfy a lower level of need before a higher; there is therefore a preponderance of needs. It makes sense that if you are very hungry or thirsty (physiological needs), you will not concern yourself with the greater development of your mind (self-actualization) until you have eaten and drunk. Such a simple step function does have its limitations. Many people do not follow the logical progression, satisfying a need at one level and then neatly moving up to the next. Maslow devised his theory with people at work in mind, and it has been used, some say too widely, to illuminate the motivation of people working at many levels and in many different kinds of work. Critics of its applicability should be reminded that for many workers the 1990s have seen a descent to a lower level of need: that of safety and security. A

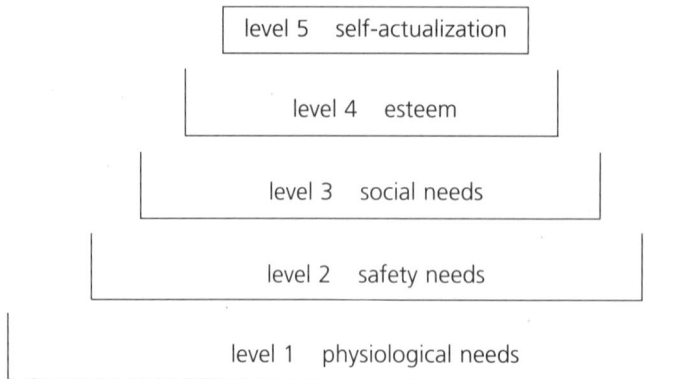

Figure 21   Maslow's hierarchy of needs

large number of people who were more concerned with higher level motivators, such as status and promotion, have reverted to a concern with the second level safety needs as they have seen colleagues lose their jobs and realize that the employment climate continues to be frosty.

Alderfer (1972) modified and extended Maslow's work on motivation, but suggested that there were three basic groups of needs: existence, relatedness and growth. This *ERG* theory of motivation classed Maslow's first two levels – physiological and safety needs – together as *Existence*, his next level – social and esteem needs – as *Relatedness* and his final level – self-actualization – as *Growth*. In addition Alderfer split motivation into two forms: chronic and episodic. Chronic motivation refers to constant underlying influences, say physical discomfort like arthritis or a lifetime ambition to become CEO of a large company. Episodic motivation occurs sporadically; hunger, for example, or the urge to diet on seeing oneself in the bathroom mirror.

Drive theory

Hull, under-reported in the literature of business and management, but valued by fellow psychologists, experimented on animals to derive his theory of motivation, originally a simple equation:

$$motivation = drive \times habit$$

and later redefined as:

$$motivation = drive \times habit \times incentive$$

He identified *priming* as a precursor to increased motivation: like the concept of pump priming, used to seed projects, Hull demonstrated that a small incentive stimulus, given to subjects early on in an experiment, resulted in an increased drive to perform the same behaviour later. It seems that priming serves as a reminder of the good or bad qualities of the incentive (Hull, 1951).

Theory X and Y

Working in the 1950s, McGregor formulated his Theory X and Y. He categorized attitudes by supervisors and management into two lists, the underlying assumptions of which are given below (McGregor, 1960). McGregor's publication of his views of managers' attitudes towards their workers caused a stir. Many companies recognized themselves with discomfort as belonging to the 'X' category and some tried to improve their human relations procedures and practices. The main problem with Theory X assumptions is that they are self-fulfilling. Regarding workers as candidates for Theory X assumptions patronizes

X	Y
People dislike work and will avoid it if they can	People do not dislike work, it is natural to expend effort in work
They are naturally inclined to be lazy	If someone feels committed to the aims of the work, they do not need coercion
Because of this, it is management's job to coerce or otherwise use external means of control to get them to do what the organisation needs in the way of output	The rewards for work can include commitment to organisational objectives
Most people want security and wish to avoid responsibility; they prefer to be directed	Under the right conditions, people will seek responsibility
	Many people have the capacity to exercise creativity in solving organisational problems
	The way industry is organised (in the middle of the twentieth century), little of the average worker's intellectual potential is tapped

McGregor's Theory X and Y

them and causes the behaviour that is feared; it removes their autonomy and trains them to be dependent and passive.

In more recent times we have been persuaded that things are now different and that Theory Y rules, not X. However, this remains only partly convincing. It seems that when times are hard in industry, there is a reversion to the tenets of Theroy X and that, even in good times, a significant number of companies operate as if these rules still apply. Conversely, companies who tell their workers that they are now empowered, implying a Theory Y culture, but who do not provide the necessary support system of an atmosphere of trust and indemnification from risk, are paying lip service to openness, while acting from the basis of Theory X.

Motivation–Hygiene theory

Working at the end of the 1950s and into the early 1960s, Herzberg (1966) surveyed a sample of 200 professional accountants and engineers in America, asking them to describe incidents or events at work which had resulted in job satisfaction or dissatisfaction. Instead of a single list of items which could be either good or bad, their responses led Herzberg to distinguish two scales of measurement: one for things which contributed positively to job satisfaction, which he termed *Motivators*, and one for incidents which did not contribute positively (apart from in the short term) but which could cause dissatisfaction if wrong; these he termed *Hygiene Factors*.

This Motivation–Hygiene theory cast strong doubt on the assumption that money was the main factor in motivating a workforce. For certain classes of worker, in this case professional people, Herzberg was able to show that the drive for money was not a motivator, only a dissatisfier if too low. Many a manager has sought to motivate a member of staff by offering a pay increase only to find that the job has not been done better nor is the worker happier after, perhaps, a short-term spurt of enthusiasm.

Hygiene factors	Motivators
DISSATISFACTION (if not met)	SATISFACTION (if met)
Company policy and administration	Achievement
Supervision	Recognition
Working conditions	The work itself
Salary	Responsibility
Status	Advancement
Relationships with colleagues	Growth

Herzberg's Motivation – Hygiene theory

Job enrichment

Job enrichment grew out of Herzberg's work. Many routine or repetitive jobs were redesigned to include more responsibility. For example, workers used to doing one simple task in a series were trained to do a wider range of tasks, or even to do every task so that they had the satisfaction of completing a component or even of making a whole product. Empowerment is perhaps the white-collar, modern equivalent of job enrichment.

Other workers in the field added to the research started by Herzberg. For example, Deci (1971), researching on what happens when you pay people to do work they would normally do for the intrinsic job interest, found that their motivation was lowered.

Attribution theory

Emerging from and building upon drive theories, attribution theories of motivation presumed that humans are 'scientific' in their assessment of the world and how their own actions might lead to a goal. If they could attribute success in a task as of their own making, they would be further motivated to do it. Conversely, if they perceived that external factors in their environment had affected the outcome and that their input was not of much or any use, they would be less motivated to continue (Heider, 1958; Kelley, 1967).

The idea that responsibility for our actions reinforces motivation makes sense. If I run for a mile in less time than ever before, I congratulate myself and envisage a future as a professional athlete. If I am then told that the track was downhill, we had a strong tail wind and record low levels of air pollution, and that several of my friends completed the mile in less time than I did, I may moderate my sense of achievement. I can no longer attribute my success to my own efforts entirely and this is likely to adversely affect my motivation in the future.

Achievement drives

Particularly interested in social motives, McClelland and other researchers working in the 1960s suggested that the motivation to achieve is a stable characteristic which predisposes people to a general tendency to approach success (McClelland, 1961). Extended by Atkinson (1964) and Feather (1967), three other variables were included:

1. The expectation of success.
2. An incentive dependent on the kind of perceived success.
3. The perception of personal responsibility for success.

If two people are generally motivated to achieve, one might desire recognition and public acclaim and the other to seek the satisfaction of a job well done; the path is different, but the objective the same.

To measure these drives, TAT or Thematic Apperception Tests were devised. These consisted of ambiguous drawings showing, for example, a man sitting, looking forwards, with a window in front of him and a picture of a woman and two children in a frame on the desk. Subjects were asked to write a story about the picture, describing what had happened before it took place, what was happening in the picture and what might happen in the future. The stories were then interpreted by psychologists to identify projected feelings from subjects. For example, if someone described the man as contemplating the successful completion of a report and its enthusiastic reception by the Board at a meeting later, this could be assumed to indicate that the subject showed achievement motivation. Presumably, someone who described him as looking out of the window and wondering if it would stay fine so that he could leave early for a turn on the golf links would score rather lower! Two criticisms of TAT tests are, firstly, that the person interpreting the test filters what they read through their own perception and motivation and, secondly, that the subject's perceptions are strongly affected by the style of the drawing and the objects represented. One of the authors, the only female in a group of 24 men on a management course some years ago, was taking the TAT test and found it hard to write an unbiased story about a man, perceived as over-formally dressed, with a military haircut, who kept a picture of a woman and two children on his desk, and nothing else!

In the later 1960s Horner posited a theory of the fear of failure, applying it to working women with high achievement drives (Horner, 1968, 1969). Perhaps a symptom of the times, this supposed difference between men and women has not been upheld in later studies (Weiner, 1992). Although our own work shows a difference on factor 1 (salary and tangible rewards) where women scored lower on average than men for Phase 1, this magnitude of difference was not replicated for the study as a whole. Another important contributor, Vroom, acknowledged the individuality of motivation. He specifically recognized the significance for appropriate work-related skills. His work is thus closest to ours, though he does not list specific motivational drivers.

Expectancy theory

In the mid-1960s Vroom suggested that people have both preferences and expectations and that their motivation is strongly affected by the interaction of these, linked to a rational attempt to achieve goals. He said that most motivational goals have two levels, a first and a second outcome: the second level is the desired end goal and the first level outcome is perceived as a necessary precursor for that goal. For example, I may have a preference to move out of the records department into public relations at work. This is my second level outcome. If many people in the public relations department have qualifications in journalism, film and media studies, I could assume that a good first level outcome contributing to my goal would be to go to college and to take an appropriate course. On the other hand, if some of the senior staff in the department are related to a senior manager in the company and I am not, my motivation is likely to be adversely affected, as I will perceive the first level outcome necessary for success to be beyond my control.

Vroom summarized his theory with an equation:

$$F = V \times E$$

where F is force (roughly the same as motivation or drive), V is valence, the strength of individual preference for an outcome, and E is the individual's expectancy (as a probability from 0 to 1) that something will lead to a first level outcome.

It is the perception of necessity for the first level outcome and the individual's assessment of their likelihood of achieving it that influences the strength of their motivation. Vroom stressed the importance of distinguishing differences between people's motivation. But, as individual preferences and expectancies differ, use of the model requires that each case be judged on its merits. You can study your own motivation, by examining your feelings, but it is less useful if you seek to establish the motivation of others. This theory raises interesting questions when managers design incentive and reward schemes. Often the pathway to reach second level outcomes is so unclear, even contradictory, that people find it hard to be motivated. Where the route to success is obscure, motivation suffers.

At the beginning of this appendix, we said that people have very effective methods of defence and rationalization, including denial, to maintain mental equilibrium. In effect, their intrinsic drives (id) become satisfied but they deny to themselves what has happened. They rationalize what the superego regards as indefensible. From a motivational point of view, people like to feel that their attitudes and actions are congruent; when they are not, they will take measures to align them. The original proponent of this phenomenon is McGuire (1966) but some very famous work was done by Festinger (1957) with his theory of cognitive dissonance.

Cognitive dissonance

Festinger's study of cognitive dissonance suggests that we like to keep our attitudes and our actions in balance. For example, if I approve of environmental awareness and think that all people should look after the planet, I am likely to experience a mixture of feelings if I do something which contradicts these beliefs: like dropping litter in an area of outstanding natural beauty. This dissonance between my attitudes and behaviour, when brought to my attention, will cause me discomfort and I will seek to dissipate it. I can either choose to deny my behaviour: 'I didn't do it', 'It was accidental', 'I was having an off-day', or to change my attitudes: 'I am not so environmentally conscious that I think one little piece of litter matters'. Whatever I do it will be motivated by my desire to bring my attitudes and behaviour into equilibrium.

Cross-cultural studies of motivation

Differences between national cultures were studied by Hofstede (1994) who classified workers at IBM according to their nationality and questioned them about their attitudes. He devised scales of orientation to such concepts as uncertainty avoidance (closely related to our factor 3, need for structure). Trompenaars and Hampden-Turner (1997) studied managers at Shell who worked in different countries. They found that cultural and motivational differences, especially for monetary reward and incentives, did occur and that it is wise to take account of such differences in devising how people are rewarded locally.

Appendix 2

The making of the Profile

This book is based on formal and informal research carried out over a period of ten years and calls on field work, survey profiling, observation, reading and experience in behavioural and training consultancy. Psychologists from the late nineteenth century through to comments from managers on our latest seminar have all been used to develop and interpret results from the Motivation Profile. Thus, over 100 years of other people's work underpins this study.

The factors

Twelve motivational factors or drivers were chosen. Five or six categories, based loosely on Maslow's work, with some deference to Herzberg, McClelland, Hunt and others, seemed too few for the level of discrimination needed. (See these authors under References at the end of the book.)

In the pilot phase of the study, undertaken in 1987 and 1988, 11 factors were tested. Apart from shuffling of order and changes in nomenclature, the big change was the addition of factor 10, creativity. This was done for two reasons: firstly, it is an activity undervalued and undersupported in business; secondly, it is becoming increasingly useful in our fast-changing world that people should be creative, even if this is only shown in its weaker forms, such as open mindedness. The final order and nomenclature of the 12 factors is given in the list below.

1. Need for high salary, tangible rewards and material goods.

2. Need for good physical working conditions and comfort.

3. Need for structure, feedback and information; the reduction of uncertainty.

4. Need for social contact: light level, many people.

5. Need for stable long-term relationships: deep level/few people.

6. Need for recognition and feedback: social significance.

7. Need to achieve and to set oneself challenging goals.

8. Need to influence and control others; power drive.

9. Need for variety and change/tendency to keep oneself stimulated.

10. Need to be explorative, creative and open-minded.

11. Need for autonomy and to develop as an individual.

12. Need for intrinsically interesting, useful and rewarding work.

For many reasons 12 factors is not an easy number. Several well-meaning consultants pointed out that they would use the Profile extensively (and return large numbers of response forms) if the complexity were reduced. One suggestion was to cut the number of factors to nine, seven or even six, which would have invalidated one of the prime purposes of the exercise: fine discrimination. To illustrate, factors 4 and 5 are often collapsed together to form a composite people-orientation need factor; the number of people whose responses show marked differences here is enough to demonstrate that some vital information is being lost by this compression. Many people who score high on factor 4 do not score high on factor 5 and vice versa. If a person scores high on factor 4 and low on factor 5, it would be a good motivational move for their work to involve contact with a wide range of other people. The constant presence, attention and social intercourse would allow them to satisfy their social needs. A colleague low scoring on factor 4 and high scoring on factor 5 would need less 'buzz' from the crowd and might even find such noise and contact disruptive, affecting concentration and work performance. They would prefer to work within a smaller work team with a membership which was stable over time and whose members they could get to know quite well.

Results and validity

The data gathered from the completion of the form are not absolutes, like bricks of a certain size or amounts of money. Therefore the statistics derived from them are non-parametric, that is they were not subject to useful analysis by hard measures or parameters. There is no point in adding up all the factor results to derive some supposed grand average score, nor in conducting statistical analyses of the chi-square type.

How valid are the findings? Let us begin with the factors themselves. Each factor represents a different scale. That is to say, they are like apples and pears which will not add up. There is little correlation between factors, the strongest correlation being 0.4. This should mean that there is little overlap between factors and that they are reasonably mutually exclusive. But anyone filling in the Profile may read any meaning they like into the words and phrases: they can project their own fears and hopes into each phrase and, although they compare their valuation of one factor with every other factor's attractions in turn, there is no way of knowing what each means to them. It would be comforting to think that a shared language guarantees commonality of understanding, but it does not. In essence, people are scoring on the basis of their own understanding. There is, as is also the case in everyday conversation, no objective standard for what the statements mean. What we are comparing is their understanding of what these motivational drivers mean to them. But, as in everyday conversation, there is a general understanding of what words mean, or at least enough of an understanding for people to draw conclusions from what has been said to them. This is the understanding on which we rely in order to make statements about people's relative preference for one factor compared with another.

The Profile was intended and is proving to be, a practical tool, best used to illuminate a much discussed, but 'soft' and difficult area of study. Like Belbin (1981), observing the actions of managers on Henley Management College's senior executive courses to derive his team roles, these factors have been tested by trial and error. Their validity has been proven by prolonged use for consulting and training in organizations.

As the people who filled in the Profile participated in subsequent workshops and seminars where their own and colleagues' results were analysed, this provided a critical and immediate measure for the face validity of the instrument. Whether or not people felt that the Profile reflected their own view of themselves was also tested, as well as the behaviour of respondents on exercises and in group work where their Profile results could be compared with their observed, and admitted, behaviour.

The people surveyed

The population for the study comprised mature, adult, professional workers and managers from the UK and overseas. By the end of November 1993 1054 responses had been received. These were sorted for completeness and accuracy, and 1000 'best' selected. This first thousand responses provided a workable and sizeable number on which to base further research. Over the period December 1993 to the start of 1998 another 412 responses were collected. These were analysed in the same manner as the first 1000. In the early part of 1998 the 'best' of both sets were collated, deriving a total of 1355 useful, complete and accurate responses. The results are summarized in Table 3 on page 275.

The Profile is truly international. The people filling in the form were from all over the world and were often very difficult to classify by nationality. The countries of origin are listed at the end of this appendix. An example illustrates the point clearly. One respondent on the database works in an international consultancy firm and was born and raised in Italy (of one Italian and one Greek parent). His work base is now Belgium (previously seven years in the USA), but he travels throughout Europe on business. He lives over the border from Belgium in France (for tax and other reasons), has an American wife and holds dual Italian and US citizenship. Such people raised interesting questions:

- Should responses from, say, Italians versus Dutch people be separated out?
- How then would nationality be decided?
- What differences, similarities or features are being sought?

The exercise seemed pointless when, for example, faced with a group of 15 respondents attending a seminar in Vienna, all working in different countries, and mostly born and having lived in a variety of other places internationally. In short, there seemed to be some benefit in deriving variations in Profile results using groups like this: seeking for 'global man or woman', but not much else.

Where there is a point, although the results were surprising, is in cases like Russia, where 24 people attended a seminar in Moscow (from Moscow work bases, many of them born and residing there). Although their results differ markedly from those of the 21 people attending in St Petersburg, this latter is a non-comparable group. Only six were from St Petersburg; most of the others flew in from places like Ekaterinburg (still Russia) and Alm Aty (Kazakhstan, formerly USSR), and were born and raised all over the former Soviet Union from the Black Sea to Sakhalin Island. It would have been interesting to carry out further analysis of the fact that these two groups differed markedly on their scores for factor 3 on the Motivation Profile, Moscow averaging high and St Petersburg very low, but after a week of further interviewing and observation, the conclusion was that, as is so often the case in this study, individual differences between people, wherever they are from or whatever industry they work in, are greater within nationality, location and workgroup (intragroup in other words) than they are intergroup or international.

This generalization is open to contest. The findings hold good for the people surveyed; they represent themselves and not their countries of origin. Other writers, such as Hofstede, Trompenaars and Hampden-Turner, who have studied cross-cultural issues and attitudes have found differences in attitudes between nationalities, which, of course, implies that there are significant similarities intra-nationally; this study has not found any similarities intra-nationally which precludes a valid search for international differences.

For the manager with a cross-cultural team it is more important to expect individual differences and to observe these, without preconception or prejudice. This view is a good, low-risk basis for managing diversity: the assumption that differences, even uniqueness, will be found.

Why a forced choice and not a ranking?

Forced choice requires people to consider four factors at a time and to choose between them, one in relation to the other. In the Profile, every factor is presented eleven times against all the other factors. It is easier to attend to four factors at a time than to cast one's mind over twelve factors, which is what would be required in a ranking exercise.

In the pilot phase, and on numerous occasions since, exercises have been used where motivational factors could be ranked in order of preference by the respondent. Invariably this produces a blunter result than the forced choice. The main difference is that the factor ranked number 1 by two people could be so important to one person that they give it 88 points, whereas the second person might only give it 37, although it still gained the highest score for them. The second difference is that there could be a vast gap between the true value of any two adjacent rankings, for example factor 2 ranked eighth might score 35 and factor 1 ranked ninth could score 12. With only so many points available for sharing between factors, choices are forced, and a series of decisions must be made yielding an indicative Profile of a person.

Why 11 points allocated to each statement?

Eleven points provides the maximum possible opportunity for discrimination and for accommodating reasonable extremes and is the maximum number intelligent people could handle in such circumstances without risk of miscalculation. Someone could give all 11 points to one element out of the four, thus increasing the range of possible scores for that factor. 132 points are, therefore, possible for any one factor, although in actuality the highest recorded score was 96 points for factor 1 (salary and tangible rewards).

Now that the Profile is on an Excel file, and scorable on computer screen, completion takes about 30 minutes and the program takes care of such problems as adding up to ensure you have allocated all 11 points to each Statement. It also checks you have allocated all 363 points, which could mean the end of the requirement for a reasonable level of mathematical ability to fill it in. This might be a shame, if it resulted in a less-numerically capable set of respondents, but the value of having the program work out the scores for the histogram outweighs it.

Some questions

Why have both positive and negative statements?

The reason was the desire to balance fast completion of the instrument (seeking emotional rather than logical responses) with slower, more considered answers. To achieve this a switch from positive to negative was used throughout. This constant series of interruptions seemed to achieve the effect required. Some people queried it and pointed out that it had caused them to hesitate each time to reassure themselves whether they were in positive or negative mode; exactly what was wanted.

Why repeat the elements?

Because the intention in the Profile is to compare each factor with every other one and to make sure that each gets an equal number of comparisons.

Why slightly change the wording of each statement?

Changing the wording of the statements means that people are not, as they move through the Profile, quite comparing like with like. The question to consider is the extent to which that change in wording affects the scoring. It does not seem to do so. There is no evidence that people are deeply affected by the semantics. The evidence is to the contrary. People have a general impression about the meaning of a statement and it is on that they register their score. They are either asked directly, 'Does this drive motivate you?' or they are asked to project their feelings 'Do you believe this drive motivates people?'. We believe projection largely reflects personal drives. The alternative, that someone can answer for others seems a strange suggestion. As for the question 'How do I know that I mean what I mean and that others mean the same?', this really is for the metaphysicist, and not for this study.

Why 33 statements?

In order to compare each factor with every other, 12 x 11 = 132 comparisons had to be made. If offering four forced choices per question, we need 132 divided by four which is 33 questions. The sheer volume of choices to be made was intended to minimize the problem that only a few might create, that of a momentary and uncharacteristic whim influencing the final score. A whim is a couple of steps away from a preference and it was hoped that repetition and concurrent variation would iron out the molehills of caprice smoothing them into a plateau of predisposition.

Table 3 presents the results of the 'best' 1355 responses. The largest range is for factor 1, salary and tangible rewards, at 96. It seems to produce the widest spread of valuation by individuals: from total indifference, a score of nil, to overwhelmingly important, at 96. The lowest range is for factor 5, relationships, at 45. Checking the responses shows that even the person who scored 45 valued two other factors more highly.

Table 3 *Results for the 'best' 1355 responses*

Factor	Range	Mode	Median
1	0–96	27	19
2	0–83	17	17
3	0–69	26	25
4	0–81	27	25
5	0–45	18	19
6	0–88	35	36
7	2–81	36	36
8	0–79	31	31
9	0–78	34	35
10	5–81	32	33
11	7–84	35	32
12	15–97	41	43

The histograms

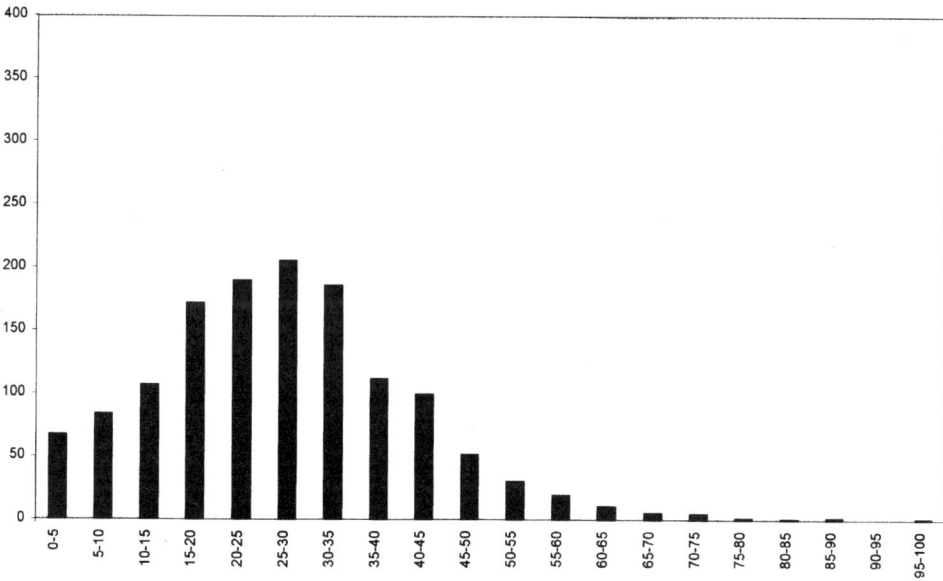

Factor 1 - money and tangible rewards
Mode 27   Median 19   Range 0 - 96

Figure 22   Factor 1: money and tangible rewards

Factor 2 - physical conditions
Mode 17   Median 17   Range 0 - 83

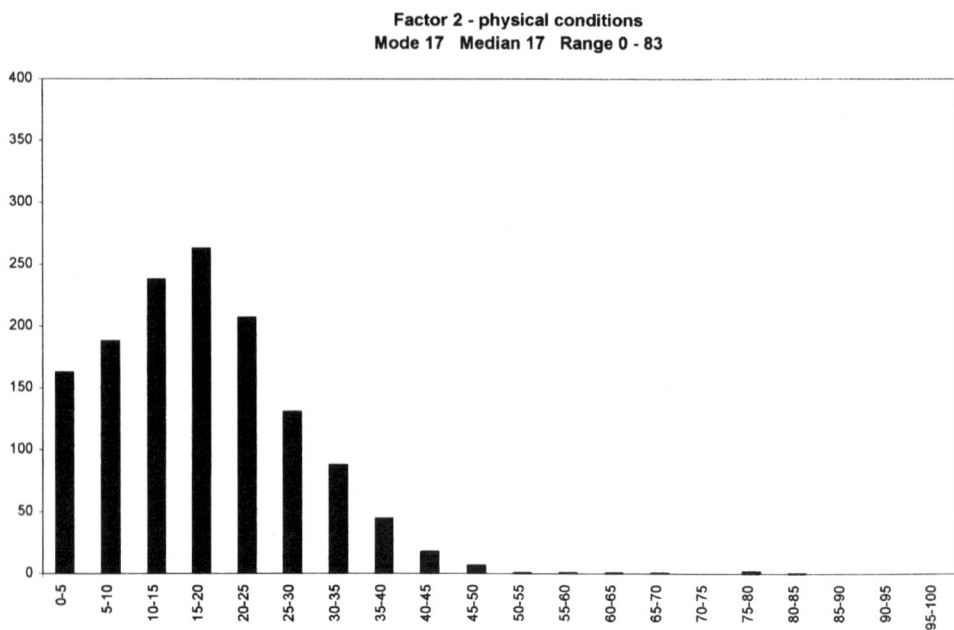

Figure 23   Factor 2: physical conditions

Factor 3 - structure
Mode 26   Median 25   Range 0 - 69

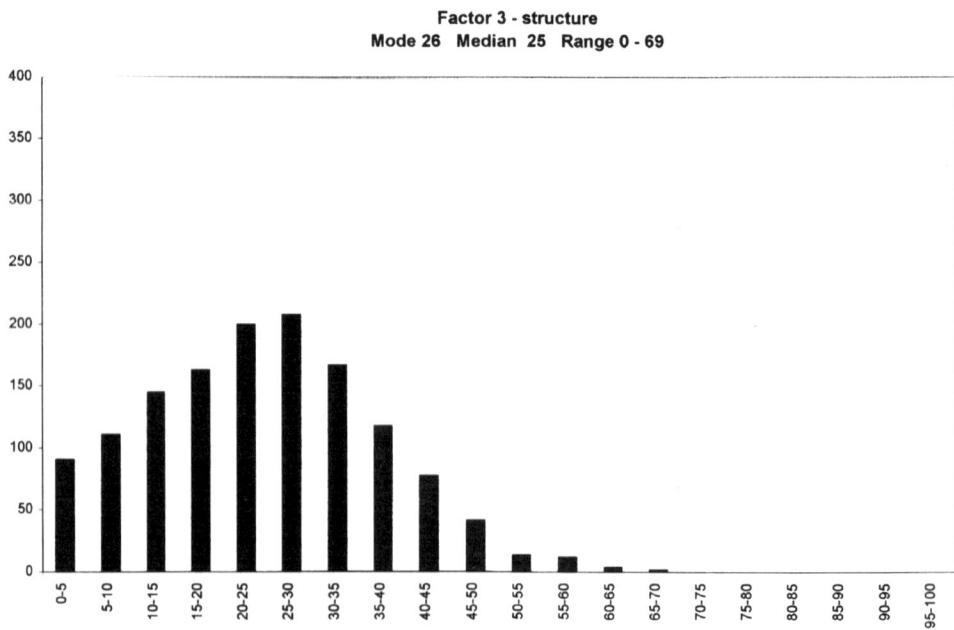

Figure 24   Factor 3: structure

Factor 4 - people contact
Mode 27   Median 25 Range 0 - 81

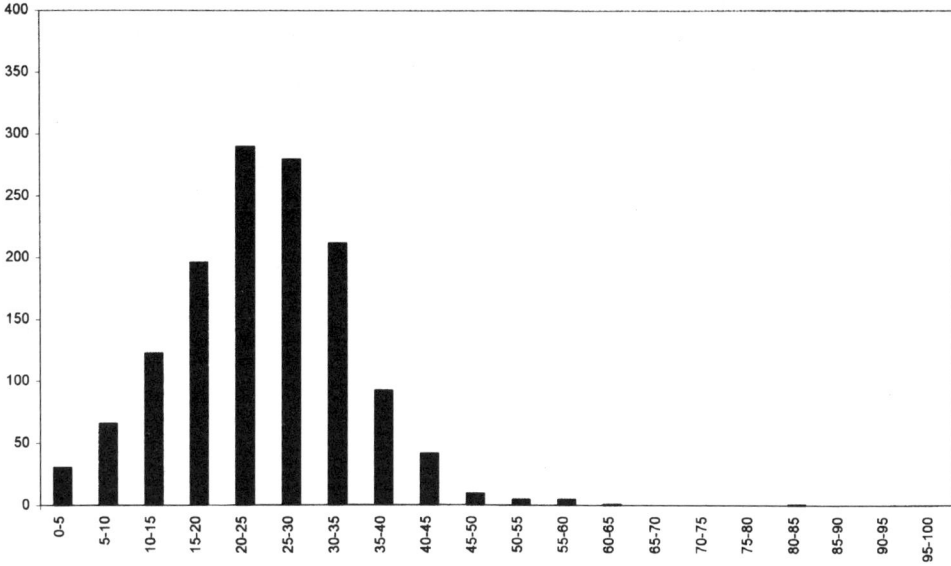

Figure 25   Factor 4: people contact

Factor 5 - relationships
Mode 18   Median 19   Range 0 - 45

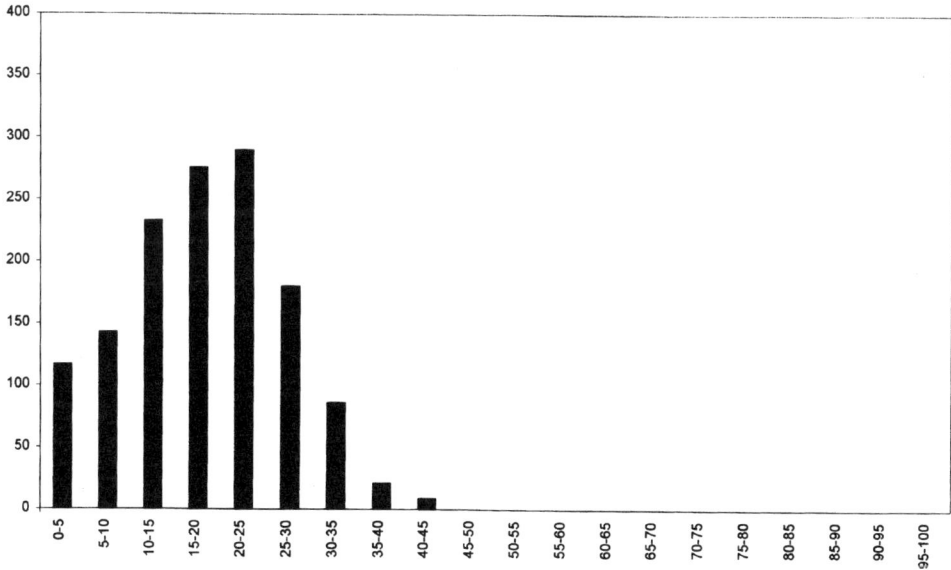

Figure 26   Factor 5: relationships

Factor 6 - recognition
Mode 35   Median 36   Range 0 - 88

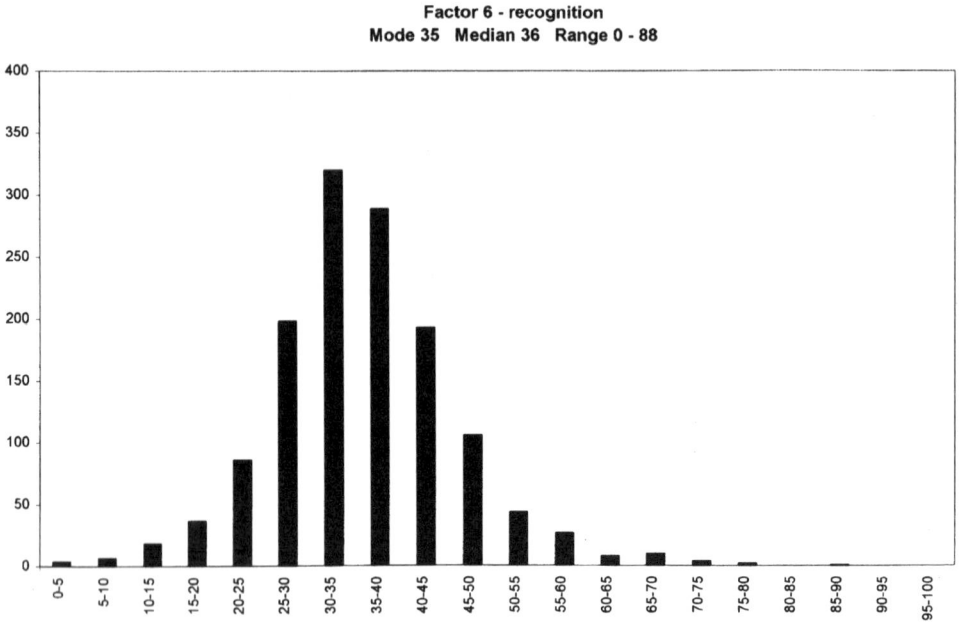

Figure 27   Factor 6: recognition

Factor 7 - achievement
Mode 36   Median   36   Range 2 - 81

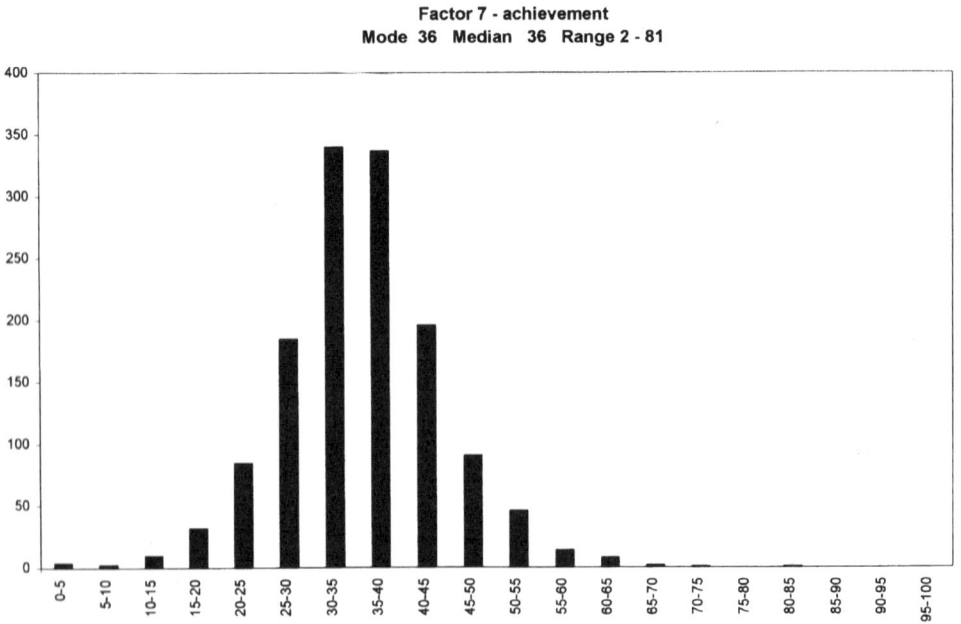

Figure 28   Factor 7: achievement

Factor 8 - power and influence
Mode 31 Median 31 Range 0 - 79

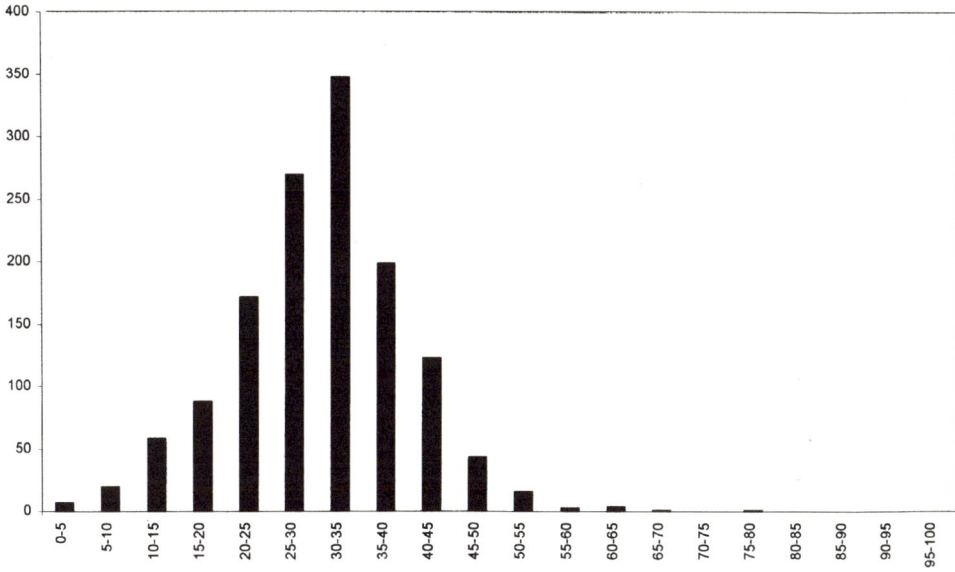

Figure 29   Factor 8: power and influence

Factor 9 - variety and change
Mode 34   Median 35   Range 0 - 78

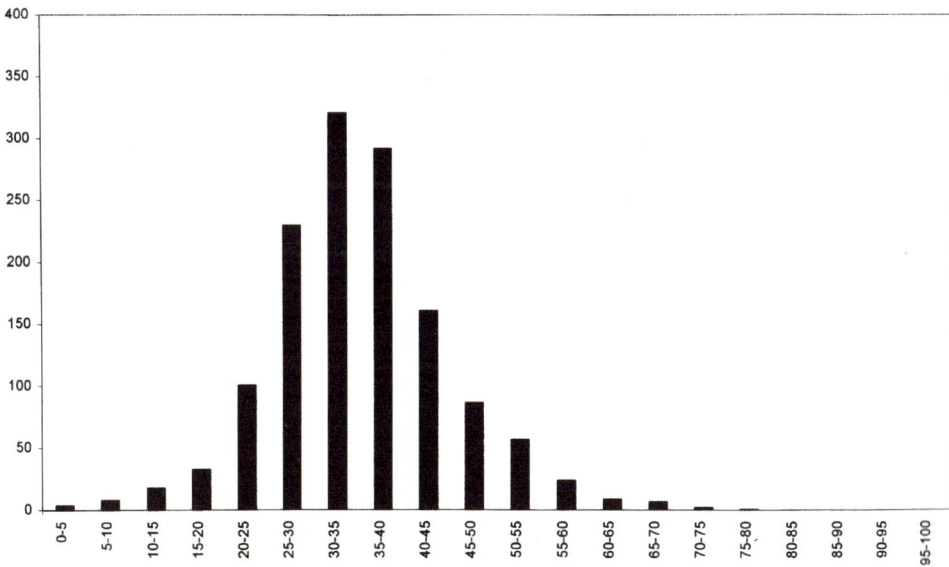

Figure 30   Factor 9: variety and change

Factor 10 - creativity
Mode 32   Median 33   Range 5 - 81

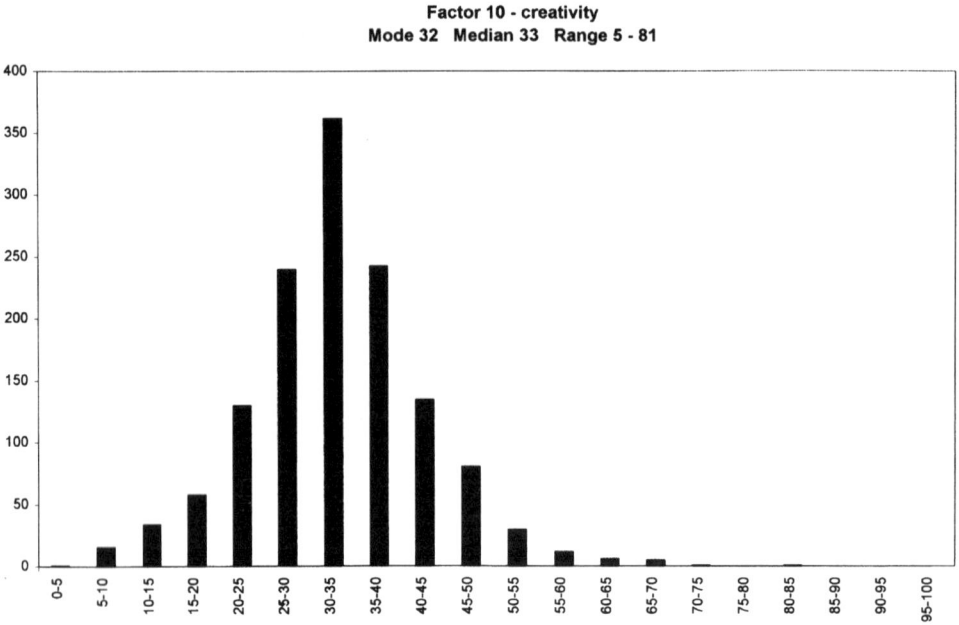

Figure 31   Factor 10: creativity

Factor 11 - self-development
Mode 35   Median 32   Range 7 - 84

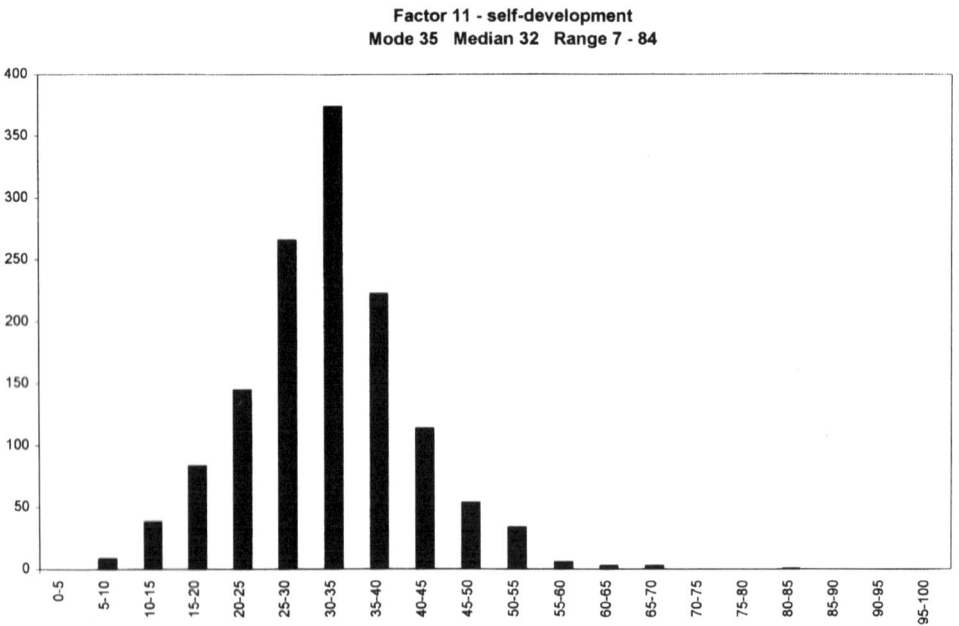

Figure 32   Factor 11: self-development

Factor 12 - interest and usefulness
Mode 41   Median 43   Range 15 - 97

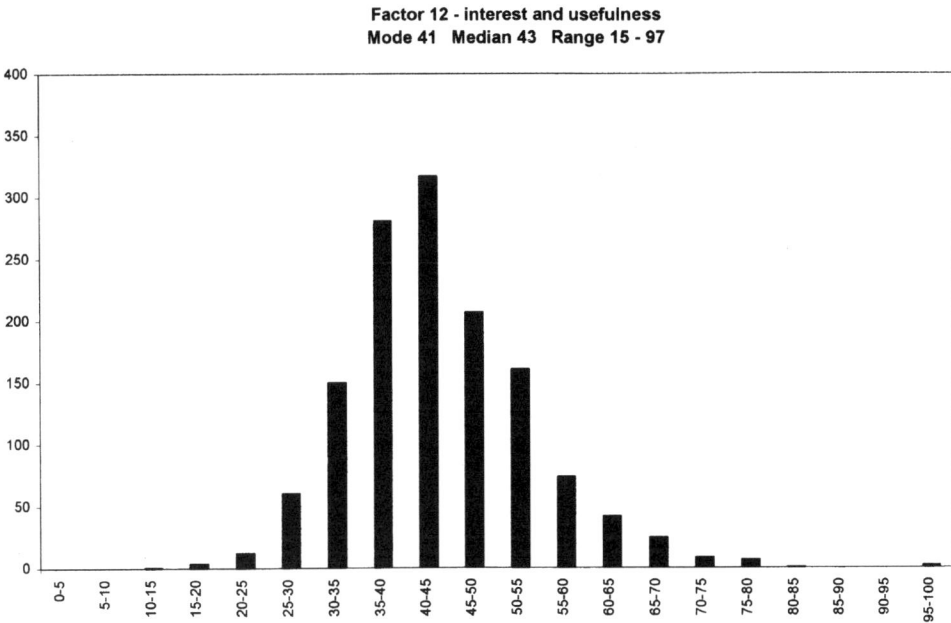

Figure 33   Factor 12: interest and usefulness

Reliability

There is tentative good news here. About 45 people who completed the Profile in one year and then repeated it two or even four years later, have shown remarkable consistency in their scores. Some of these people have made considerable life and career changes in the period between the two responses; and yet only slight variation has occurred. On seven occasions when people filled it in after a period of three or four months the same consistency seems to occur. The Profile seems to be internally consistent and reliable over time. Further work is being undertaken on this issue.

At least one factor does seem to change over time and circumstance: the need for structure (factor 3). This is covered in the chapter on Structure. Factor 1 (need for money and tangible rewards) seems to be similar.

Honesty

Do people fill it in honestly? Probably, yes. As it is designed for people with high intelligence, and the stated purpose is to help them to understand themselves and their approach to work better, there is little incentive to lie. We did not include the kind of 'dissembler spotting' questions that some instruments use: like 'Have you ever told a lie? YES or NO', or 'Have you ever wished your partner could be thrown from a tall building?' Such questions, intended to trap the respondent who is being a little (or very) evasive, add up to a dissembling score which gives the marker (assumed to be someone other than the respondent) a good idea of how much confidence to place in the honesty of the replies. Unfortunately, our population of managers and professionals can recognize such questions from two miles away, rendering them useless. On this Profile, if someone wants to lie, they lie.

The Profile has been designed to encourage honesty. Its length, with 132 phrases to be compared, and the repetition of those phrases, means that even those who try, in the early stages, to appreciate the underlying thrust of each phrase and to weigh it up carefully against what logic might tell them they should value, begin to flag. The sheer tedium of comparison and the mesmerizing repetition cause them to suspend rational thought and to proceed more quickly, with luck projecting feelings – 'gut reaction' – rather than logic, into their responses. And they are asked to do just this in the instructions at the beginning of the Profile.

But for those about to be offered or refused a job on the strength of their answers, too much is at stake for casual completion. If a manager uses the Profile for selection, transfer or job promotion, there is no guarantee of honesty from the respondent and so, as we explain in the chapter on Selection, we increase the complexity of the process so that cheating is not practicable. This problem is common to all who use psychometric tests for selection; no one has yet produced a cheat-proof, foolproof test that cannot be distorted by someone clever and determined enough to do so.

Do time and circumstance affect the score?

This cannot yet be tested directly because we do not have a large enough sample of people who have completed the Profile at different times and in different personal circumstances. Nevertheless, there is some circumstantial evidence in that the research was conducted in two phases, one of 1 000 responses in 1989 to 1993 and a second of 412 responses from 1994 to 1998. Particularly factor 3, the need for structure, scores for which might be expected to rise during a time of disruption and change, coupled with a strong further weakening of the traditional employer/employee bond and of the expectation that workers would remain with one organization for most of their working life. Despite these social changes, no such rise is evident in the results; in fact the median remains the same and the mode lowers slightly from 27 to 25. It is possible that time and circumstances affect the scores, but we are not able to point to firm evidence either way until more work has been done.

Although taken from a different set of people tested at a different date some broad conclusions can be drawn from the results. The lack of variation from the first Phase to the second could either reassure us that we have some measure of reliability in the instrument or merely indicate that the study does not show that people are feeling unsettled by the supposed insecurities and uncertainties of modern working life.

Use of the Profile overseas

Countries where the Motivation-to-work Profile has been completed by nationals and used on training seminars in that country, are listed below.

Abu Dhabi	Latvia
Albania	Macedonia
Austria	Norway
Belgium	Pakistan
Bulgaria	Russia
Dubai	Sweden
Estonia	Switzerland
Germany	Syria
India	United Kingdom
Jordan	Ukraine

The Profile has also been used extensively in the UK on groups of managers and professionals made up of mainly British nationals and on mixed groups, where the country of origin may have been known, but the exact nationality of the participant open to question. Page 271–2 offers a good example of this classification difficulty.

References

Alderfer, C.P. (1972), *Existence, Relatedness and Growth and Human Needs in Organisational Settings*, London: Collier Macmillan.

Atkinson, J.W. (1964), *An Introduction to Motivation*, Princeton, New Jersey: Van Nostrand Reinhold.

Basowitz, H., *et al.* (1955), *Anxiety and Stress*, New York: McGraw-Hill.

Belbin, R.M. (1981), *Management Teams: Why They Succeed or Fail*, London: Heinemann.

Blake and Mouton, J. (1964), *The New Managerial Grid*, Gulf Publishing.

Blanchard, K. and Johnson, S. (1983), *The One Minute Manager*, London: Fontana.

Boam, R. and Sparrow, P. (1992), *Designing and Achieving Competency – A Competency Based Approach to Developing People and Organisations*, Maidenhead, UK: McGraw-Hill.

Cooper, C.L., Cooper, R.D. and Eaker, L.H. (1988), *Living with Stress*, Harmondsworth, UK: Penguin Books Ltd.

Deci, E.L. (1971), 'The effects of externally mediated rewards on intrinsic motivation', *Journal of Personality and Social Psychology*, **18**, 105–115.

Feather, N.T. (1967), 'Valence of outcome and expectation of success in relation to task difficulty and perceived locus of control', *Journal of Personality and Social Psychology*, **7**, 372–386.

Festinger, L. (1957), *A Theory of Cognitive Dissonance*, Stanford, California: Stanford University Press.

Freud, S. [1915], (1934), *A General Introduction to Psychoanalysis*, New York: Washington Square.

Goleman, D. (1996), *Emotional Intelligence: Why it Can Matter More than I.Q.*, London: Bloomsbury Publishing Plc.

Grove, A.S. (1983), quoted in 'My turn: breaking the chains of command' *Newsweek*, 3 October 1983, p. 23.

Heider, F. (1958), *The Psychology of Interpersonal Relations*, New York: John Wiley.

Herzberg, F. (1966), *Work and the Nature of Man*, Cleveland, Ohio: World Publishing Company.

Hofstede, G. (1994), *Cultures and Organizations: Software for the Mind*, London: HarperCollins.

Honey, P. and Mumford, A. (1992), *The Manual of Learning Styles*, Maidenhead: Peter Honey Publications.

Horner, M.S. (1968), 'Sex Differences in Achievement Motivation and Performance in Competitive and Non-competitive Situations, PhD, University of Michigan.

Horner, M.S. (1969), 'Fail: bright women', *Psychology Today*, **3**, Nov. 1969, 36–38.

Hull (1951), *Essentials of Behaviour*, New Haven, CT: Yale University Press.

Hunt, J. (1981), *Managing People at Work*, London: Pan Books Ltd.

Industrial Society (1996), *Managing Best Practice*; Management Competencies No. 21, March 1996, London: Industrial Society.

Kelley, H.H. (1967), 'Attribution theory in social psychology', in D. Levine (ed.), *Nebraska Symposium on Motivation*, Lincoln, Nebraska: University of Nebraska Press.

Lazarus, R.S. (1976), *Patterns of Adjustment*, New York: McGraw-Hill.

Leavitt, H.J. (1986), *Corporate Pathfinders*, Homewood, Illinois: Dow Jones Irwood.

Le Doux, J. (1992), 'Emotion and the limbic system concept', *Concepts in Neuroscience*, **2**.

McClelland, D.C. (1961), *The Achieving Society*, Princeton, New Jersey: Van Nostrand Reinhold.

McGregor, D. (1960), *The Human Side of Enterprise*, New York: McGraw-Hill.

McGuire, W.J. (1966), 'The Current Status of Cognitive Consistency Theories', in S. Feldman (ed.), *Cognitive Consistency*, New York: Academic Press.

Martin, P. and Nicholls, J. (1987), *Creating a Committed Workforce*, London: Institute of Personnel Development.

Maslow, A.H. (1943), 'A theory of human motivation', *Psychological Review*, **50**.

Matthews, V. (1997), 'Case Study on Waterstone's', *The Financial Times*, 6 August, p. 10.

Mayo, E. (1949), *The Social Problems of an Industrial Civilization*, London: Routledge and Kegan Paul.

Revans, R. (1983), *The ABC of Action Learning*, 2nd edition, Bromley: Chartwell-Bratt.

Robinson, G.M. (1986), writing in *Handbook of Management Development*, 2nd edition, Aldershot: Gower, p. 317.

Roethlisberger, F.J. and Dickson, W.J. (1939), *Management and the Worker*, Cambridge, Massachusetts: Harvard University Press.

Roffey Park Management Institute (1994), *Career Development in Flatter Structures*, Horsham, UK: Roffey Park Management Institute.

Rycroft, C. (1968), *Anxiety and Neurosis*, Harmondsworth, UK: Penguin Books Ltd.

Schein, E. (1985), *Organisational Culture and Leadership*, San Francisco, California: Jossey Bass.

Seligman, M.E.P. (1975), *Helplessness: on Depression, Development and Death*, San Francisco: Freeman.

Stafford-Clark, D. (1967), *What Freud Really Said*, Harmondsworth, UK: Penguin Books Ltd.

Trompenaars, F. and Hampden-Turner, C. (1997), *Riding the Waves of Culture: Understanding Cultural Diversity in Business,* 2nd edition, London: Nicholas Brealey Publishing Limited.

Tuckman, B.W. and Jensen, M.A.C. (1977), 'Stages of small-group development revisited', *Group and Organisation Studies*, **2**, (4), 419–427.

Vroom, V.H. (1964), *Work and Motivation*, New York: Wiley.

Vroom, V.H. and Deci, E.L. (eds) (1970), *Management and Motivation: Selected Readings*, Harmondsworth, UK: Penguin Education, Penguin Books Ltd.

Wallach, M.A., Kogan, N. and Bem, D.J. (1962), 'Group influence on individual risk taking', *Journal of Abnormal and Social Psychology*, **65**, 75–86.

Weiner, B. (1985), 'An Attribution theory of motivation and emotion', *Psychological Review*, **92**, 548–573.

Weiner, B. (1992), *Human Motivation: Metaphors, Theories and Research*, London: Sage Publications Ltd.

Yerkes, R.M. and Dodson, J.D. (1908), 'The relation of strength of stimulus to rapidity of habit formation', *Journal of Comparative Neurology and Psychology*, **18**, 459–482.

Index

The 12 motivation factors which form the subject of this book are referred to many times in this Index. Their correct form of reference is listed below.

Motivation Factors

1 money and tangible rewards
2 physical conditions
3 structure
4 people contact
5 relationships
6 recognition
7 achievement
8 power and influence
9 variety and change
10 creativity
11 self-development
12 interest and usefulness

Ending the Blame Culture

Michael Pearn, Chris Mulrooney and Tim Payne

What do we know about making mistakes? What kind of mistakes do people make? Where are they most prone to make them? What kind of lessons do we learn from our mistakes? Are some types of mistakes more helpful to us than others? Can we learn to harness mistake-making as a powerful source of learning?

This book is about mistakes and what we can learn from them. It faces up to, and explains how organizations can escape from 'blame cultures', where fearful conformance and risk avoidance lead to stagnation, to 'gain cultures' which tolerate and even encourage mistakes in the pursuit of innovation, change and improvement.

Ending the Blame Culture was written on the back of systematic analysis of the content of over 200 accounts of real mistakes within businesses and organizations, ('My Biggest Mistake', *The Independent on Sunday*). This analysis provides both insight and understanding into the type of mistakes made, the context they were made in and how they helped learning and development. As a result the authors are able to distinguish between intelligent and undesirable mistakes: those which should be tolerated and those which must be avoided. The result is a book which gives sound advice on how individuals learn, practical measures that organizations can adopt to enhance learning through better management of mistakes, and the promotion of a culture which supports and fosters experimentation and risk taking.

Gower

The Excellent Manager's Companion

Philip Holden

This is for every manager who aspires to excellence in everything they do, but wonders how they'll ever find the time ...

With *The Excellent Manager's Companion* in your desk drawer, you'll be equipped with succinct guidance on today's most talked-about business issues. And you'll be able to pepper your conversation with pertinent quotations, and even know which books to turn to when you really do need more detailed guidance on a specific topic.

Twenty-one chapters look at key topics, ranging from corporate culture to customer orientation, and from innovation to influencing people. Each chapter is organized around standard sections, which makes 'dipping' into the book quick, easy, and rewarding.

Sections are:

• questions for self-analysis
• a step-by-step guide to best practice
• the ten 'don'ts'
• pertinent quotations
• summaries of key books and articles
• a case study
• a glossary of terms.

Philip Holden's lively *Companion* combines expertise with entertainment, with a supporting cast that ranges from Walt Disney to Confucius, and from Dilbert to Drucker. This book is guaranteed to appeal to busy managers in all sectors.

Gower

The Gower Handbook of Management

Fourth Edition

Edited by Dennis Lock

'If you have only one management book on your shelf, this must be the one.'

Dennis Lock recalls launching the first edition in 1983 with this aim in mind. It has remained the guiding principle behind subsequent editions, and today *The Gower Handbook of Management* is widely regarded as a manager's bible: an authoritative, gimmick-free and practical guide to best practice in management. By covering the broadest possible range of subjects, this handbook replicates in book form a forum in which managers can meet experts from a range of professional disciplines.

The new edition features:

- 65 expert contributors - many of them practising managers and all of them recognized authorities in their field
- many new contributors: over one-third are new to this edition
- 72 chapters, of which half are completely new
- 20 chapters on subjects new to this edition
- a brand new design and larger format.

The Gower Handbook of Management has received many plaudits during its distinguished career, summed up in the following review from *Director*:

'... packed with information which can be used either as a reference work on a specific problem or as a guide to an entire operation. In a short review one can touch only lightly on the richness and excellence of this book, which well deserves a place on any executive bookshelf.'

Gower

Gower Handbook of Management Skills

Third Edition

Edited by Dorothy M Stewart

"This is the book I wish I'd had in my desk drawer when I was first a manager. When you need the information, you'll find a chapter to help; no fancy models or useless theories. This is a practical book for real managers, aimed at helping you manage more effectively in the real world of business today. You'll find enough background information, but no overwhelming detail. This is material you can trust. It is tried and tested.'

So writes Dorothy Stewart, describing in the Preface the unifying theme behind the Third Edition of this bestselling *Handbook*. This puts at your disposal the expertise of 25 specialists, each a recognized authority in their particular field. Together, this adds up to an impressive 'one stop library' for the manager determined to make a mark.

Chapters are organized within three parts: Managing Yourself, Managing Other People, and Managing the Business. Part I deals with personal skills and includes chapters on self-development and information technology. Part II covers people skills such as listening, influencing and communication. Part III looks at finance, project management, decision-making, negotiating and creativity. A total of 12 chapters are completely new, and the rest have been rigorously updated to fully reflect the rapidly changing world in which we work.

Each chapter focuses on detailed practical guidance, and ends with a checklist of key points and suggestions for further reading.

Gower

How to Design and Post Information on a Corporate Intranet

Bryan Hopkins

Whatever the potential of an intranet for your organization, it's only ever going to be as effective as the information that you post onto it.

Whether you are trying to give staff access to information, communicate with them more proactively, or provide them with training and development, you need to be extremely rigorous in deciding what should (and shouldn't) be posted; how to present it and how it will work.

Bryan Hopkins' book provides you with a step-by-step process that you can follow and adapt to suit any of your own projects. Refreshingly, it assumes that you have limited computer skills and explains: what an intranet is; how to define your need; how to gather and structure the information; how to design and programme your pages using Microsoft® FrontPage™; how to monitor the quality of your work and evaluate its effectiveness.

You may be a training designer, involved in corporate communication, or simply representing your department in the project team responsible for your organization's intranet - either with or without the help of external consultants. This book will show you how to create an intranet web site, carrying information that people will want to use, starting from a blank sheet of paper and taking you through to the evaluation of a fully functioning site.

Gower

Impro Learning

How to Make Your Training Creative, Flexible and Spontaneous

Paul Z Jackson

Impro Learning is the first training book to treat creativity as the doorway to success - and provide the keys to unlock it. Drawing on sources as diverse as theatre, accelerated learning, sports, co-operative games and psychology, Paul Z Jackson reveals practical methods for enhancing all aspects of training, from joining instructions and bonding to detailed course design and evaluation. The emphasis throughout is on participation and results, and the text is packed with warm-ups, energizers, team exercises and innovative processes. As Peter Kline says in the Foreword, '... what Paul Jackson has to offer us is probably the most essential and basic ingredient of the new approach to corporate training that is beginning to emerge all over the world'.

This pioneering book will enable you to:

• design and deliver training programmes that achieve demonstrable results
• improve your skills as both a platform presenter and a group facilitator
• apply the principles of learning to broaden the range of training you can offer
• enhance your confidence and the ways you project it.

In short, *Impro Learning* offers simple yet powerful techniques for developing both yourself - as a trainer and a person - and those you train.

Gower

A Learning Approach to Change

Ken Griffiths and Richard Williams

Constant change is a given for most companies today. What differs is the scale, and the ability of people and organizations to deal with change in a positive, learning environment. Training must adapt too, to respond to the different learning styles of a new generation whose learning needs are the result of working in delayered, leaner, empowered organizations.

Griffiths and Williams look at the implications for training and development, drawing on their first-hand experience of being with IBM during an extensive reengineering programme. Using IBM's widely respected Systems Approach to Education as an example of a successful scheme, the authors discuss a range of issues, including the principles of adult learning, the design and operation of a skills management system, and trends in schools and universities. With the aid of checklists, questions, summaries, 'food for thought' and numerous real-life examples, they show how to improve corporate performance through organized learning. The book underlines the vital importance of linking learning with business needs and evaluating it like any other investment.

This book will appeal to anyone with responsibility for initiating, influencing, designing or implementing training programmes to support organizational change, and to anyone questioning the ability of current programmes to answer today's needs.

Gower

Managing the Training Process

Putting the Principles into Practice
Second Edition

Mike Wills

What they said about the first edition ...

'It is about time that professional trainers had a book that contains all they need to know, written in a clear concise and thought-provoking way. This is it.'
IT Training

'I wish it had been available at the time I became a trainer.'
Leslie Rae, The Training Officer

A comprehensive practical guide to managing all aspects of training, from programme creation to implementation and monitoring success rates. It offers flexible strategies for adapting training to meet the demands on today's professionals. The book takes into account all the complexities of modern business practices and how trainers and training managers should plan and then implement an overall training process in their organization.

This new edition retains popular features of its predecessor, for example, the flow chart structure, and some of the original themes which have now been developed further. It also covers some of the latest developments in the ever-changing world of training and development, including quality assurance of training suppliers; training self-audits; using managers and others to deliver training; the line manager's role in the training process; the relationship of the training process to the learning organization; the use of competencies in the process; training networks; and the Internet and training.

Gower